The New Basic Training for Trainers

W9-AUT-286

An Info-line Collection

Volume 3

Info-line is a series of "how-to" reference tools; each issue is a concisely written, practical guidebook that provides in-depth coverage of a single topic vital to training and HRD job performance. *Info-line* is available by subscription and single copy purchase.

1640 King Street
Box 1443
Alexandria, VA 22313-2043
PH 703.683.8100, FX 703.683.8103
www.astd.org

ISBN 156-286-150-6

Library of Congress Catalog Card No. 98-70076

Printed in the United States of America.

The New Basic Training for Trainers

An Info-line Collection

Volume 3

Editor
Cat Sharpe

Graphic Production
Anne Morgan

Lesson Design and Development

Issue 8906

Lesson Design and Development

Editorial Staff for 8906

Editor
Susan G. Butruille

Revised 1999

Editor
Cat Sharpe

Contributing Editor
Ann Bruen

Contributing Consultant
Chuck Hodell

Lesson Design and Development

In their book *Developing Vocational Instruction,* authors Robert F. Mager and Kenneth M. Beach once described a lesson plan as "the instructional prescription, the blueprint that describes the activities the student may engage in to reach the objectives of the course." Mager and Beach wrote the book for vocational teachers more than 40 years ago, but their description still applies. Then as now, it is as relevant for those in the training field as it is for educators.

In a training context, the trainer or facilitator follows lesson plans as a prescription or blueprint to guide learners in performing the "training objectives." David R. Torrence, in his article "Building a Lesson Plan," describes a lesson plan as both a *strategy* and a *ready reference:*

- As a *strategy,* the lesson plan is "a sequential set of events that leads to a desired goal."

- As a *ready reference,* the lesson plan is "a checklist of the necessary information to effect the set of events. A lesson plan summarizes who will conduct the instruction, to whom the instruction is directed, and what, where, when, why, and how instruction will take place."

Info-line No. 8905, "Course Design and Development," covers the overall design of a course—the big picture. This issue narrows the focus to zoom in on the details of designing and developing the actual lesson plans within the course design.

Lesson design and development represent the final refinement of course design and development, contained within the design and development phases of instructional systems development (ISD). The five basic ISD phases, all of which interrelate, are:

1. Analysis.

2. Design.

3. Development.

4. Implementation.

5. Evaluation.

Lesson plans are developed within the conventional ISD model, in which the trainer or facilitator has a larger role. Learning plans are developed with the competency-based ISD model, which is more learner centered and individualized. This issue concerns mainly the conventional ISD model structure, which moves from courses to units to lesson plans to activities.

Refer to *Info-line* No. 9706, "Basics of Instructional Systems Development," for a complete examination of ISD principles and methods. For further information on the competency-based model, see *Info-line* No. 8905, "Course Design and Development," and the section of this issue that provides information on individualized instruction and learning plans. (For a discussion on the roles that designers and facilitators fill in lesson design and development, see the sidebar *Designers and Facilitators: Who Does What?*)

Process and Structure

Lesson design, like any other element of ISD, is not static. Nor is there any one way to do it. But to produce a good lesson plan, you will generally do the following things:

1. Specify the title of the lesson and write a one-line description of the lesson.

2. Based on the course objectives, state the lesson objectives, specifying the following:

   - the conditions under which the objectives will be achieved (equipment or material to be used)

   - performance (observable behavior) expected

   - criteria used to judge satisfactory performance

3. For each objective, design a posttest, stating how the learner will be tested or evaluated for achievement of the objective. Each posttest should match the conditions of each objective and should contain instructions and specific items to be tested.

Designers and Facilitators: Who Does What?

The training designer and the instructor or facilitator often play different roles in lesson design and development. It is not unusual, however, for the same person to design and present the training program. This is especially true in organizations with small training departments.

It is important to know which person is responsible for certain decisions in the ISD process. In lesson design and development, the designer outlines the lesson, suggests approaches to topics, determines instructional periods and breaks, and selects and prepares major instructional material such as tests and guides.

The chart below, adapted from *Principles of Instructional Design*, shows how responsibility may be divided between designer and facilitator in lesson design and development.

General Division of Responsibility

Lesson Designer	Instructor/Facilitator
Chooses major strategies.	Selects details of strategies and implements presentation.
Selects major training aids.	Implements use of major training aids; chooses and implements use of minor training aids.
Designates number of instructional periods and break points.	Selects and implements structure and timing with instructional periods.
Selects and prepares participants' handouts, such as exercise sheets, data sheets, instructor and learner guides.	Implements use of materials—detailed selections and timing.
Selects principal components of content and evaluation.	Selects and implements ways to stimulate interest, motivate, and present material.

4. Outline how the performance objectives will be achieved in the following areas:

- content
- instructional methods, media, and techniques
- student activities

5. Build in evaluation to determine learners' progress during the course. Posttests will show whether or not the learner can perform the objective *after* the learning event (summative evaluation); while feedback during the learning event will check learners' progress *during* the learning event (formative evaluation).

6. Create the lesson plan (strategy), specifying learning activities, time allotted, and materials used.

Not all lesson plans will look alike. For one thing, their design depends on whether learning will be:

- cognitive (knowledge)
- psychomotor (skills)
- affective (attitudes or values)

Use the material presented in *Lesson Plan Variations* on the next page for a more complete understanding.

Once the designer goes through the design steps, he or she will have a lesson plan that includes the following components:

■ *Course and Lesson Title*
These should provide the purpose and conceptual framework of the lesson so that participants and their supervisors will be able to determine what will be taught and whether or not it is applicable to their learning needs.

■ *Time and Date*
This information must provide employees and managers sufficient lead time for planning purposes in the event that they need to make arrangements for their normal workload to be temporarily covered by someone else.

Lesson Plan Variations

The *Develop a Lesson Plan* module of the *Professional Teacher Education Module Series* shows model lesson plans based on whether learning objectives are informational (knowledge), manipulative (skills), or problem solving/managerial (attitudes).

The **informational (knowledge)** format has these components:

- unit title
- lesson topic
- objectives
- introduction
- method (technique)
- learning activity
- resources
- evaluation
- summary

The **manipulative (skills)** format has the following components:

- unit
- lesson
- job
- aim (objective or purpose)
- tools and equipment
- materials
- teaching aids
- references
- four-step method (preparation, presentation, application, test)*
- suggested reading for students

The **problem-solving/managerial (attitude)** format has these components:

- unit
- lesson topic
- objective
- instruction
- introduction (identification of the problem—informal; statement of the objective—informal)
- method (key questions to ask to identify factors; factors to be identified)
- resources (list of resources for students to use in locating information needed to solve problem)
- summary (draw conclusions to the problem)
- evaluation

*For further information about the four-step method, see *Info-line* No. 8808, "Basic Training for Trainers."

■ *Objectives*

Develop the lesson objectives from the course and unit objectives. These are the most important elements in the lesson plan. Objectives should specify what the learner will do or know as a result of the lesson, the conditions under which the performance will be accomplished, and the criteria for judging performance or understanding of the skill or knowledge.

■ *Posttests*

List the posttests the learners will be expected to perform as a result of training. Tie each posttest to an objective. Examples of types of posttests include: true-false, essay, multiple choice, performance, demonstration, and standardized. (For more information on this topic, see *Info-line* No. 8907, "Testing for Learning Outcomes.")

■ *Materials and Media Lists*

Make a detailed checklist of supplies and equipment needed for conducting the lesson, such as projector, screen, tools, paper, pens, lights, outlets, extension cord, adapter, extra bulb, flipcharts, films, computers, and so forth. Include instructor and learner guides, texts, name tags, participant rosters, and job aids.

■ *Time Frames*

Somewhere in the lesson plan, often in the left-hand margin, list the expected duration of each activity within the lesson plan. Each activity should last not less than five minutes, or more than one hour. Plan for breaks, listing the duration of the break.

■ *Introduction*

The introduction orients learners by informing them of the following:

- lesson objectives

- content of posttests

- how the lesson relates to their jobs

- how the lesson relates to previous knowledge and present skills

The introduction also motivates learners by arousing interest and attention through:

- a brief demonstration
- a funny story or interesting anecdote
- provocative questions
- background information

■ *Content*

Based on the objectives, develop a list of topics and subtopics. Topics are arranged in the following sequence:

- known to unknown
- simple to complex
- concrete to abstract
- big picture to details

Teaching or learning points to be covered during the lesson are then developed from the sequenced list of topics and subtopics.

■ *Trainer Activities*

This component lists the techniques used by the trainer or facilitator to guide the learner toward achieving the objectives. Examples of these techniques include: lectures, demonstrations, films, discussions, or records or tapes. For further information, see *Selecting Instructional Techniques and Materials* on the next page.

■ *Learner Activities*

This component lists what the learners will do to achieve the learning objectives. Examples include the following: practice, role play, fill out a form or worksheet, participate in a discussion, read out loud, demonstrate, brainstorm, debate, research, write.

■ *Summary*

The summary serves several purposes by doing the following:

- reinforcing major concepts
- relating themes
- drawing conclusions or generalizations
- clarifying or expanding major concepts

■ *Evaluation and Feedback*

Summative evaluation takes place with some kind of posttest, while formative evaluation checks ongoing learning through periodic question-and-answer sessions, discussions, self-evaluations, and so forth. (See the job aid at the end of this issue.)

Instructional Techniques and Materials

Before choosing techniques and training materials, the designer must consider many factors. These include the following items:

■ *Instructional Objectives*

Instructional techniques and activities must match the objectives—whether they involve cognitive learning (knowledge), psychomotor learning (skill), or affective learning (attitude):

- Cognitive learning involves mental processes and the acquisition of knowledge.

- Psychomotor skills involve manipulation of objects or machinery based on mental decisions. Training techniques include demonstration—practice, simulation, and mock-ups.

- Attitude involves motivation and perceptions. Training activities include role play, discussion, and brainstorming.

For a more complete discussion of how people learn, see *Motivational Principles* sidebar.

■ *Cost or Budget*

Designers must always keep in mind cost benefit when determining training media and activities. Does the effectiveness of the activity in helping learners meet learning objectives justify the expense?

■ *Lesson Content*

Techniques and media must be consistent with the lesson content.

Selecting Instructional Techniques and Materials

The chart below matches some training techniques and instructional media with the three categories of learning (knowledge, skills, and attitudes—KSA). Use the chart only as a guide.

Technique/Activity	Knowledge	Skills	Attitudes
Assigned reading and research	X		X
Brainstorming	X		
Buzz group	X		X
CD-ROM	X	X	X
Computed-based instruction	X	X	X
Critical incident	X	X	X
Demonstration/practice		X	
Field project	X		X
Field trip	X		X
Flipcharts	X		X
Games	X	X	X
Guided discussion	X		X
Handouts	X	X	X
Job aids		X	
Lecture	X	X	X
Manuals	X	X	X
Panel	X		
Role play		X	X
Simulation		X	
Video	X	X	X
Web-based instruction	X	X	X

Motivational Principles

Understanding how people learn is an integral part of planning and writing a lesson plan. What motivates adults to learn? Six basic motivational principles apply within the context of planning and writing a lesson: relevance, conceptual framework, learning outcome, method, evaluation, and primacy or recency.

■ *Relevance*

This principle addresses the relevance of the lesson for the trainees. It is usually covered in the introduction part of the lesson plan and tells trainees what benefit they will derive from the lesson.

■ *Conceptual Framework*

This consists of the main ideas and secondary ideas of the lesson. It provides two important things. First, it tells trainees where they are going during the lesson. Second, it creates gaps in the trainees' minds that must be filled. When the instructor tells a trainee that he or she will talk about three things and then names those three things, he or she creates gaps, which can be powerful learning tools. By filling the gaps, the instructor provides closure in the trainees' minds, a subconscious force that can be used as part of the strategy for learning.

■ *Learning Outcome*

This principle tells trainees what they must be able to do at the end of the lesson, under what conditions, and how well. Knowing the expected outcome reduces trainees' anxiety.

■ *Method*

The method tells trainees how they will learn. It should cover all the methods that will be used in a particular class, such as lectures and demonstrations.

■ *Evaluation*

One of the most important things learners want to know is how they will be tested. When describing the evaluation of trainees' learning, the instructor should cover the method of evaluation and when it will occur. This also tends to decrease trainees' anxiety.

■ *Primacy or Recency*

Research shows that people tend to remember best the first and last things they see or hear. The course developer should keep this principle in mind when determining the sequence of teaching points and for planning reinforcement of what was taught in the middle of the lesson.

Adapted from "Lesson Plans—Strategies for Learning" by Michael R. Toney, Training & Development, *June 1991.*

■ *Learners' Knowledge and Expectations*

Learners will come from different ages and backgrounds as well as varying levels of experience and knowledge. Training activities must meet their needs while avoiding the extremes of being overly simple or too complicated. Trainers must consider the learners' level of comfort with different activities.

■ *Trainer's Experience and Capability*

The trainer should be comfortable and experienced with the training technique. If he or she has not tried a particular technique before, sharing that information with the learners can help enlist their support.

■ *Time Availability*

Expected duration of training activities must realistically fit within time constraints.

■ *Facilities, Equipment, and Material*

Even such constraints as fixed row seating can greatly affect the choice of training and learning activities, and the availability of equipment obviously affects the choice of training media.

See *Info-line*s No. 8808, "Basic Training for Trainers," and No. 8602, "Alternatives to Lecture," for listings and explanations of various training activities and techniques. See *Info-line* No. 8804, "Training and Learning Styles," for explanations of various training and learning styles.

Incorporating Evaluation

When building evaluation into a lesson plan, it is helpful for the designer to be familiar with the four classical steps in evaluation outlined by Donald L. Kirkpatrick in *Evaluating Training Programs:*

1. Reaction.

2. Learning.

3. Behavior.

4. Results.

Reaction, or Level 1, evaluation tests how well participants liked a training program. This is the easiest—and most common—form of evaluation, usually done by questionnaire. This type of evaluation focuses heavily on the trainer in terms of subject, techniques used, and performance. Here are some sample questions:

- Did the course, lesson, or session address your needs?

- How well did the trainer convey the objectives?

- Was the trainer well prepared?

- Did the trainer hold your interest?

- Did he or she adequately cover the subject?

- How well did the trainer summarize the subject?

- What was your most valuable experience during the session? The least valuable?

The evaluation form should be phrased to allow the respondent to answer as briefly as possible—for example, ask for a rating from 1 (poor) to 10 (excellent). The form should include space for additional comments.

Learning, or Level 2, evaluation is harder than Level 1. Evaluation of learning should, of course, be based on learning objectives. (See the sidebar *Choosing Evaluation Techniques* for a list of some common evaluation techniques used to measure learning.) Kirkpatrick emphasizes the importance of building in pretests and posttests when measuring learning, as well as using control groups and statistical analysis in analyzing and interpreting results.

Behavior, or Level 3, evaluation is harder yet to measure. One way to measure on-the-job behavior is by an attitude survey—getting feedback on the participant's behavior from the participant, that person's peers, supervisors, and subordinates.

Results, or Level 4, evaluations measure what happens because of training. Such results as reduction of costs, increase in production, and reduction of turnover often can be measured by a comparison of records. Other, more elusive effects, such as quality, can be assessed through interviews, questionnaires, and other techniques. For a thorough discussion of evaluations, refer to *Info-lines* No. 9813, "Level 1 Evaluation: Reaction and Planned Action"; No. 9814, "Level 2 Evaluation: Learning"; No. 9815, "Level 3 Evaluation: Application"; and No. 9816, Level 4 Evaluation: Business Impact."

Evaluation Tips

When you are building evaluation into your lesson design and development, you may find it helpful to do the following:

- Allow enough time for participants to complete evaluation forms. Do not let the participants take the forms home; they are hardly ever returned.

- Build in "processing time"—time for participants to reflect on and discuss their own experience during the session.

- Try to include the same number of questions about strengths and weaknesses of the learning event.

- Allow for quick, on-the-spot evaluations throughout the course—even if it is simply asking the participants, "How are we doing?"

- Build in frequent written feedback. The trainer can prepare a written summary of evaluations and discuss them at the beginning of the next session.

Choosing Evaluation Techniques

The chart below matches some evaluation techniques with the three categories of learning (knowledge, skills, and attitudes).

Technique/Activity	Knowledge	Skills	Attitudes
Demonstration/performance test		X	
Essay	X		
Interview			X
On-the-job observation		X	
Oral presentation	X		
Paper and pencil test	X		
Questionnaire			X
Role play		X	X
Survey			X

- For written evaluations, give participants the option of remaining anonymous.

- Design written forms so that responses can be tabulated and quantified.

- Instead of having participants fill out the entire evaluation form at the end of the session, allow breaks after each topic to jot down reactions.

- Evaluations should be kept for future reference.

For further information, see *Info-lines* No. 9705, "Essentials for Evaluation," and No. 8808, "Basic Training for Trainers."

Guidelines for Design and Development

When designing and developing lessons, you should focus on several broad areas of concern: the learning process, timing and flexibility, participant involvement, creative learning experiences, retention and transfer of knowledge, and automated instructional design.

The Learning Process

A basic understanding of the learning process will guide the designer in narrowing down lesson content and activities in the lesson plan. The learning process, as explained by Lawrence Munson in *How to Conduct a Training Seminar*, can be described in six general phases.

1. Motivation.
Learners need to see "what's in it for them"—how they can benefit personally from the learning process.

2. Explanation.
Objectives and learning activities should be presented clearly and in a logical sequence.

3. Demonstration.
The trainer or subject matter expert demonstrates the skill to be learned, or, particularly in the knowledge or affective domain, provides an example or illustration.

4. Self-evaluation.
Learners should assess their own learning, both during the course (formative evaluation) and afterward (summative evaluation).

5. Application.
Learners must be able to apply ideas and skills learned when they return to their jobs.

6. Feedback.
Learners need to know how they are doing. The lesson design should provide for feedback during the course and at its conclusion.

Timing and Flexibility

Management of time must be built into the lesson plan, allowing flexibility for unforeseen circumstances, and for varying the pace according to participants' learning styles and speeds. Here are some tips for timing and flexibility:

- Training time should not exceed six to seven hours a day, excluding breaks. Generally allow for two 10-minute breaks before lunch and two after lunch. Each learning period should not exceed an hour.

- Be clear what the learning objectives are and plan time accordingly.

- Prioritize activities according to their importance: "A" for critical, "B" for should be done, "C" for nice to do. This way the trainer can add or subtract activities according to the learners' receptivity, pace, or such unexpected events as electrical failure or a class emergency.

- Allow enough time for learners to become proficient in each objective before moving on to the next.

- Keep in mind the attention span of learners; for example, attention span for a video will be much greater than for an audiotape. Lecture periods should not last more than 10 minutes at a time.

- Concentrate on techniques that allow the most time for learner participation; too much instructor-led "busy work" wastes the learners' time.

- Mix group activities with individual events for variety and maximum effectiveness.

- Allow for periodic transitions to summarize previous material and set the stage for what comes next.

- Consider individualizing instruction or inviting learner participation in designing some segments within the lesson.

Participant Involvement

The more participants are involved with their own learning, the faster and better they will learn. Here are some ways to increase their involvement:

- Punctuate lecture periods with question-and-answer sessions, quick quizzes, and other forms of feedback.

- Consider giving brief, learner-involved assignments, such as self-assessment quizzes, before the learning event. This allows for instant feedback from the beginning.

- More advanced and time-consuming reading assignments before the learning event can allow more time for class discussion and group activity.

- Ask participants what their expectations are—either in writing or orally. This increases interest level while giving the trainer an indication of whether or not the learning event will meet expectations.

- Allow plenty of time for questions, and build in opportunities to turn learners' questions into learning activities.

- Depending on the skill level of the trainer and the participants, responsibility for lesson design may be shared. Working with the basic course or lesson design, participants may themselves fill in learning activities they feel will best help them to reach their learning goals.

Creative Lesson Design

Involving participants in lesson design can lead to some creative learning experiences. The trainer and participants can negotiate all or part of a design as it relates to:

- goals
- objectives
- tasks
- time frames
- values and norms
- evaluation

Some creative teaching or learning activities to consider include the following:

- visualization
- guided imagery
- drawing
- journal keeping
- listening to music
- coaching

For ideas on building creativity into lesson design, see *Info-line*s No. 8901, "Discovering and Developing Creativity," and No. 8902, "15 Activities to Discover and Develop Creativity."

Retention and Transfer of Knowledge

If participants cannot remember what they have learned in training and relate new skills and knowledge to the job, training has failed. Strategies for ensuring retention and transfer of knowledge to the job include building into the lesson plan ways to do these things:

Review material periodically. Using the new skill or knowledge periodically and relating it to something new enhances retention.

Generalize knowledge. Change the context in which the new skill or knowledge is applied; for example, use new computational skills in a different way.

Build in feedback. Getting feedback through games, role-playing, demonstration, and other techniques tests understanding as well as retention. Asking participants to critique or evaluate themselves periodically also ensures retention and tests understanding.

Ask questions. Build in question-and-answer sessions to get immediate feedback.

Automated Instructional Design

Do not overlook the ever-increasing advances in computer technology for designing and developing instructional materials. Examples of uses of automated systems include media selection, evaluation, materials design and development, flow charting, script writing, content development, simulation, testing, and front-end analysis.

Individualized Instruction

Individualized instruction can constitute a whole course or part of a course, depending on any number of factors. A program or lesson designer can use individualized instruction to complement group instruction by designing portions of the course or lesson for self-instruction. Individualized instruction is a key part of competency-based instruction (CBI).

When should the designer consider individualized instruction? Likely situations include the following:

Differences in learner needs or capabilities. Participants' work experience or skill levels may differ widely. Or learners may have vastly different learning styles or learning rates.

Budget considerations. Once materials are developed, the costs of implementing individualized instruction are generally lower than trainer-led instruction.

Schedules. Sometimes workers are on different shifts, which makes scheduling group instruction difficult.

Characteristics of individualized instruction include some distinguishing features:

- The course is divided into learning modules or units, with each module containing assigned reading, study guides, and possibly a programmed textbook. Learning plans are contained within each module and often worked out cooperatively between learner and instructor.

- Pretests are used for initial diagnosis of learner knowledge and skill to determine efficient use of time and resources.

- Lectures and demonstrations are used sparingly, if at all.

- Learners themselves control how quickly they master the program or module.

- Frequent self-assessment helps learners to assess what they have mastered and what they still need to know.

- Both summative and formative evaluations can be built into the program.

- The role of the instructor becomes that of a guide, rather than teacher.

- Records of the learners' progress can be recorded on computers to follow progress and for future reference.

There are more advantages of individualized instruction in addition to those outlined above, and they include:

- Participants take responsibility for their own learning.

- Individualized instruction focuses on mastering a task, rather than on instruction. Learners can test their mastery of a skill when they feel they are ready.

- Learners progress at their own speed without disrupting the pace of the class as a whole.

On the other hand, there are some disadvantages to individualized instruction:

- Learners may not be able or motivated enough to work through the program independently.

- Independent study can be lonely; it will not work with people who need the stimulus of others in order to learn.

- Evaluation can be more difficult because periodic oral feedback and other techniques are limited.

- There can be logistical problems, such as what to do with learners who complete the program way ahead of others, or those who cannot handle the material.

Learning Package Components

The designer, often in conjunction with the learner(s), develops learning packages for individualized instruction. Learning packages, or modules, generally consist of the following elements:

- a cover page
- an introduction
- directions
- performance objectives
- learning activities and materials
- a performance evaluation or assessment

The learning plan generally consists of a description of the following:

- learning goal or objective
- skills to be developed
- proposed start date
- proposed completion date
- date(s) to be rated

Both learner and instructor sign the learning plan.

The "Instant" Lesson Plan

When the time to create a lesson plan is limited, trainers can create an effective, complete, and internally consistent plan by including four basic elements:

- an introduction—consisting of the overview, the lesson objectives, the teaching methods to be used, and the evaluation

- the core of the training—essential course content, demonstration, practice, and feedback (in sufficient detail to enable a substitute trainer to give the class)

- an opportunity to ask questions—allowing the learners to ask questions and provide the trainer with immediate feedback on the effectiveness of the lesson

- a summary of what has been learned—a restatement of the main ideas, application to the work place, and testing to reveal learners' strengths and weaknesses

This approach to lesson design and development addresses the few essential requirements that will create learning environments that benefit learners and save the trainer time. Ideally, however, the lesson plan developer will have sufficient lead time to carefully follow the conventional ISD structure outlined above in order to create the most effective learning experience for trainees.

References & Resources

Articles

Broadwell, Martin M., and Carol Broadwell Dietrich. "How to Get Trainees Into the Action." *Training,* February 1996: 52-56.

Downs, Sylvia, and Patricia Perry. "Can Trainers Learn to Take a Back Seat?" *Personnel Management,* March 1986: 42-45.

Eline, Leanne. "Choose the Right Tools to Reach Your Training Goals." *Technical & Skills Training,* April 1997: 4.

Mullaney, Carol Ann, and Linda D. Trask. "Show Them the Ropes." *Technical & Skills Training,* October 1992: 8-11.

Quinlan, Laurie R. "The Digital Classroom." *Techtrends,* November/December 1996: 6-8.

Tate, Ted. "Lesson Planning." *Successful Meetings,* March 1998: 118.

Toney, Michael R. "Lesson Plans—Strategies for Learning." *Training & Development,* June 1991: 15-18.

Wircenski, Jerry L. "Improving Your Questioning Skills." *Technical & Skills Training,* May/June 1996: 25-27.

Yelon, Stephen, and Anne Wineman. "Efficient Lesson Development." *Performance & Instruction,* August 1987: 1-6.

Yelon, Stephen, and Lorinda M. Sheppard. "Instant Lessons." *Performance Improvement,* January 1998: 15-20.

Books

Briggs, Leslie J. (ed.). *Instructional Design: Principles and Applications.* (2nd edition). Englewood Cliffs, NJ: Educational Technology Publications, 1991.

Earl, Tony. *The Art and Craft of Course Design.* New York: Nichols, 1987.

Gagne, Robert M., and M. Driscoll. *Essentials of Learning for Instruction.* (2nd edition). Boston: Allyn and Bacon, 1988.

Hamilton, James B. *Develop a Course of Study.* Athens, GA: American Association of Vocational Instructional Materials, 1985.

———. *Develop a Lesson Plan.* (2nd edition). Athens, GA: American Association of Vocational Instructional Materials, 1984.

Kirkpatrick, Donald L. *Evaluating Training Programs.* San Francisco: Berrett-Koehler, 1994.

Lynton, Rolf P., and Udai Pareek. *Training for Development.* (2nd edition). West Hartford, CT: Kumarian Press, 1990.

Mager, Robert F. *Making Instruction Work.* (2nd edition). Atlanta: Center for Effective Performance, 1997.

Mager, Robert F., and Kenneth M. Beach Jr. *Developing Vocational Instruction.* Belmont, CA: Fearon Publishers, 1968.

Munson, Lawrence. *How to Conduct Training Seminars.* (2nd edition). New York: McGraw-Hill, 1992.

Nadler, Leonard. *Designing Training Programs.* (2nd edition). Houston: Gulf Publishing, 1994.

Yelon, Stephen. *Powerful Principles of Instruction.* White Plains, NY: Longman Publishers, 1996.

Info-lines

"Basic Training for Trainers" No. 8808 (revised 1998).

Butruille, Susan. (ed.). "Course Design and Development." No. 8905 (revised 1998).

Callahan, Madelyn R. (ed.). "Alternatives to Lecture." No. 8602.

Gryskiewicz, Stanley S. "Discovering and Developing Creativity." No. 8901 (revised 1997).

———. "15 Activities to Discover and Develop Creativity.." No. 8902 (revised 1997).

Hacker, Deborah G. "Testing for Learning Outcomes." No. 8907 (revised 1998).

"Improving White Collar Productivity." No. 8809.

Kirrane, Diane. (ed.). "Training and Learning Styles." No. 8804 (revised 1998).

Plattner, Francis. "Instructional Objectives." No. 9712.

Russell, Susan. "Effective Job Aids." No. 9711.

Waagen, Alice. "Essentials for Evaluation." No. 9705.

Job Aid

Sample Lesson Plan

Course title: _____

Lesson title: _____

Time and date: _____

Objective(s):

_____
_____
_____
_____
_____
_____
_____

Posttest(s):

_____
_____
_____
_____
_____
_____
_____

Notes: time, transitions, key points	Introduction	Content/teaching points	Instructor activities	Learner activities	Summary

Materials:

_____

_____

_____

_____

_____

_____

Evaluation plan:

_____

_____

_____

_____

_____

_____

Notes/comments:

_____

_____

_____

_____

_____

_____

_____

_____

_____

_____

_____

_____

Job Aid

Lesson Plan Checklist

This checklist will help the lesson designer check for missing elements, relevance, and clarity:

☐ The lesson plan clearly states one or more learning objectives.

☐ Lesson objectives are based on the unit or course objectives.

☐ Objectives state conditions under which the objectives will be achieved, and criteria by which achievement of the objectives will be measured.

☐ Posttests are stated in terms of objectives.

☐ The introduction contains information that motivates participants and orients them to the lesson objectives.

☐ The number of teaching points is appropriate to meet the objectives within the allotted time frame.

☐ Teaching and learning activities and techniques are based on learning objectives.

☐ The lesson plan employs a variety of teaching and learning activities.

☐ Teaching and learning techniques are relevant to learners' needs and learning domain (whether knowledge, skills, or attitudes).

☐ Learners are given ample opportunity to participate and to apply what they learn.

☐ Instructional media are appropriate for the learning domain, budget, and learner needs.

☐ The summary reinforces and pulls learning points together.

☐ Time frames and transitions are noted.

☐ Both summative and formative evaluation are planned for each learning objective.

☐ Ample time is allowed for participants to process their own experiences.

☐ Segments within the lesson plan are long enough to accomplish the objective, and short enough to say within learners' attention span.

☐ Content is prioritized to provide flexibility.

☐ The lesson plan provides for individualized learning (if needed).

Task Analysis

Issue 9808

Task Analysis

AUTHOR:

Alice K. Waagen, Ph.D.
Waagen and Associates
1557 Hiddenbrook Drive
Herndon, VA 20170-2817
Tel: 703.834.7580
E-mail: aaw5@aol.com

Alice Waagen has over 16 years experience in designing and implementing corporate training. She has developed full systems of training measurement and evaluation, including cost of training, training volume and activity, training customer satisfaction, and ROI. Dr. Waagen holds M.S. and Ph.D. degrees in education.

Editor
Cat Sharpe

Associate Editor
Sabrina E. Hicks

Production Design
Anne Morgan

ASTD Internal Consultant
Phil Anderson

What is Task Analysis?

Once, long ago, working for an organization was a marvelously predictable thing. People entered the workforce after they completed whatever level of schooling their aptitudes, inclinations, and finances dictated. They began at the bottom rung of the mythical career ladder, whether that was as a floor sweeper in a manufacturing plant or as a mailroom clerk in the service sector.

Jobs in those days were well defined and documented in formal job descriptions delineating those knowledge, skills, and abilities—or KSAs—required for success in the position. Well-defined career ladders meant you always knew your current place, future opportunities, and even where you would go if job performance or political mayhem required a backward step.

With jobs and job progression so well defined, the course developer's task was equally well structured. Different models for structured course development, like the instructional systems development (ISD) model, proliferated. Such ISD models as the ADDIE (that is, analysis, design, development, implementation, and evaluation) model offered a wonderfully concrete, step-by-step approach to developing training. The ADDIE model begins with front-end analysis and concludes with evaluation, with multiple steps and substeps in between. (See the model on the following page.) One of the critical front-end analysis steps is task analysis.

Task analysis is defined as the systematic identification of the following items, which are necessary to perform any job:

- specific skills
- knowledge tools
- conditions
- requirements

In the past, instructional designers relied on formal job descriptions as the basis for beginning a task analysis. The job descriptions, which often were written after the completion of a job analysis, defined the specific tasks and duties of the position. The designer's job, in essence, was to translate the requirements of the job, as noted in the job analysis and job description documents, into training materials and then to train employees to successfully perform the job.

This process has no flaws in its logic. Indeed, it is still followed in many organizations as a way to develop the support materials and programs needed to ensure optimal job performance. But more and more, the business mantras of improved speed, performance, and process all but do away with the formal definitions of jobs and the rigidity of organizational job tables and progression steps.

Noticing this change, William Bridges, in his innovative book *JobShift*, writes, "There are no more jobs, only work to be done." The rigid job structures of the past have all but been eliminated from many of today's forward-thinking organizations. Employees are expected, indeed required, to perform multiple jobs, which are, in reality, tasks merged from many jobs into one. Few document these new "jobs," for when they put keystroke to paper, employees find that business exigencies require them to stop performing certain tasks and start performing all new ones.

Where in the chaos of fluid job roles and responsibilities does that leave task analysis? Is performing a task analysis a thing of the past, gone the way of the keypunch machine? No, task analysis still has an important place in the development of sound training programs. What has changed is not the need for documenting the required actions that ensure top job performance but the sources of information the developer examines to determine the job or tasks to be trained.

This issue of *Info-line* describes the value and utility of good task analysis—specifically how to analyze work and work processes using various task analysis methods. It will describe how to plan task analyses as well as provide guidelines to ensure that your research stays focused and produces results. Case studies are provided to illustrate how training practitioners apply the principles of analysis to create various training deliverables.

The ADDIE Model of ISD

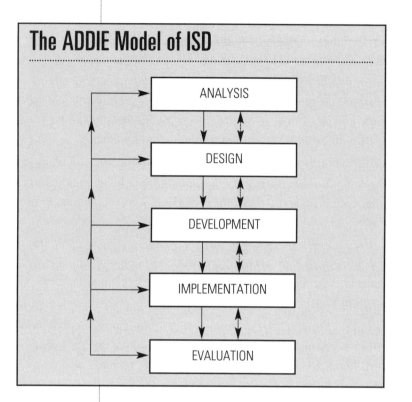

ANALYSIS

DESIGN

DEVELOPMENT

IMPLEMENTATION

EVALUATION

Jobs Versus Processes

The thrust of total quality management (TQM) and reengineering movements centers on improving processes to increase efficiency and effectiveness. Some organizations that adopted TQM define work totally in terms of processes, not jobs. TQM encourages all employees to understand their place in the total, end-to-end, process and to strive to continually improve the effectiveness of the process. In these quality-based organizations, an employee's job might entail performing one segment of a larger process or many segments of multiple processes.

The fundamental difference between job- and process-based work is the degree of change in process-based work. Continuous quality improvement requires employees and their work teams to constantly question the efficiency of how they perform and to correct their actions so that they can improve the overall process.

What does this mean to task analysts? Primarily, it means that they can be less reliant on printed documentation about jobs. In organizations, the formal job descriptions that once defined the duties of the job have all but been abandoned. Job duties are more often documented in process charts and

process descriptions. When functioning in a process-based work environment, trainers faced with developing task or process training should do the following things:

- Shift their orientation and language from *jobs* to *processes*.

- Search out all process documentation as the basis for development work.

- Ask to join process improvement teams early in their work to pinpoint the needed training.

- Be active participants in process improvement teams. (As teams redesign work, trainers can provide valuable input on how easy or difficult the new process will be to train and communicate.)

- Constantly think of speed—ways to shorten and improve the training development process itself. (For example, use existing documents, like process flowcharts, as job aids rather than create new ones.)

Undertaking a Task Analysis

To perform a useful and valid task analysis, you must know the basic steps to follow and what methods of gathering data are most effective and appropriate for your assignment. Once the up-front planning is completed, use the following guidelines to help you reach a successful conclusion to the task analysis process.

First Steps

Task analysis can differ in complexity and scope. For instance, you could accurately document a simple set of tasks by interviewing current employees, if they were performing the tasks successfully to performance standards. On the other hand, it could take many interview and data-gathering sessions to identify all the components of a complex job or a position that was undergoing change and did not currently exist in a well-understood manner.

Regardless of the level of complexity, task analyses share the following fundamental steps:

1. Identify the major or critical outputs of the job. This will help you identify the major tasks and task groupings.

2. Break down the major tasks into subtasks or steps. You have completed the task breakdown when you can achieve the goal or result of the task by completing all the steps or subtasks.

3. Determine the type of all tasks and subtasks:

   - Knowledge tasks—require the trainee to acquire knowledge, information, or understanding. These tasks are also known as cognitive tasks.

   - Skills tasks—require a change in behavior or an action on the part of the trainee. These tasks are also called action tasks or behavior tasks.

4. Collect all data necessary to document the tasks and subtasks. Using a variety of data sources increases the validity of the data. Make sure each task has a discernible output or result.

5. Validate the data. You can confirm information derived from interviews by direct observation. Likewise, you can validate observation logs by reviewing with subject matter experts (SMEs). Direct observation or employee reviews can verify formal job descriptions or job analyses.

6. Obtain review and approval of task analysis from client, training management, or other management in your organization. Provide management with the opportunity to modify the scope of the tasks, if needed.

7. Finalize the reporting of the task analysis. The format you choose depends on the end use of the data. For the final result, you can generate any tables, flowcharts, and narrative descriptions in the detail needed.

8. Distribute your findings to management for final approval. Once approved, your task analysis is complete.

Task Analysis Planning Checklist

The proper design of a training program depends on a comprehensive task analysis. The key to writing accurate learning objectives is to specify *what* is to be learned, based on identifying the individual tasks the learner needs to perform.

Careful up-front planning is critical to the success of the task analysis. Planning ensures that you are gathering the right amount of data: Too much data gathering results in redundant data sets and wasted time; too little, and you may lack the full picture of the job or process you are documenting. Use the following checklist to increase your chance of producing good results.

☐ What is the end result of the task analysis? Is it strictly training development, or will the data generated also be used for performance appraisal criteria or job description copy?

☐ Has anyone ever researched this job before? Has a job analysis been performed? Job aids developed? Any other documentation that will help in the analysis?

☐ What is the relationship you have with the client? Do you have a formal status-reporting agreement? Have you specified procedures for communicating project delays, problems, concerns, or issues?

☐ Who will be trained? How many? Where are they located? What are the time frames and deadlines for the deliverables?

☐ What is the background knowledge or skill level of the audience? Are they complete novices to the tasks, or have they some experience to draw on for the learning?

☐ What is the nature of the tasks to be analyzed? Are they skill (behavior) based? Knowledge (cognitive) based? Both?

☐ How will you collect the data? Direct observation, interviews (individual or focus groups), review of existing documents, questionnaires, surveys?

☐ How will you verify the data for accuracy? Do you have subject matter experts (SMEs) who can help with this?

☐ How will you organize your results? For yourself? For your client?

Task Listings

Task listings or inventories are accurate task statements describing the work activities of employees in specific occupational areas. This format specifies the actual job tasks. It involves a process of organizing the tasks, determining their importance, detailing the steps, and putting them in proper sequence. Here is an example of a task listing:

Task Listing Sheet

Job: Receptionist

Tasks:
(In order of importance)

1. Answers telephone.

2. Greets clients.

3. Receives mail.

4. Calls office personnel to inform them that their visitors have arrived.

5. Updates office telephone directory and receptionist relief schedule.

6. Assists with other departments' administrative duties.

When to Use Task Listings

You can use task listings when you need to accomplish the following things:

- discover different jobs and tasks, their relationships to each other, and the requirements for successful performance of the task

- develop task descriptions for all jobs in the occupational area

- identify training that should be modified or completely eliminated (outmoded or irrelevant information may be identified and cut from the curriculum)

- identify and structure jobs into career fields

- determine the tasks critical to sound vocational or technical education programs

- determine critical tasks for occupational competency and certification tests

- illustrate the range of activities to provide a basis for trainees and supervisors to form realistic perceptions of the job

How to Prepare Task Listings

Prepare a form for the task listing; choose a simple, straightforward format for easy use in recording data. The form should provide space for the task description and any other information necessary for your analysis, such as level of difficulty, degree of importance, and frequency of performance. Then follow these guidelines:

1. If you are reporting the prevalence of tasks, indicate how often they are performed during the job performance. Focus only on frequency rather than on other factors, such as importance and level of difficulty.

2. Record the actual number of times the task is performed within a set period of time (per day, week, or month) or record general frequency (the task is performed frequently, occasionally, or rarely). Either approach will help you decide on the sequence of lessons, range of subject matter, and the amount and scope of practice exercises.

3. If time is the most important feature of your study, use a modified task-listing approach and arrange the information in a timeline format showing each task as it occurs during a performance.

4. Show that some tasks are more important than others by listing them in the order of their importance.

5. Research by looking at the job description, talking with employees, or observing employees as they perform actual work. This kind of investigation will help you select relevant content for your course.

6. List all the tasks that are part of the job.

Advantages

Task listings have a number of advantages. They are inexpensive; data can be quantified; and information regarding the size of the workforce, the numbers performing specific tasks, and the descriptions of work and workers are readily available. Finally, computers easily store, organize, analyze, and report quantifiable information.

Disadvantages

Disadvantages to this method of data gathering include the fact that task listing is very time consuming and can be tedious if the particular job is extremely detailed. The technique works most effectively when the job being studied is linear and requires the trainees to make only a few simple decisions.

Data Collection Methodology

How you collect data for a task analysis can vary widely depending upon the needs of the organization, the time allotted for the task, and the nature of the information to be identified. The following sections describe methods you can use to collect data for a task analysis.

Observations

When directly observing employees performing tasks in the work setting, do the following:

- Make sure that you explain to the employees, their supervisors, and union representatives the purpose of your observation.

- Explain that the work performed during the observation period must be done exactly as it is always done, not modified because of the observer.

- Take notes on each work task and element.

- Use the observation data to validate findings obtained through other data-gathering methods.

Individual Interviews

This method employs direct questioning of employees, their supervisors, and other employees with significant involvement in the task performance. Following are some useful points to remember:

- These interviews can be highly structured, using standard questions for each interview, or open ended, asking respondents to narrate how they perceive a task is performed.

- You may choose to ask questions about how employees currently accomplished the work, as well as gather information about improving the performance of the tasks.

- You can use interviews to clarify ambiguous or confusing information obtained from documents or observation.

Group Interviews

This method involves direct questioning of several individuals in the same position to acquire consensus data about how employees perform the tasks. You can also use it to interview a team that has more than one person responsible for completing a given task or series of tasks. These interview sessions are also called focus interviews and facilitated research sessions.

When using group interviews, remember the following guidelines:

- Encourage employees to analyze and discuss various aspects of the job, especially areas that are problematic or difficult to perform.

- Use group interviews to determine how cooperative and interdependent roles contribute to accomplishing goals.

Printed Materials

Many printed materials such as job analyses, university or technical training materials, job descriptions, and technical manuals include information about jobs or processes. When using them to collect data, follow these guidelines:

- Be aware that job descriptions may be written to justify pay levels or job titles and may not accurately reflect how employees perform the work.

- Look for rich sources of information outside of your organization—such as benchmarking studies, professional journals, or academic publications.

- Use printed information to supplement other methods. If using information from outside of the organization you are studying, verify that they follow similar job and task standards.

Sample Task Criticality Rating Form

Measure the importance of the specific task to the overall process or job by assigning ratings as shown in the form below.

Task	% of Total Job (All must add up to 100%)	Time (in minutes/day)	Relative Importance Scale (1 = low importance, 5 = high importance)				
Perform basic statistical calculations	5	10	1	2	3	4	5
Analyze data using statistical packages	5	15	1	2	3	4	5
Report results to management	5	5	1	2	3	4	5
Propose corrective action	2	5	1	2	3	4	5

Questionnaires

When using prepared question-and-answer formats (checklists, surveys, polls) that focus on detailed information about various work activities, perform the following:

● Design the questionnaire with the help of an SME to ensure that the questions are focused and accurate.

● Test the questionnaire with a sample group of employees to verify that its directions are clear and easy to understand.

● Use the questionnaire to gather data from large numbers of geographically dispersed employees or to add validity to data gathered from other methods.

Checklists

Providing respondents with checklists from which to choose the tasks they perform in their jobs can be useful tools, but they involve some precautions:

● Use of checklists requires extensive preliminary work involving questionnaires, interviews, or observations to identify tasks.

● The checklist method requires recognition rather than recall. This is simpler for respondents and less time consuming if used also as a questionnaire. The information gathered may be limited, however, particularly in relation to task sequencing, relationships between tasks, and employee-machine interactions.

Diaries

The diary method for collecting data requires participants to organize activity schedules and to follow schedules by keeping logs and records of their daily activities. When using this method, remember the following:

● This method may be time consuming and disruptive.

● You can use diaries to determine the frequency of task performance.

Prioritizing and Classifying Tasks

Often direct observation or interviews yield long lists of tasks being performed. You need to prioritize or classify these tasks to facilitate moving to the next step of the process—whether it be training design or job redesign. Prioritizing tasks also helps to indicate if you have overlooked any tasks or if the list is incomplete. Use the following factors to prioritize tasks:

● time spent completing task

● frequency of task execution

● importance of task to overall process or job (also known as a *task criticality rating*)

Use task criticality ratings to accomplish the following items:

● Capture critical behaviors that are required to perform the task.

● Develop criteria for designing a training program.

● Determine the parts of the training program that should be emphasized, further developed, shortened, or eliminated.

● Establish operating procedures and policies regarding specific behaviors (such as, handling customer complaints).

● Generate helpful suggestions and recommendations for equipment design or modification.

You should take other factors into account when using criticality ratings. Ratings of importance are subjective and determined by the background experience or point-of-view of the rater, but using multiple raters can minimize the subjectivity factor.

The previous page has an example of a task criticality rating form that you can use to assess the importance of a task to the whole process.

Sample Process Flow

The following diagram depicts the tasks needed to be executed to begin the task analysis phase of a curriculum development project.

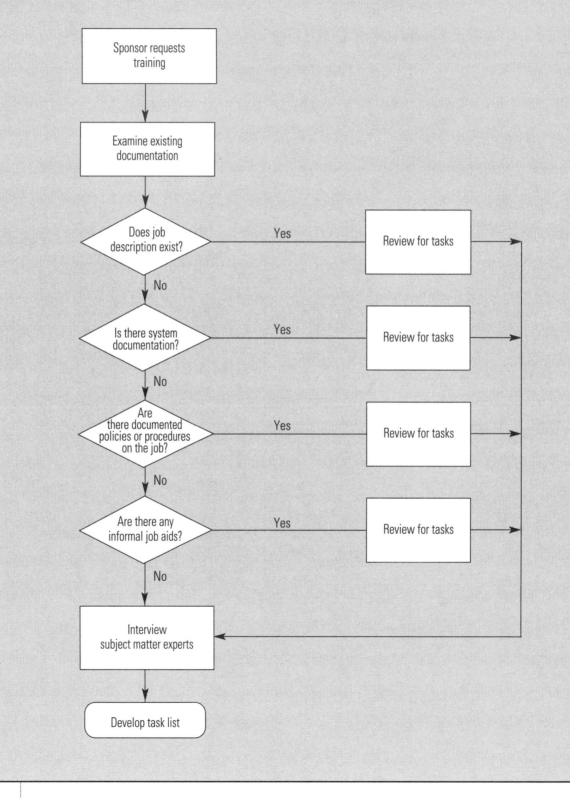

Collecting and Organizing Data

Two additional data-gathering techniques will be useful to you: critical incident technique and process mapping. You can use these methods to gather, organize, and display data as well as to indicate any data gaps or missing information.

Critical Incident Technique

Critical incident technique uses the individual or group interviews to document tasks surrounding a critical incident in the workplace. Most task analysts use this method of data collection after a perceived serious failure of job performance results in employee or customer injury, equipment malfunction or damage, or other event determined to be critical to the business.

Frequently, critical incident investigations appear on the news after air or rail transportation accidents. Once an accident occurs, federal agencies like the Federal Aviation Administration (FAA), Federal Rail Administration (FRA), or National Transportation Safety Board (NTSB) rush to the accident scene and sift through both physical and verbal evidence to determine the cause of the mishap. The focus of these investigations centers on two factors: human or mechanical error. The human errors are detected by interviews structured around questions like "What did you do? What next? When?"

If the source of the error is determined to be performance, employees require new or upgraded training to ensure that the performance shortfall is corrected. Task analysts can use the investigation documents as well as perform further critical incident interviews to determine the tasks needed to be trained.

Some considerations for using critical incident technique are as follows:

- Stress that respondents describe only actual events, not "What did they want to do?" but "What did they really do?" You are trying to document actual job performance and current techniques, not how people envision performing the task.

- Do extensive prework before the interviews to identify all possible critical incidents.

- Try to interview at least five different sources for each incident. Remember, you are recording their recollections of how they responded to circumstances at the time of an incident. With more sources, it is less likely that subjective information will sway you.

- As always, be extremely wary that the outcome of the investigation will be a recommendation for more training. Objective, unbiased research may indicate that mechanical failure or inefficient work processes caused the incident. Additional training will not "fix" these problems, and another accident may occur.

Process Mapping

Process mapping is a visual tool used to systematically describe actions and behaviors in a sequential flow. A process flow or map presents a clear and logical visual representation of all the tasks and steps involved in the execution of a particular process. Unlike a simple task list, process maps are beneficial in that they graphically demonstrate decision points and their multiple selections, thus allowing "branching" of the tasks into separate paths, depending upon the outcome of the decision (see the sample process flow on the following page). Process mapping allows the task analyst to record multiple outcomes of decisions and is an ideal technique for documenting knowledge or cognitive tasks.

The foundation of process mapping is the depiction of an *input,* the *process* or *action* taken on the input, and the *outcome* or *result* of the action. Information for the process map can come from direct observation of the tasks or from interviews with top performers.

You can create process maps by following these steps:

1. Assemble a group of top performers or employees who are experts in the process.

2. Use a meeting room with white boards, flipcharts, or large pieces of paper attached to the wall. Have chairs facing these media.

Process Mapping

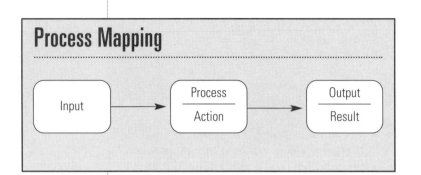

3. Brainstorm the inputs to the process—all people, materials, activities, or resources that are used in the process. Write each input on a separate note card.

4. Define the outputs from the process, including any financial, material, and people resources. Write each output on a separate note card.

5. Map the activity flow, including the "What happens?" and "Who does it?" Write each activity on a separate note card. Have participants arrange the note cards in sequential order and pencil in the direction of the flow between notes.

6. Use separate shapes to denote actions versus decisions. Usually, an action is depicted in a rectangle, while a decision is shown as a diamond.

7. Annotate each process step with who is responsible for the step, the time it takes to complete the step, where the step is performed, or any other relevant information.

8. Review with the team the final flow for any changes or adjustments.

Guidelines for Writing Task Analyses

Task analysis can require a considerable investment of time, energy, and resources. Get the most from your analysis project by following these suggestions.

For your first draft of the analysis, describe the tasks as they currently exist. Do not include any suggested improvements or "what if" proposed changes to the process. Annotate these items in an appendix or footnote and have SMEs or expert reviewers verify.

Include all elements or work activities that are the employee's responsibility regardless of how long or how often they are performed. Tasks that can take only minutes to perform can be as vital to the job as those that take months to complete.

Describe tasks according to the policies, procedures, and performance (output) standards of the company or organization.

Get management verification that employees are performing tasks according to standards. Be mindful of company policies, safety rules, or procedures as you document how employees perform the task. You may unearth some work practices that are actually in violation of these rules.

Study the task, not the employee. Characteristics of individuals, their education and background for example, are irrelevant to the analysis unless successful performance of the task requires knowledge or skills acquired from the education.

Distinguish between human activity and other kinds of work (such as machine operation). Employees manipulate controls—push buttons, turn dials, pull levers—so that machines will perform assorted tasks like drilling, sawing, photocopying, and so forth.

Distinguish between an employee's tasks and the team's tasks. If developing public relations materials is the objective of a group effort, consider the individual functions involved: Analyze tasks involved with individual production, research, visual art, marketing, and management position.

Study all process flowcharts if your organization has undertaken any process reengineering work. They can be good high-level breakdowns of how work is accomplished.

Research any information systems projects that have been done to automate the function you are examining. Data flow diagrams and information flow diagrams document the flow of information and work and can contain valuable information.

Note the amount of action or behavior tasks. If the job is primarily physical, you can document it quickly and accurately by videotaping it. You can then translate the video into a text document or use it as a future training aid.

Case Studies

One serious consideration of any task analysis work is *time.* Traditional analysis work, based on multiple interviews and document analysis, takes considerable time and resources. As stated earlier, one of the real enemies of a lengthy analysis is the speed of change. In many organizations, training development cycles have shrunk from months to weeks to days.

When tasked with developing and delivering training within a day or week, an analyst can use various techniques to reduce analysis time without affecting the quality of the final piece. The following case studies are real-life examples of development efforts shortened by the use of creative analysis techniques.

University Program Development

Gloria Holland, Ph.D., of the Center for Instructional Advancement and Technology at Maryland's Towson University, was asked to develop new degree and certificate programs that epitomized academic excellence in research and theory and also provided students with the KSAs that would ensure them employment in their field upon graduation.

The **goal** was to design—from the bottom up—credit programs, which defined the end employers as key stakeholders in the development process, and to build strong ties between the university and its business partners.

Techniques

Local business organizations were contacted and asked to identify an internal SME in the specific field of study. This expert, collaborating with colleagues, described and prioritized specific workplace abilities graduates needed for success. The ability lists served as the first draft of the task listings.

Business experts then participated in a facilitated session during which participants consolidated and transferred the ability lists to note cards and grouped them under categories. Redundancies were eliminated, and dialogue began regarding priorities or task descriptions. The business experts and their academic partners reached a final consensus on the task list and descriptions. Next, the academics used this guidance as the basis to develop the curriculum.

Rapid Analysis Tips

- Provide worksheet formats and guidance to individual experts.

- Use facilitated consensus techniques in group meetings to allow analysts to shorten the data-gathering phase.

- Identify redundant tasks easily by grouping under categories.

- Discuss and resolve priority conflicts quickly.

Using a facilitated meeting technique shortened the original process—based on individual interviews—from months to a half-day.

Computer Training Support

John Keim of Computer Learning Centers, Inc. was asked to design a curriculum to train non-computer users to staff computer help desks. The overall **goal** was to develop a seven-month-long curriculum of progressive courses supporting the KSAs required for an entry-level position at a computer help desk. For the graduates of this program to be placed in positions with area employers, Keim had to design the curriculum around the specific needs of these employers.

Techniques

To start, an analyst went to the Help Desk Institute to acquire names of experts in the field—actual practitioners able to describe all of the nuances of the job. These experts became the base team members. Because it was vital to have input from managers who hire program graduates, this team also included help desk supervisors from the local business community.

The Developing a Curriculum (DACUM) methodology of design analysis was employed to create the curriculum. During the DACUM session, a facilitator led the group through a series of brainstorming exercises to determine the exact tasks and duties required by a help desk individual.

The team stated the behavioral outcomes of the tasks as well as task frequency, criticality, and degree of difficulty. They then grouped similar tasks, wrote overall objectives, and organized the objectives into individual courses. The tasks and objective groupings were then handed off to the developer for lesson plan and course material development.

Rapid Analysis Tips

- The team followed DACUM task charts, which allowed them to be aware of what content preceded and followed their own content. This enabled the team to provide links between the classes, providing a cohesiveness to the curriculum.

- Industry experts used in the design work enabled the team to view course content from a customer's point of view. The importance of customer service skills, such as defusing anger, listening, and stress reduction, did not occur to the more technically focused team members but were clearly identified by the expert employees.

- Group-facilitated sessions to map the program's design, rather than build the curriculum course by course, reduced the course development time to two days.

Law Enforcement Training

Ken Hayes, of Wackenhut Services, Inc., in Aiken, South Carolina, had the task of developing a basic skills and knowledge course for newly hired law enforcement state troopers that met both state and Department of Energy requirements.

Techniques

An initial draft of the task list was developed, based on reviewing existing documentation (for example, work orders and required regulations) and interviewing employees and management. In a facilitated session, Hayes asked SMEs to review the task list and determine whether the task was performance or knowledge based. Subtasks with related KSAs were also noted for every task.

Next, each main task was posted to a wall. Experts were grouped according to tasks that fit their backgrounds and experience. Then an analyst coached them on developing instructional objectives for each task. Once appropriately sequenced, the expert teams and training staff worked independently to develop lesson plans and training materials.

At one point, an older, obsolete course was examined for relevant content. When the experts matched objectives of this course against the final task/skill/knowledge matrix, they discovered that more than 30 percent of the existing course material was irrelevant.

Rapid Analysis Tips

- Using a facilitated session that paired the instructional design team with the appropriate SME enabled the team to move very quickly from initial task listing to training development.

- Using a structured approach to develop content and objectives, analysts were able to identify and eliminate the "nice to know" information from the curriculum and concentrate solely on what was needed to perform the job.

Aviation Inspector Training

Jennifer Guitard, of Tecsult Eduplus, Inc., Halifax, Nova Scotia, was tasked with developing competency profiles of skills, knowledge, and attributes of several types of Transport Canada inspectors. The overall **goal** of the analysis was to conduct an intensive and detailed competency inventory (a task list structured by skills and subskills that lists the knowledge and attribute components of each skill) of aviation transportation inspectors—identifying common elements in order to train them as a group. A follow-on activity was to employ competency inventories as a means of training in specific areas.

Techniques

The analysis team began by reviewing all known documentation on aviation inspection, which included the following items:

- current regulations
- past task analyses
- checklists
- job aids

The team—usually in pairs, one representative from central headquarters and one from a regional office—then interviewed inspectors. Using this information, the team compiled a competency inventory. Once all task lists were compiled, the team performed an in-depth content analysis, looking for common elements. These elements formed the basis inspectors' course, followed up by courses specific to inspector type.

Rapid Analysis Tips

- Interviewing groups of inspectors concurrently provided richer material than from single or paired interviews.

- Interview location influenced the quality of the responses. Those conducted at headquarters had a more serious demeanor than those at the regional offices, where inspectors were in their own work environment and unable to mentally "escape" from their day-to-day tasks.

References & Resources

Articles

Ahlers, Robert. "Automated Task Analysis for Training Development." *Bulletin of ASIS,* August/September 1990, pp. 11-14.

Clifford, James P. "Manage Work Better to Better Manage Human Resources." *Public Personnel Management,* Spring 1996, pp. 89-102.

DeSalvo, Gerald L. "Write It Right." *Security Management,* May 1991, pp. 81-83.

Elliott, Paul. "Power-Charging People's Performance." *Training & Development,* December 1996, pp. 46-49.

Fetterman, Harry E. "Certifying Instructors In-house." *Technical & Skills Training,* August/September 1996, pp. 10-15.

Gayeski, Diane M., et al. "Getting Inside an Expert's Brain." *Training & Development,* August 1992, pp. 55-62.

Korotkin, Arthur L. "A Taxonomic Approach to Integrating Job Analysis with Training Front-end Analysis." *Performance Improvement Quarterly,* vol. 5, no. 3 (1992), pp. 26-34.

Miller, Janice A., and Diana M. Osinski. "Training Needs Assessment." *SHRM, White Paper,* 1997.

Reynolds, Angus. "The Basics: Job/Task Analysis." *Technical & Skills Training,* November/December 1994, pp. 5-6.

Rogers, James L. "Helping Clients Make Training Decisions." *Performance & Instruction,* July 1996, pp. 24-27.

Romano, Gerry. "Successful Task Analysis: All Questions Asked." *Technical & Skills Training,* October 1990, pp. 37-43.

Smith, Teresa L. "Job-related Materials Reinforce Basic Skills." *HRMagazine,* July 1995, pp. 84-90.

Still, Tim. "Training on a Tight Budget." *Technical & Skills Training,* February/March 1994, pp. 29-32.

Books

American Society for Training & Development. *The Best of Needs Assessment.* Alexandria, Virginia: American Society for Training & Development, 1992.

Bridges, William. *JobShift: How to Prosper in a Workplace Without Jobs.* Reading, Massachusetts: Addison-Wesley, 1995.

Lock, Edwin A., and Gary P. Latham. *A Theory of Goal Setting & Task Performance.* Englewood Cliffs, New Jersey: Prentice-Hall, 1990.

Patrick, J. *Training: Research and Practice.* San Diego: Academic Press, 1992.

Rothwell, William. *Mastering the Instructional Design Process: A Systematic Approach.* San Francisco: Jossey-Bass, 1992.

Swanson, Richard A. *Analysis for Improving Performance Tools for Diagnosing Organizations and Documenting Workplace Expertise.* San Francisco: Berrett-Koehler, 1994.

Zemke, Ron, and T. Kramlinger. *Figuring Things Out.* Reading, Massachusetts: Addison-Wesley, 1982.

Info-lines

Austin, Mary. "Needs Assessment by Focus Group." No. 9401 (revised 1998).

Butruille, Susan (ed.). "Be a Better Job Analyst." No. 8903.

Callahan, Madelyn R. (ed.). "Be a Better Needs Analyst." No. 8502 (revised 1998).

———. "Be a Better Task Analyst." No. 8503 (out of print).

Kirrane, Diane. "The Role of the Performance Needs Analyst." No. 9713.

Plattner, Francis. "Instructional Objectives." No. 9712.

Sharpe, Cat (ed.). "Basic Training for Trainers." No. 8808 (revised 1998).

———. "Course Design and Development." No. 8905 (revised 1997).

———. "Write Better Behavioral Objectives." No. 8505 (revised 1998).

Practice Task Analysis

Task analysis is the systematic identification of all the elements necessary to perform a job. The work and work processes that make up your analysis will determine what training programs need development. Practice doing a task analysis by using the exercises and worksheet.

Task Analysis Exercises

Gaining real experience with analysis without having to worry about someone evaluating your performance is easy. Try performing some sample field exercises to get your analytical skills honed.

1. Complete a task analysis for a simple, everyday household job like loading the dishwasher or making a bed. Have a "top performer" in your home verify the accuracy of your analysis work by using the task list to perform the job.

   _____

   _____

   _____

   _____

   _____

   _____

   _____

   _____

   _____

   _____

2. Complete a task analysis for a more complex task for which you have no experience, like tuning a car or painting a house. Interview at least two or three subject matter experts (SMEs) to gather task data. Have these SMEs review your analysis work for accuracy (or, if possible, use your analysis work to train a new employee!). Now, take this approach into the workplace. Select a simple office task (like mail distribution) and analyze it.

   _____

   _____

   _____

   _____

   _____

   _____

   _____

   _____

   _____

   _____

Job Aid

Task Analysis Worksheet

1. List the primary elements of the task or skill.

_____
_____
_____
_____
_____
_____
_____

2. Sequence the tasks in performance order.

_____
_____
_____
_____
_____
_____
_____

3. List any skills or knowledge needed to perform the tasks (prerequisites).

_____
_____
_____
_____
_____
_____
_____

4. Describe the desired outcome of performing this job. _Be specific. This information will be used to develop evaluation methods for your analysis._

_____
_____
_____
_____
_____
_____
_____

The 3-5-3 Approach to Designing Creative Training

Issue 9609

The 3-5-3 Approach to Designing Creative Training

AUTHOR:

Sophie Oberstein
Sophie Oberstein
1555 Beechnut Circle
Maple Glen, PA 19002
Tel.: 215.619.7929
Fax: 215.619.7935
E-mail: Soberstein@aol.com

Sophie Oberstein is an instructional designer and corporate training specialist, focusing on analyzing organizational training needs and customized interventions. She holds an MS in Human Resources and postgraduate certification in training and development. She also has authored numerous articles.

Reprinted 1999

Editor
Cat Sharpe

Production Design
Anne Morgan

The 3-5-3 Approach to Training

The 3-5-3 Approach was developed to encourage trainers to think creatively when designing training interventions. Training programs resulting from the use of this approach are generally more effective because they are more engaging and more memorable than traditional programs. This is because it encourages trainers to think "out of the box," or in ways that they are not usually inclined to think about developing a new training curriculum.

Once developed, different uses for this simple idea-generating technique become apparent. The 3-5-3 Approach can be taught to participants in a training program on creativity or problem solving. It also can be used for activities like naming a new course, determining when and how to get evaluations completed, or coming up with debriefing questions.

Benefits of Creative Training Programs

The 3-5-3 Approach was developed along the lines of thinking that creativity expert Edward De Bono describes this way: "If the purpose of chance in generating new ideas is to provide one with something to look at which one would not have looked for, then there may be methods of encouraging this process." That is, people may already recognize the need to go beyond the ideas that are comfortable or usual for them but may not have a model for structuring this exploration. The 3-5-3 Approach provides a framework to encourage and to contain our expanded thought process.

The reasons instructional designers need to shift their thinking out of their ordinary mode are much the same as those that trainers use for calling upon their participants to think "out of the box"—to come up with better solutions to problems or to experience greater success.

Why should trainers think about new ways to accomplish their objectives? Here are some of the goals corporations use to encourage creative thinking among their employees.

■ *Provide Exceptional Customer Service*
Often one must think in new ways to satisfy customer needs. For example, at Nordstrom department store, the story goes, a customer wanted a blue shirt with a white collar. Nordstrom didn't sell that particular style but did sell white shirts and blue shirts. To meet the customer's need, Nordstrom employees took the collar off of a white shirt and had it sewn on a blue shirt. Likewise, being creative in training design helps trainers meet participant needs. People learn in different ways, so thinking of several creative alternatives can lead to participant and customer satisfaction.

■ *Reinforce Company's Innovative Reputation*
Organizations often tout the creative accomplishments of their employees in order to prove that they are on the cutting edge. Likewise, your training programs can be on the cutting edge if you incorporate new ways to accomplish your objectives. This will, in turn, allow your training organization to be recognized as innovative and will further professionalize your position.

■ *Save Time and Money*
Frito-Lay reported reaping "hundreds of millions of dollars in savings and improved productivity" as a result of a sweeping creativity enhancement in the mid-1980s. In the same way, thinking creatively about how you format your training programs means you waste less of your organization's money or your learner's time. Unusual approaches keep you motivated because your work is more interesting. Stale ideas in business can create loss of time, money, and motivation. Stale ideas in a training program take away your audience's motivation. As philosopher Emile Chartier says, "Nothing is more dangerous than an idea when it's the only one you have."

■ *Promote Organizational Change*

The training department is often seen as the change agent or the change communicator in an organization. If you want to help participants become comfortable with change, you have to model your willingness to change. If training is about change, the programs themselves ought to model new ways of doing things.

■ *Maintain a Competitive Advantage*

In May 1986, *Training* magazine reported: "Uniqueness is required for a company to establish a permanent market position. The key to uniqueness is creativity." Change, upheaval, and restructuring are going to be with us for good. Organizations must be agile and so must their training efforts. If trainers wish to compete, they must be ready to see things in new ways and to offer the organization unique ideas and solutions.

■ *Provide Professional Development*

Many companies have realized the tangible benefits of offering employees professional development opportunities. If a company has committed to making this type of investment, the professional development programs offered must be effective. A creative training program is critical to adult learning and increases the chances that learning will be remembered and therefore transferred.

The 3-5-3 Approach

It is not a phenomenon limited to trainers. Most people, as soon as they have one solution to a problem, stop thinking about the problem. And in today's high-pressure work environment, that first solution may just do the trick. But what if there is a better solution than the one you came up with— one that costs less, is more reliable, or is easier to implement? One that better communicates the information you wish to impart? That is where failing to go further than your initial response can have negative consequences.

When a trainer gets stuck in a rut—choosing to use the same two or three training methods for every training program—harmful effects can result when participants don't perform better on the job after the trainer's intervention. Trainers who cannot choose between the wealth of training methods in existence may also fall back on old ways. But there is a simple method for breaking out of your patterns or for choosing among the multitude of techniques. That method is summarized in scientist Linus Pauling's statement: "The best way to get a good idea is to get lots of ideas." The way to develop a wider range of training options is to think past your first answer. The 3-5-3 Approach is a structured method for thinking this way.

First, pick out a particular training issue or problem. Now, with that in mind, go through the steps—3, 5, and 3.

3: The First Three Training Methods

In a nutshell, describe the first three training methods or instructional strategies that come to mind, then disregard them.

It is instinctive. Someone comes to you with a training need and your mind starts devising a program to fill the performance or knowledge gap that prompted the request. Often you are asked to put this program together under tremendous time constraints. The ideas you come up with then, on first being asked, are often the ones you end up using for your ultimate program. And these may not be bad ideas. They may, in fact, be ideas that have worked well in the past, have been well received by participants, and have been easy to implement quickly.

So this first step—just jotting down the first three ideas that come to your mind—shouldn't take much time to think about. The only thing you need to do during this initial step, in addition to listening to your natural thought process, is to imagine or make notes about how your three initial ideas would work. In other words, in response to a request for an interactive program on a company's employee benefits package, don't just think that you will play a game; imagine what kind of game

Model 1: Embracing a New Company Philosophy

The challenge that the training designer has to face in this model is how to get employees to embrace a new company philosophy that is not expected to be easily adapted.

3: Describe the First Three Training Methods or Instructional Strategies That Come to Mind, Then Disregard Them

Mini-lecture. Deliver a short presentation on the new company philosophy stressing to the employee the benefits of working in this new way.

Brainstorm benefits in small groups. Divide the participants into three subgroups. Assign each subgroup one of the following topics:

- Benefits of the new philosophy to me.
- Benefits of the new philosophy to the customer.
- Benefits of the new philosophy to the organization.

Have each subgroup brainstorm responses to its assigned topic and report back to the large group.

Think about the philosophy from another perspective. Ask participants to put themselves in the customer's shoes and to think about what kind of company philosophy would be important to them as customers of the organization.

5: Describe Five Additional Methods of Delivery

Create an advertising campaign. Divide participants into subgroups and have each subgroup prepare a print or audio advertisement promoting the company's new philosophy. Have each subgroup share its advertisement.

Hold a staged debate. Have another facilitator take the con side in a debate about the value of the new philosophy while you take the pro side.

Do a "stump the expert" activity. This variation on a debate has participants listing their own objections to the new philosophy and challenging you in the role of expert to defend the new philosophy.

Have participants defend the philosophy. This is the same as the "stump the expert" activity except that the participants take on the role of defender to your scripted anticipated objections.

Let participants create a philosophy. Give participants some details about the current situation that caused the need for a new philosophy. Have them try to come up with a philosophy that they would have proposed. Compare the philosophy they create with the real one.

3: Structure a Previously Generated Method

The last idea in Step 5 (**Let participants create a philosophy.**) allows participants to appreciate the situation that led up to the creation of the new philosophy. The following ideas also ask participants to explore the present environment in hopes that it will lead them to appreciate the new philosophy.

Put philosophy in the context of existing problems. Have participants identify problems in the current work environment. Discuss how the problems negatively influence their performance or motivation. Share the new philosophy and ask for ideas on how it will help relieve some of the current problems.

Put philosophy in the context of current customer service. Have participants imagine that after every customer interaction they currently have, they can go home with the customer and hear what the customer is saying about the company. What is the customer unhappy with? Then have them imagine the same thing after the new philosophy is in place. Is there any change in how customers perceive the company and its work?

Put philosophy in the context of current job satisfaction. Ask participants to share with the group their best and worst work experiences. Have them compare the different philosophies and values that were in place during each of the experiences. Ask them how the new philosophy might help create more positive experiences and less negative ones.

you will play. Would it be a *Jeopardy* game, with questions grouped by the different types of benefits available; or would it be a game of *$25,000 Pyramid*, where each player has to describe several benefits to a partner in order to get that person to name them? Thinking about your first idea in some detail will help make the next step in the 3-5-3 Approach easier because it will intrinsically start you thinking about multiple ideas.

The ideas you come up with in the first and second steps of this approach can be as idealistic or unrealistic as you wish. If there is anything worthwhile about an "out-there" idea, you will have a chance to bring it back to earth during the final step. Often, if you dream of how you would design a training program in an ideal situation, you can come pretty close to that ideal.

The last part of this step is to put aside the three ideas you have just generated. Isn't that a waste of time? Didn't you just come up with three very viable options for your program? You might have. But the first three ideas that come to your mind are not always your most creative. These are the old standbys, and you want to get beyond them.

Now you can think about other ways to accomplish your program objectives with less pressure—you have already created three options that you can always fall back on. So you can go on to the next step feeling confident that you will be able to meet your requester's desires.

5: Five More Methods

Now you will want to describe five additional methods of delivery. Why come up with eight ideas when only one will be used? Imagine an invention—a pen perhaps. Wouldn't you like to know that several ideas about its design, usefulness, and safety had been tested before it was manufactured and before you purchased it? Don't you want to have more than one choice about which one you purchase? Generating so many ideas has a similar purpose. You want to know that you have exhausted your inventiveness and come up with the best possible response.

Unlike the designs for pens that are discarded before the final design is produced, the ideas you think of using the 3-5-3 Approach don't go to waste. They might inspire you—or be usable just the way they are—in the future.

You are also less likely to censor yourself when you know that you have to fill in eight idea "slots." Because it is a challenge to complete this step of the 3-5-3 Approach, you will consider ideas that you might not have had you not been trying to achieve this quantity.

Once again, each of the ideas generated during this step should be completely thought out and can be as imaginative or unrealistic as you wish. At the end of this step, you should have eight ideas in mind or on paper. The last step will allow you to look at one of your ideas in more detail.

3: Structure One Method

Take at least one of your previously generated ideas and describe three ways to structure it. During this final step, you will be able to examine one of your previous ideas more closely and perhaps revise it so that it is practicable given your budget, time, and resources. The first two steps help you get your instructional strategy lined up; this final step lets you get your activity mapped out. Hopefully, this step also will get you excited about at least one of the new ideas you have generated.

Just select one of the eight ideas you have had so far. Even if you go back to your very first one—the idea of playing a game about employee benefits— this step will ensure your game is the best you can create. You are now going to think about three additional ideas for games beyond your first idea.

Case Study: Sharing Participant Expectations

You are about to pilot a training program that you are proud of. The objective of the program is to provide senior management with the skills they need to coach their employees. A few days before the pilot is scheduled, however, you realize that you don't really want to start off this program in the same way you have started other programs in the past. Particularly, you don't want to have participants share their expectations with you for the program in the same old way—asking each participant one at a time to state their expectations for the program and to chart all of their responses.

How do you have participants share their expectations about the coaching program? Use the 3-5-3 Approach to generate some alternatives.

3: Describe the first three training methods or instructional strategies that come to mind, then disregard them.

_____

_____

_____

5: Describe five additional methods of delivery.

_____

_____

_____

_____

_____

3: Take at least one previously generated method and describe three ways to structure it.

_____

_____

_____

_____

_____

_____

_____

After you have completed this case study, refer to _Model 2: Expectations for a Coaching Program._

If the game you thought of in the first step was *Jeopardy,* you might now think about making employee benefits into a game of bingo, go fish, or trivial pursuit. Bingo would require participants to block out squares on a card with the names of benefits that the instructor was describing. Go fish might have participants hold on to question and answer cards. A participant could read the question on the card to another participant who would either give the card with the answer to the person who asked or tell that person to "go fish." Trivial pursuit would use questions like the ones used in *Jeopardy,* but they would be presented in a board game format. Because many organizations overuse *Jeopardy* (initial idea), one of these other games might be better received.

And that's all there is to the 3-5-3 Approach. Think of three ideas and set them aside, think of five more ideas, and then develop the idea you like best into three additional approaches.

This whole process may take some time at first, especially if you are not used to pausing when a training request is first presented to you. As you continue to use it and it becomes more natural, the 3-5-3 Approach can actually save time that might be spent developing or piloting an idea that does not work out or that isn't as good as it could be. More experienced trainers may even eliminate the actual development of the first three ideas, if the information generated at that stage is not leading to actual methods.

The approach can also be used for processes other than selection of instructional methodologies. You can use it, for example, to determine how to sequence a program, how to present results to management, or how to determine which stress-reduction program your department should invest in. You can also teach the 3-5-3 Approach in creativity workshops as an idea-generating or a problem-solving technique.

Overcoming Design Obstacles

Despite the many benefits of thinking creatively when designing a training intervention, there are many potential obstacles to doing so:

Participant resistance ("You're not getting me to draw pictures!")

Facilitator resistance ("I'm not comfortable presenting creative material.")

Designer resistance ("Won't creative approaches steer us away from program objectives?")

Limited time and budget ("I don't have time to design new programs. Why reinvent the wheel?")

Organizational resistance ("My organization's culture does not encourage creativity.")

■ *Participant Resistance*
This can be expected when training approaches require them to put themselves on the line or to do more work than a conventional method might call for. Always be prepared with an alternative to the creative technique. For example, in an introductory exercise, have participants draw what creativity looks like to them. Tell those who don't want to draw that they can simply create a collage of words, or if even that idea isn't appealing, they can write out their definition of creativity.

If you still encounter resistance, either address it with the individual or talk to the group. Ask participants if they have any ideas about why the program is structured the way it is. Talk about the benefits of doing the activity the way it was designed. This is no different than a discussion you would have with any group of resistant participants. It is not specific to the fact that the program is being presented in a creative manner.

■ *Facilitator Resistance*
When you design a creative program for other facilitators to present, you may encounter resistance. It is actually better to hear these complaints up front than to hear none, and then find out later

Model 2: Expectations for a Coaching Program

Note: The ideas that follow are not meant to be correct responses against which you should compare your own responses. The objective of the case study is that you use the 3-5-3 Approach in response to a training need. Each time you use it, it will become easier, and the ideas you create will be more rewarding. These ideas are provided to give you another example of how the 3-5-3 Approach can be used and to help build up your storehouse of training methods.

3: Describe the First Three Training Methods or Instructional Strategies That Come to Mind, Then Disregard Them

Go around the room asking for expectations. Write them on a flipchart.

Have participants give you an index card stating what they hope will happen in the program and what they are afraid will happen in the program. This idea works best if the course is a multisession one. You can have participants share these cards with one another. You can compile them and hand out a master list at the following class session and hold a discussion at that time.

Have participants visualize the end of the session. Ask participants to imagine that the program is over. Ask them to reflect on what was the best thing they learned during the program. Prompt them to start their reflection with words like, "I'm so happy that we accomplished . . ." or "The best thing about this program for me was . . ." Keep them speaking as if the program had occurred in the past tense.

5: Describe Five Additional Methods of Delivery

Brainstorm expectations of a coach. Ask participants which parts of a coach's role they want to learn today. Because this is a training program on coaching, tie it in to reviewing the program expectations. Talk about what you expect a sports coach to do and then ask what they would need help doing as a coach in a business setting.

Have participants interview each other, then group themselves by common expectations. Ask participants to discuss "cocktail-party style" what their expectations are for the program. After about 10 minutes, ask them to group together with others who had similar expectations.

Create an ad for the course they really want to take. Have subgroups create posters advertising a course on your topic that they would really like to take. What promises does the program make? What will they get out of it? After subgroups have presented their "ads," the instructor should show an already prepared ad for the current course and a comparison can be made.

Have group write behavioral objectives for the program. Work together to create behavioral objectives for the program. You may just adapt these for the remainder of the workshop or you may use them as a comparison to the actual program goals.

Play "expectations bingo." Set up bingo cards that have different expectations someone might have for the program in each box. Ask the group at large to call out their own particular expectations. Participants should mark off the expectations raised if they match what is on their card. The card could list expectations that will be met or those that won't.

3: Structure a Previously Generated Method

Go around the room asking for expectations and write them on a flipchart. This is perhaps the most common way trainers currently get at expectations. In order not to be too off-putting for instructors, change the kinds of questions asked.

Ask, "Why did you choose to come to this class?"

Ask, "When you told people you were coming to this class today, how did you describe it to them?" In other words, how did you feel about coming here? What good points did you list for your friends? If you told your friends you thought coming here would be a drag, why? What do you think will be bad about this program?

Ask, "How could this class fail?" Use this information to make sure it doesn't.

Model 3: Thinking Out of the Box (A Meta Example)

Just as some learners learn visually and some learn by doing, for some program designers the 3-5-3 Approach will not be the most appropriate method to encourage creative thinking. This section will once again illustrate how the 3-5-3 Approach can be used, and it will also provide readers with eight additional ways that trainers can start thinking "out of the box."

3: Describe the First Three Training Methods or Instructional Strategies That Come to Mind, Then Disregard Them

Create a mind map. Put an objective of the program in a circle in the middle of a piece of paper. Let your thoughts flow freely using this method of branching out from the center. Write down anything that comes to mind about the objective or how to accomplish it. Do the same for the rest of the program objectives.

Conduct research. Several sourcebooks exist describing unique training activities. Some of these are listed in the "References & Resources" section at the end of this issue. Ask your peers for their ideas or attend a program on the same topic offered by another institution to get ideas for your own programs.

Revisit your objectives. Continually go back to the program objectives and ask yourself what activities you can create that will achieve the objective.

5: Describe Five Additional Methods of Delivery

Imagine a "fantasy" workshop. Imagine that there are no limits to how much you could spend on your program, no limits on how many trainers would be available, and no other impediments at all. Design the program you would lead in that context. Then adapt it for your current situation.

Play "devil's advocate." Ask yourself, "What can I do to ensure that participants will not learn this content?" Then, whatever it is, do the opposite.

Create lists. List all the factors that are important to you in the design of the program (for example, time, resources, variety of approaches, motivation). Then list all the topics you would like to cover. Compare the two lists and see if each topic meets your criteria in the factors you are concerned with.

Have one idea per hour all day long. Brainstorm in stops and starts. Keep the topic in the back of your mind all day, stopping hourly to record a new idea. Some creativity theorists believe that the pauses are when real innovation happens.

Follow your participants back to work. Imagine the participants back on the job the day after your training program. What will they be doing? How will they use what you have taught them? Design a program that mirrors the next day at work.

3: Structure a Previously Generated Method

The second idea in Step 5 (**Play "devil's advocate."**) looks at how to be creative in the design of a training program from another perspective—the devil's advocate. The following ideas also ask users to imagine they are wearing a different "hat" when approaching the problem.

Put on the hat of negativity. Design the program as you normally would. Upon completion, ask yourself a series of questions like the ones that might come from the most resistant participant. For example, ask: "What's boring about this idea?" "What will go wrong?" "What will participants complain about?" Design around these ideas.

Put on the organization's hat. Take a training program you have created and ask yourself a series of questions from the point of view of the most demanding client. For example, ask:

- "Is this program worth my money?"

- "Will going through the program mean the participants can do what I want them to?"

- "Will this program be perceived as a perk by my employees?"

Design around these issues.

Let the idea wear hats. Take the perspective of the activity you have designed. Say your idea is to create a game. Let the game ask such questions as:

- "If I weren't a game but a puzzle, how would I work?"

- "What about if I were a role play?"

- "What about a lecture?"

Pick the iteration that sounds the best after imagining the answers to these questions.

that your creative activities are not being used in the classroom. You can help ensure that the facilitators do present the program in the creative manner in which it was designed by anticipating facilitator resistance and addressing it in the train-the-trainer session.

Instructor resistance occurs frequently, particularly if the facilitator will be a subject matter expert rather than a trainer, and can result from not knowing how the activity will work, the confusion a creative activity can cause, or the work it takes to set up. Make sure the trainers have seen the activity in its entirety. Give them a chance to practice facilitating it while you observe. Once again, talk about the benefits of presenting this way—for instance, in terms of learner retention. Discuss their comfort level in leading the activity and perhaps set up a gradual schedule so they don't have to facilitate the activities alone in the beginning.

■ *Designer Resistance*

Other designers can derail your creative impulses. People who are not as creative as you won't see the good in your idea right away. These people need to be assured that you have not forsaken the program objectives in designing your creative activities. The concerns of other training designers may be justified. If an idea is too "out there" or doesn't replicate behavior that the participant will ever be asked to do on the job, it might not be the right program. Creative activities should never derail the learning; they should only enhance it.

Designers are also concerned with the sequence and flow of the training program. Your creative approaches should not be jarring for participants. Activities should be varied so that after something especially creative, participants have a chance to come back to a more traditional approach. One creative activity right after another can cause loss of effect.

■ *Limited Time and Budget*

This is an objection liable to be raised by anyone involved in the project—from the subject matter experts, to trainers, to participants. Designers must be shown that the creative approach can make difficult material more readily understandable or that it can make the objectives come alive so that less time will be spent on long lectures. Organizations need to know that the money they spend on creative programs is well spent. The more you can demonstrate measurable, bottom-line results of training, the more organizational commitment to future creative efforts you will receive. Participants may feel that an interactive program takes more time away from their jobs than a more traditional program. The opposite is often true. Some creative techniques (for example, multimedia, case studies, peer coaching) actually require less time away from the work site. When training sticks, as creative programs often do, less time is needed for refresher or reinforcement training.

■ *Organizational Resistance*

Organizational resistance is difficult to counter. One of the main problems is that the organization cannot visualize what your finished program will look like until you show it to them. The more you can share your plans, the benefits to the participants, and the benefits to the organization, the better. Showing how creative training programs at other companies in your industry have increased sales or generated acclaim can be extremely helpful; for example, NJ Transit's creative approach to teaching participants about safety got national recognition—not for the trainers but for the organization. Make sure you ask members of the organization to sit in at your pilot so they can see how your crazy-sounding idea really looks. Make sure you have enough time after the pilot to make changes based on any feedback you receive.

Using the 3-5-3 Approach

People in every occupation can get in a rut. Some don't even realize that their standard mode of operation has become stale. For trainers, who are expected to be innovative and engaging, the use of old ideas can be particularly noticeable. The 3-5-3 Approach can be used to create a spark of innovation in your training programs. This approach is just one way to expand your thinking. It is a framework in which you can experiment with going beyond your initial approach.

People need first to recognize the benefits of designing creative training programs for themselves, for their participants, and for their organizations. But beyond recognition, they must actually learn how to accomplish this goal. For people who don't consider themselves naturally creative, it can be especially difficult. But creativity can be fostered by the right environment, and learned like any other skill. Once you have made a commitment to thinking outside of your "box," you are on your way. The 3-5-3 Approach can take you from awareness to reality.

Quiz: How Creative Is Your Current Training Design?

Complete this self-assessment to get a sense of how creative your programs are now. Scoring and suggestions follow.

1. What is your own assessment of your creativity? Use the following scale to rate yourself:

   1—not at all creative
   2—a bit creative
   3—creative
   4—extremely creative

2. Answer *yes* or *no* to each of the following questions. (If your answer is "sometimes," answer *yes*. If your answer is "rarely," answer *no*).

	Yes	No
Are there areas in your work or your life in which you consider yourself a risk taker?	☐	☐
Can you be comfortable when you do not have an answer in a problem situation?	☐	☐
Do you have a positive attitude about new ideas?	☐	☐
Do you make decisions based on your intuition rather than the facts presented?	☐	☐
Do you practice active listening?	☐	☐

3. List up to three different ways each to accomplish the following training activities:

   Learn participant names:

   _____
   _____
   _____

   Form subgroups:

   _____
   _____
   _____

   Spice up lectures:

   _____
   _____
   _____

4. How important do you feel creativity is in designing training interventions? Use the following scale to rate your feeling on its importance.

   1—Not at all important; the content is all that matters.

   2—A bit important; all program objectives should be met first.

   3—Important; creative approaches make learning fun.

   4—Extremely important; participants don't get as much from a noninteractive program as they do from a creatively designed one.

5. Answer *yes* or *no* to each of the following questions. (If your answer is "sometimes," answer *yes*. If your answer is "rarely," answer *no*).

	Yes	No
Do you participate in any creative pursuits (for example, read or write fiction, draw, dance, play instrument)?	☐	☐
Do you attend any artistic programs (for example, operas, plays, dance performances)?	☐	☐
Do you know and tell jokes?	☐	☐
Do you like crossword puzzles or riddles?	☐	☐
Do you collect anecdotes or stories?	☐	☐
Do you make analogies easily?	☐	☐

6. List up to five different ways to ask the following question: **What did you get out of today's program?**

   _____
   _____
   _____
   _____
   _____

Quiz: How Creative Is Your Current Training Design? *(continued)*

7. Answer *yes* or *no* to each of the following questions. (If your answer is "sometimes," answer *yes*. If your answer is "rarely," answer *no*).

	Yes	No
Do your peers/supervisors tell you that your efforts are creative?	☐	☐
Do your participants give highly positive ratings on evaluations of your more unusual activities?	☐	☐
Do your programs get described as interactive or memorable?	☐	☐

8. Answer *yes* or *no* to each of the following questions. (If your answer is "sometimes," answer *yes*. If your answer is "rarely," answer *no*).

	Yes	No
Have you attended workshops on creativity or right-brain thinking?	☐	☐
Is there anyone whose work you admire for its creativity that you are in regular contact with?	☐	☐
Do you read books or articles on creative thinking?	☐	☐

9. List up to five different answers to the following question (answers will not necessarily be correct): **How can you measure the height of a skyscraper?**

_____

_____

_____

_____

_____

10. Answer *yes* or *no* to the following questions. (If your answer is "sometimes," answer *yes*. If your answer is "rarely," answer *no*).

	Yes	No
Have you ever rearranged the furniture in your classroom (for example, taken away chairs, put chairs in a circle or a V-shape)?	☐	☐
Do you ever play music or hang artwork in a training room?	☐	☐
Do you have participants change seats or form new groupings during a training program?	☐	☐
Do your brainstorm lists typically contain eight or more items?	☐	☐
Do you run at least one true pilot before rolling out a program?	☐	☐
Do you set aside time for creative thinking about each training program you design?	☐	☐
Do you ever attend training programs on topics similar to the ones you deal with?	☐	☐

Quiz: How Creative Is Your Current Training Design? *(continued)*

Scoring

1. If you answered…   Assign yourself a score of…

1 0
2 1
3 2
4 3

Your own perception of how creative you are can have a strong positive or negative impact on the programs you design and on your creativity. Not only artists and musicians with natural-born talent are creative. If your score on this item is 1 or 2, remember that creativity is a learned skill. Like any skill, there are barriers to overcome in order to learn it. A negative self-perception is one of those barriers.

2. Assign yourself one point for each *yes* response.

Creativity flourishes when one is able to function without all the answers. The need to be right all the time is the biggest obstacle to new ideas. If your score on this item is three or lower, you may want to practice deferring judgment and living with uncertainty for a time until the right approach presents itself.

3. Add up all of the ideas you generated on this item and subtract 3.

Learning participant names, forming subgroups, and moving away from standard lectures are just three of the elements that are common to most training programs. Just because these factors are the same does not mean you must go about completing them in the same way for every program. If your score on this item is 4 or lower, try to vary the way you present common material. Ask your peers or read training sourcebooks for new ideas on how to accomplish the regular elements (for example, learning guidelines, housekeeping, going over the objectives or agenda) that are contained in most training programs.

4. If you answered…   Assign yourself a score of…

1 0
2 1
3 2
4 3

Many creative people fight off their own creative impulses under the assumption that the work environment is not the place for these to surface. Others feel creative approaches take away from the program content. These beliefs are discussed in the section "Overcoming Design Obstacles." If your score on this item is 0 or 1, ask your peers or supervisors if they have had success with creative approaches or read articles on the benefits of creativity in training before you write off utilizing creative approaches to learning.

5. Assign yourself one point for each *yes* response.

While indulging in creative pursuits or diversions in your spare time is not a requirement to be creative in training design, it can open your mind to new ways of doing things. If your score on this item is 3 or lower, give your mind a workout occasionally by taking a pottery class, doing a jigsaw puzzle, or attending an opera.

6. Add up all of the ideas you generated on this item and subtract 1.

If you have ever asked a group a question and received back only blank stares, you know that the way you ask a question can affect the response. If your score on this item is 1 or 2, try sitting down before your next training program to come up with new ways of asking for the same information.

7. Assign yourself one point for each *yes* response.

While self-perception is important, it is often not as accurate as the perception of an objective outsider. If your score on this item is 1 or 2, or if you couldn't answer this question because you didn't know what others thought of your creativity, ask for feedback. Feedback is a big part of creativity—you have to put your ideas out for review, as outrageous as they might seem. Don't be hurt if they are shot down, but if they are accepted by reviewers, chances are you should pilot them with a group.

Quiz: How Creative Is Your Current Training Design? *(continued)*

8. Assign yourself one point for each *yes* response.

Creativity is something that often gets pushed to the side in today's stressful and demanding work environment. If you have outlets to continue to learn about and nurture your creativity, you are ahead of the game. If your score on this item is 1, try tapping into some sources to inspire and refine your creative impulses.

9. Assign yourself one point for each answer you generated.

Your ability to think concretely about abstract issues, or programs that have yet to be designed, is crucial. Answering questions about measuring the height of a skyscraper can help you break out of your normal mode of thinking to be able to generate real possibilities. Some possible answers to the problem include: measuring the shadow of the building and constructing a geometric equation to determine the skyscraper's height; holding a weighted piece of string from the roof and measuring the string; measuring one floor of the building and multiplying by the number of floors; comparing the building with a building whose height you already know; or looking at the architect's blueprint of the building before it was constructed. If your score on this item is 3 or less, practice with this kind of question some more. Ask yourself, for example, how many miles of subway track there are in your city or how many people are born in the world each day.

10. Assign yourself one point for each *yes* response.

Creativity extends beyond design. Even if you are facilitating a course someone else has written, there are opportunities for you to imprint it with your own creative approaches without touching the content. If your score on this item is 4 or lower, you might want to start experimenting with making other people's programs more creative so that you can then do it with your own.

Overall Score

40–46

If your score is in this range, your current training design may be too creative. Beware of going off the deep end and leaving your participants behind. They might see that your ideas are great and your mind is active but be confused as to what they are expected to do or how it all fits together. You can use the 3-5-3 Approach to limit your design impulses that may go beyond what is useful.

30–40

If your score is in this range, you have achieved a level of creativity that it is effective and exemplary. It is a level that recognizes that being creative is not in conflict with program objectives or content but that it has its own importance. As such, your efforts are probably a mixture of fun, interactive, and creative techniques balanced with the important components of good content. You can use the 3-5-3 Approach if you ever do find yourself in a rut—even creative people often need to alter their perspective.

20–30

If your score is in this range, your training design has probably been well received and your design efforts are probably quite well executed. You may wish, however, to spice things up for yourself and your participants by challenging yourself to be even more creative. Get feedback from peers, participants, and supervisors on what you are doing right now and then take those things a little further. You can use the 3-5-3 Approach to help you expand your creativity.

Less than 20

If your score is in this range, your training design is probably not as effective or engaging as it could be if you were to vary your approach. The first thing you might need to do is look at creativity as a skill that you can learn. You may need more exposure to the benefits of creativity for you and for your participants, or you may simply need to set aside more time to experiment and try to get comfortable with new techniques. You can use the 3-5-3 Approach to get started.

References & Resources

Articles

Ashkenas, Ron. "Real Innovation Knows No Boundaries." *Journal for Quality and Participation,* November/December 1998, pp. 34-37.

Caropreso, E.J., and R.A. Couch. "Creativity and Innovation in Instruction Design and Development: The Individual in the Workplace." *Educational Technology,* November/December 1996, pp. 31-39.

Caudron, Shari. "Corporate Creativity Comes of Age." *Training & Development,* May 1998, pp. 50-55.

Cocks, J. "Let's Get Crazy!" *Time,* June 11, 1990, pp. 40-41.

Ditkoff, Mitchell. "Ten Skills for Brainstorming Breakthrough Thinking." *Journal for Quality and Participation,* November/December 1998, pp. 30-33.

Feder, Brooke, and Richard Feder. "How to Turn Normal People into Stark, Raving 'Ideators.' " *Training & Development,* November 1997, pp. 11-12.

Flynn, Gillian. "Think Tanks Power Up Employees." *Personnel Journal,* June 1996, pp. 100-108.

Gordon, J., and R. Zemke. "Making Them More Creative." *Training,* May 1986, pp. 30-45.

Handley, C. "Why Frito-Lay Is Cracking with New Ideas: Use of the 'Creative Problem Solving' Process Is Paying Off at the Snack Food Giant." *Purchasing,* May 3, 1990, pp. 84A2/3.

Jones, Michael. "Getting Creativity Back into Corporate Decision Making." *Journal for Quality and Participation,* January/February 1997, pp. 58-62.

Kiely, T. "The Idea Makers: The Importance of Creativity Training in Business." *Technology Review,* January 1993, p. 32 (9).

Liebman, S. "The 3-5-3 Approach to Creative Training Choices." *Training & Development,* February 1995, pp. 11-13.

Lizotte, Ken. "A Creative State of Mind." *Management Review,* May 1998, pp. 15-17.

Markides, Constantinos. "Strategic Innovation." *Sloan Management Review,* Spring 1997, pp. 9-23.

McDermott, Brian, and Gerry Sexton. "Sowing the Seeds of Corporate Innovation." *Journal for Quality and Participation,* November/December 1998, pp. 18-23.

Stern, Sam. "How Companies Can Be More Creative." *HRMagazine,* April 1998, pp. 59-62.

Sweetman, Katherine J. "Cultivating Creativity: Unleash the Genie." *Harvard Business Review,* March/April 1997, pp. 10-12.

Verberne, Tom. "Creative Fitness." *Training & Development,* August 1997, pp. 68-71.

Wise, R. "The Boom in Creativity Training." *Across the Board,* June 1991, pp. 38-42.

Books

Albrecht, K. *The Creative Corporation.* Homewood, IL: Dow Jones-Irwin, 1987.

Biech, Elaine. *The ASTD Trainer's Sourcebook: Creativity and Innovation.* New York: McGraw-Hill, 1996.

De Bono, E. *Lateral Thinking: Creativity Step by Step.* New York: Harper & Row, 1970.

———. *Six Thinking Hats.* Boston: Little, Brown, 1985.

Edwards, B. *Drawing on the Right Side of the Brain: A Course in Enhancing Creativity.* New York: St. Martin's Press, 1989.

Eitington, J. *The Winning Trainer.* (2d edition). Houston: Gulf, 1989.

Kuhn, R. (ed.). *Handbook for Creative and Innovative Managers.* New York: McGraw-Hill, 1988.

Michalko, Michael. *Cracking Creativity: The Secrets of Creative Genius.* Berkeley, CA: Ten Speed Press, 1998.

Ray, M., and R. Myers. *Creativity in Business.* New York: Doubleday, 1986.

Scannell, E., and J. Newstrom. *Even More Games Trainers Play.* New York: McGraw-Hill, 1980.

———. *Games Trainers Play.* New York: McGraw Hill, 1980.

———. *More Games Trainers Play.* New York: McGraw Hill, 1980.

Silberman, M. *101 Ways to Make Training Active.* San Diego: Pfeiffer, 1995.

Thiagarajan, S. *Take Five: A Participatory Strategy for Better Brainstorming.* Amherst, MA: HRD Press, 1995.

Vance, Mike, and Diane Deacon. *Think Out of the Box.* Franklin Lakes, NJ: Career Press, 1995.

Von Oech, R. *A Whack on the Side of the Head.* New York: Warner Books, 1983.

Wujec, T. *Five Star Mind.* New York: Doubleday, 1995.

Job Aid

How to Select Your Best Approach

The 3-5-3 Approach results in the creation of multiple ideas on how to present the same content during a training program. Several factors must be considered before an instructional designer can determine the best idea he or she has generated. These factors include the culture of the organization, the cost of the idea, the resources available, and the comfort level of the facilitator. This checklist will help you to evaluate the ideas you have created so you can select the best one.

Assign each of the alternatives you devised using the 3-5-3 Approach to one of the numbers on the top row of the chart. For each idea, place a mark in the box below it if it meets the criteria in the far left column. Total the number of marks underneath each idea. You can either use the idea with the highest score or revise another idea to bring it to a more desired state.

	3			5					3		
	1	2	3	1	2	3	4	5	1	2	3
This idea meets program objectives.											
I have the time to develop this idea.											
I have the materials necessary to develop this idea (video, computers, demo equipment).											
I have the necessary resources (budget, space, trainers).											
The organization will like the idea.											
Participants will feel comfortable doing this.											
Participants will like it.											
I feel comfortable doing this.											
I like it.											
It fits in with the rest of the program.											
There is time in the program to do it.											
It is interactive and hands-on.											
It is unusual for me—a stretch.											
It meets the needs of several learning styles.											
It is not too confusing to explain.											
Total											

The material appearing on this page is not covered by copyright and may be reproduced at will.

Make Every Presentation a Winner

Issue 8606

Make Every Presentation a Winner

AUTHORS:

Jerry L. Wircenski
College of Education
Department of Technology &
    Cognition
University of North Texas
P.O. Box 311337
Denton, TX 76203-1337
Tel. 940.565.2714
Fax: 940.565.2185
E-mail:
    wircensk@tac.coe.unt.edu

Richard L. Sullivan
Director of Training
JHPIEGO Corporation
Brown's Wharf
1615 Thames Street,
Suite 200
Baltimore, MD 21231-3447
Tel. 410.614.3551
Fax: 410.614.0586
E-Mail: rsullivan@jhpiego.org

Editorial Staff for 8606

Editor
Madelyn Callahan

ASTD Staff Consultant
Eileen West

Revised 1998

Editor
Cat Sharpe

Contributing Editor
Ann Bruen

Winning Presentations

In business, presentations are a fact of life, particularly in the field of training and development. They can range from brief presentations before management to a series of talks that constitute a training program. The three critical areas for successful presentations, say experts, are planning, delivery, and follow-up.

Planning includes understanding the audience; assessing training needs and establishing objectives or goals for the presentation; researching the topic; designing the instruction; and matching facilities to program requirements. Delivery includes the presenter's style and ability to involve participants in meaningful learning activities and should follow fundamental guidelines for verbal and nonverbal communication, questioning and reinforcement, group interaction, and the appropriate use of humor. Follow-up includes the presenter's availability to provide feedback during the training, assistance to participants on the job, and evaluating transfer of learning.

This issue of *Info-line* will introduce you to techniques for planning, presenting, and following up your training to better ensure learning transfer.

Planning

Effective presenters plan every detail to ensure the success of their presentations. Areas to consider during planning are audience profile, training needs and objectives, the most effective training approaches, and required training facilities.

Audience Profile

Developing an audience profile means becoming familiar with your intended audience. During this critical phase of the planning, consider the following suggestions:

- Get a sense of who your audience is by asking about their education, background, and experience. Other useful information includes median age, job titles, and cultural orientation.

- Find out about your participants' interests and abilities. This can help you develop relevant instruction to meet your participants' needs.

- Determine the gender and cultural mix of the audience.

- Identify any issues or topics that should be avoided when addressing your audience.

- Find out if any members of your audience can serve as special resources—perhaps as a discussion leader or facilitator for break-out sessions.

- If possible, survey your audience to find out about their preferred learning styles. This information can help you select instructional strategies and materials.

Topic Research

Topic research involves educating yourself thoroughly in the content and subject matter of your presentation. This includes gathering library research, consulting subject matter experts (SMEs), surveying learners, analyzing corporate files, and so forth. During this phase of the planning process, consider the following suggestions:

1. Review training goals and objectives to better focus your research directly on training content.

2. Think of ways to conduct your research effectively. Some examples include interviews with subject matter experts, direct observation, surveys, questionnaires, corporate files, and production/waste records.

3. Using research and an audience profile, select an effective and appropriate instructional approach. Many approaches are available to presenters. These include case studies, discussions, demonstrations and practice, games and simulations, role playing, and small-group activities. Your selection of one or more of these approaches will depend on other audience- and program-related variables such as your objectives for the presentation, audience needs, and time limits.

4. Draft a presentation plan that includes goals or objectives, suggestions for introducing the topic, an outline of the presentation content, and outlines for participant activities.

Preplanning Countdown

To make sure your investment of time and energy is worth your efforts, do some preliminary thinking and organizing. The following questions will help you make the best choices for preparing a successful presentation:

1. Who are your participants? Do they share the same background and level of experience?

2. Have participants attended presentations similar to yours? Do they have any knowledge or skills that pertain to the topic of your presentation?

3. How many participants will attend the presentation? How will you use this information for selection of instructional strategies, meeting room, facilities, and materials?

4. How were the participants selected to attend the presentation? Have they volunteered, or were they required to attend?

5. What are the participants' preferred learning styles? Do most prefer lectures, demonstrations, simulations, group activities, or a combination of these approaches?

6. Do some participants have special learning needs? Do any have visual, hearing, or mobility difficulties? How will you accommodate these learners?

7. What are the goals of the presentation? Have you developed objectives to inform them of what they are expected to know and do after the presentation?

8. How much time will you have for the presentation? Will you include a question-and-answer period?

9. How well do you know your subject area? How will you research and prepare for your presentation?

10. How much will the presentation cost? Will you need to add to the budget to buy or rent audiovisual equipment? Is your presentation cost effective?

11. Do you have the support of management? Will managers and supervisors reinforce the training back on the job? How will you assist them in following up?

5. Develop a "catchy" title for your presentation that reflects its purpose. For example, instead of calling your presentation "Computer-Aided Design," how about a title like "Egad! It's CAD!—Exploring Computer-Aided Design."

6. Always rehearse your presentation. Even a short run-through is preferable to walking in cold.

Facilities Planning

The most dynamic presenter can fail in poorly prepared facilities. Even when the presenter is aware of the participants' backgrounds and has comprehensive instructional plans, the presentation may still fail if, for example, it is delivered in an overcrowded, hot room. Consideration of the physical environment is a crucial part of the planning process. Here are some suggestions for establishing a comfortable physical and social environment:

- Determine your size requirements. How big should the facility be to accommodate your audience?

- If you require break-out rooms, arrange for the appropriate number.

- Make sure all rooms are accessible to all participants. Are the rest rooms located nearby, and are they accessible to all participants, including those with disabilities?

- Try to make the room comfortable. Is it relatively free of distractions and noise from adjoining rooms and hallways? Can the climate controls in the room be adjusted?

- Determine your lighting requirements? Where are the controls? Can the room be dimmed as opposed to darkened?

- Determine what type of support media you are going to need? Don't forget to place a request for a microphone, if needed.

- Ensure that the furniture—tables, chairs, and desks—are comfortable and appropriate for the learning. Do you need a podium and table up front for your handouts and materials?

- Arrange the room in a way that suits your objectives and presentation format. Some examples include U-shaped or horseshoe, classroom style, circle, multiple tables, and theater style. (For more information see *Info-line* No. 8504, "Succeed in Facilities Planning.")

- Schedule enough time for meals, breaks, and phone calls, and have refreshments such as coffee, tea, water, and soft drinks available throughout the session.

Delivery

Even with solid research, good planning, and excellent facilities, some presentations still fail. Why? The presenter may not have a good, relaxed delivery style. Without that skill, participants quickly lose interest and become bored. Delivery style is important because presentations are primarily trainer centered. Three areas that presenters can work on to improve their delivery are verbal and nonverbal communication, questioning and reinforcement, and humor. But, first, they need to put the participants in a receptive mood.

Introduction Techniques

The introduction should both explain the topic of your presentation and capture the audience's attention. Do not attempt the second without covering the first. Remember, if your attention grabber does not tie into your topic, you will only confuse and distract the audience. Here are some suggestions for working up an interesting and effective introduction:

- State the purpose or goal of your presentation. All audiences want to know your objective(s).

- Make your introductions relevant to real-life experiences. This helps participants grasp the content of your presentation by relating it to something they understand.

- Ask questions to stimulate thinking on the topic of your presentation. Besides stimulating the thought process, this technique helps participants develop a focus on the topic. These might be rhetorical questions or a show of hands.

An On-Site Checklist

Before participants arrive, be sure to allow enough time to check the following:

☐ Locate the temperature and ventilation controls and regulate them so the environment is appropriate for your audience and equipment.

☐ Make sure the lighting is adequate. Know where the controls are so you can adjust the lighting easily for visual displays.

☐ Check the size of the tables to make sure there is sufficient space for participants to work with training materials.

☐ Test all audio, video, and demonstration equipment to be sure it is in working order.

☐ Check microphones to make sure they operate correctly and be sure you know how to adjust the volume.

☐ If you are using a writing board, be sure it is clean and that chalk or pens are available.

☐ Hang any posters, charts, or visuals applicable to your session. Make sure that these can be seen clearly from any location in the room.

☐ Set up a display of instructional material, projects, work samples, or other items relating to your presentation.

☐ Check information boards to make sure they are up to date with schedules, announcements, and other training-related notices.

☐ When appropriate, place name cards and training materials on tables before participants arrive.

☐ Have back-up supplies handy such as extra pens, paper, tape, and flipchart pads.

Caution: Introduction Ahead

A good introduction will get you started in the right direction. Here are some suggestions for preparing a strong beginning and getting your participants involved:

Give participants a clear picture of your presentation by discussing your objectives in the introduction. Use an overhead projector or blackboard and list each objective neatly and in simple terms.

Describe the activities and assignments you will expect participants to perform. Make sure they understand what will be expected of them—group tasks, projects, and other outcomes.

Describe in specific terms what participants will be expected to do during the presentation, in between sessions, and after the training. Should they take notes as you speak, bring assignments to each session, do outside reading and research, and so forth?

Explain the nature of the evaluation system you have planned. Tell them if they will have an opportunity to critique the presentation and your performance and how you will be evaluating their performance.

Give trainees a specific schedule outlining due dates for their assessments. Participants need to plan their time so they can complete and submit their work on time and to the right source.

Explain how you plan to deliver your presentation. Describe your approach. Will you be giving an illustrated talk, demonstration, group presentation, or another approach? When participants know how you intend to provide the information, there are fewer delays caused by misunderstandings and surprises.

Keep your personal introduction short and to the point. Avoid reading your entire résumé, focusing on your numerous accomplishments, ad-libbing, or starting with "I started work back in 1967. . . ."

- Share a personal experience or anecdote that is universal. You will spark participant interest if they have experienced something similar. But limit your "war" stories; too many can turn off interest.

- Create interest with an imaginative visual. Weekend comic strips or editorial pages are full of motivational tools. Remember to check the copyright laws, and if necessary, ask artists for permission to use their work.

- Make a provocative statement. When applicable, this technique generates comments and discussion to help introduce your topic. Be careful with this one! It can also turn off your audience if not handled well.

- Give a unique demonstration. This works well with technical topics. You can then proceed from the introduction to explanations of the "why" and "how" of your demonstration.

- Use an interesting or famous quotation, or perhaps turn this quotation around just a bit to fit your topic. For example: "Ask not what work teams can do for you, but what you can do for your work team."

- Relate the topic to previously covered content. Perhaps the speaker who preceded you has established the groundwork for your presentation topic. (For additional information, see *Info-line* No. 8911, "Icebreakers.")

Verbal And Nonverbal Communication

In any presentation, how you say something is just as important as what you say. Experts have observed that the techniques used to communicate information often determine whether or not the information is received. To improve your presentations consider these suggestions for re-sharpening verbal and nonverbal communication skills.

Verbal

Pay attention to the sound of your voice. Your projection—the pitch, tone, and volume of your voice—is crucial for effective delivery. Vary the pitch, tone, and volume to draw emphasis to key points. For example, voice inflection can capture and hold participant interest. Beware of sounding monotone; that is the easiest way to lose your audience. Avoid the use of repetitive words or phrases such as "OK," "ah," "now," "like," and "Do you know what I mean?" Try to break bad habits such as unconscious long pauses between sentences and using "um" or "uh" while pausing. Talk to, not at, your participants. Deliver key words and concepts slowly. Less important material can be covered more quickly. The recommended rate of speech is about 110 to 113 words per minute.

Begin by capturing the attention and interest of your audience. The first moments of your introduction should set the tone of your presentation. They should make your audience want to know more about the topic. Examples of effective introductions include the following:

- a provocative statement

- a unique demonstration

- an illustration of how the topic relates directly to work experiences

- a topic-related visual

Communicate on a personal level with your participants. Be sure to pronounce and spell words that are difficult or technical. Reinforce this by writing out new words on a board or flipchart. Accept and praise ideas offered by participants. These individuals should feel very positive about being involved in your presentation. Your acceptance of ideas and observations will encourage others to get involved and contribute to the presentations.

Emphasize key points through relevant examples, questioning techniques, appropriate application activities, and the use of visuals. Use sufficient and relevant examples to assist participants in understanding the subject of the presentation. Examples should relate to work activities, personal experiences, or current events. Make logical transitions between topics. If transitions are too abrupt, participants may get confused and lose interest. Topics should be in logical sequence with smooth transitions between each one.

Nonverbal

Dress appropriately for the presentation. First impressions are important. Experts say participants often form an opinion about a presenter based solely on appearance.

Use eye contact to "read" participants' faces to detect comprehension, boredom, or lack of understanding. From the participants' standpoint, eye contact with the presenter is essential in order to make them feel they are part of the presentation. Arrange the training area for maintaining optimal visual contact.

The effective use of body language and gestures contributes to communication—to emphasize, show agreement, and maintain audience interest. Important points about body language to remember include the following:

Use quick, positive, and energetic movements of the hands, arms, and head. Keep the attention of your audience by making your movements unpredictable. Walk rapidly, but alter the pace of your stride as you make points and reinforce them. Coordinate movement and gestures with your delivery.

Pay attention to unconscious body language. Some gestures and movements that can distract your audience include fidgeting, pacing, and jiggling keys or coins in pockets.

Observe your audience's body language. Facial expressions, down-turned eyes, fidgeting, or slouching are signals of boredom, disinterest, or lack of understanding.

Use positive facial expressions. These include smiles, expressive eyes, looks of concern, empathy, and encouragement. Look at your face in the mirror. How do you communicate feelings and emotions? How do you use your eyes, eyebrows, and mouth to express yourself?

Never sit behind a desk or stand behind a podium or lectern during your presentation. This establishes a barrier between you and your participants. Put more life into your presentation by moving freely about the room and down the aisles. Presenters who sequester themselves behind the podium and venture out occasionally to the writing board or flipchart appear less than enthusiastic.

Walk toward participants as they respond to your questions. This encourages them to continue. As a participant responds, nod your head slowly to show you understand what they are saying, approve of their comments, and invite them to continue.

To be effective, demonstrate enthusiasm about your subject and presentation. Remember, sincere enthusiasm is contagious; it generates interest and positive feelings. Illustrate your points with visuals such as real models, mock-ups, transparencies, videotapes, slides, computers, posters, charts, flipcharts, work samples, or writing boards. Besides being worth a thousand words, pictures lend variety and creativity to a presentation, making it more interesting and stimulating.

Give clear directions for all activities so that participants have the opportunity to apply the new information and practice new skills. Participants should not at any point be wondering what is next, what they are supposed to be doing, or how they should be conducting activities. Because training sessions are designed to provide participants with an opportunity to acquire new knowledge, skills, and attitudes, presenters must plan for appropriate application or follow-up activities that may take place during the session or back on the job.

Provide closure to main segments of your presentation by drawing together the main points in a good summary. Summaries should be complete and brief, and they should provide an opportunity for participant feedback. They can be used for clarification at points during the presentation as well as at the conclusion of the presentation. (For more information, see *Info-line* No. 9409, "Improve Your Communication and Speaking Skills.")

Questioning And Reinforcement

Questioning provides participants with an opportunity to display their understanding of key points. Participants' responses not only tell you how effective your presentation is but also indicate how to adjust your delivery. When posing questions, you can address participants by name and involve them in the presentation. Questioning also gives you the opportunity to provide the positive feedback and reinforcement that are essential for effective learning.

Advantages

The use of questioning and reinforcement is helpful for the following reasons:

- It involves all participants in the presentation.

- It stimulates and motivates participants.

- It provides participants an opportunity to display their understanding of the topic.

- It promotes active, not passive participation.

- Participants have an opportunity to apply the knowledge and skills you have presented.

- Responses to questions provide feedback to the presenter as to the effectiveness of the delivery.

- The questioning process helps you evaluate individual performance.

- Questions create variety in presentations.

Levels of Questions

Low

Memory: The participant is required only to recall or recognize information.

Comprehension: The participant demonstrates an understanding of the material or the idea being presented; discovers relationships between facts; makes generalizations; or explains meanings.

Application: The participant solves practical problems through the use of ideas, principles, or theories.

to

Analysis: The participant solves a problem by breaking it down into its component parts and determining the relationships between them.

Synthesis: The participant solves a problem by using original, creative thinking; and composes or combines parts or elements to form a whole.

High

Evaluation: The participant makes judgments on specific criteria rather than opinions.

Disadvantages

There are, however, some aspects of questioning and reinforcement that can detract from your presentation:

- The overuse of low-level or short-answer questions may not challenge the participants.

- Questioning can be time consuming.

- Some participants may not wish to get involved in the interaction process.

- Some participants may attempt to dominate the interaction process.

Questioning and Reinforcement Tips

Carefully formulate questions during the planning process and use the following guidelines:

1. Write questions at a variety of levels, from the simple *yes/no* kind to those that require more thought. Questions such as "Why?" and "What is your opinion?" stimulate a lot of discussion.

2. Phrase questions carefully. Avoid ambiguous or vague questions since they may confuse participants and cause them difficulty in responding.

3. Make questions short enough to remember. When questions are too long, presenters have to repeat them.

4. Design questions to focus on key points or concepts of the presentation. Do not waste time asking about secondary or less important information. You want to be sure participants comprehend the most significant material.

5. Design questions so they do not suggest the answer and state them in a way that eliminates guessing.

6. State questions clearly for the entire group. Pause for a volunteer response or direct your questions to specific participants. Address participants by name, and then ask your questions.

7. Repeat participant questions and responses, especially if you are addressing a large group. This ensures that everyone can hear. It also gives the presenter an opportunity to clarify questions and responses and provides positive reinforcement to the participant.

8. On occasion, handle participant questions by pausing and then redirecting the question to another participant. This involves more participants in the discussions and creates more interaction.

Humor

Humor and laughter help improve, maintain, and enhance participant interest. Camaraderie begins to develop when presenter and participants share a pun, story, or other common experience. Humor fosters a "team" atmosphere and promotes a positive learning experience. You can integrate humor into your presentations in the following ways:

- Use topic-related cartoons, stories, puns, and anecdotes to emphasize and reinforce points throughout your presentations.

- Maintain a file of humorous stories, pictures, drawing, and related materials.

- Avoid humor that might offend or alienate your participants.

- Practice telling stories *before* your presentation.

- Laugh *with* not *at* others.

- Laugh at yourself, particularly when a story or pun flops. This puts your audience at ease and indicates you are comfortable with the group and self-confident about your presentation.

Follow-Up

Follow-up requires the presenter to be available for instructional feedback and performance evaluation both during training and in the work place.

During Training

Effective presenters often find that participants want to discuss various features of the presentation before, during, and after sessions. When presenters make themselves accessible to participants, they can resolve individual questions and concerns. By being available for feedback, presenters help to tie the session together, summarize important points, and provide closure. Here are some hints for making yourself accessible to participants:

- Take the time to greet and talk with participants as they gather before the presentation actually begins.

- Remain in the room during breaks to answer questions and interact with participants.

- Stay after the presentation ends to address individual questions and concerns.

Instructional Feedback

Presentations or training sessions that require assignments, projects, or evaluations give the presenter an opportunity for keeping participants apprised of their progress. Here are some suggestions for giving feedback on learning:

- Give participants clear written and oral instructions for all assignments and activities.

- Return participant assignments and materials with positive written and oral comments and suggestions. It is important to include encouraging remarks and reinforce participants' successes, particularly for participants who are experiencing difficulty.

- Return all assignments and materials promptly. Participants are anxious to know about their progress and begin working on weak performance areas. If you wait too long, they may lose enthusiasm.

- If appropriate, use a progress chart to map participants' activities and accomplishments.

- When session activities yield products such as projects, written material, or action plans, invite the authors to display or discuss their work. This motivates participants, and the materials serve as samples of satisfactory work products.

In the Workplace

Some presenters reinforce training with follow-up activities in the workplace. For example, on-the-job training or coaching would be effective follow-up activities for a variety of jobs, from management to manufacturing. Besides on-the-job training and coaching, presenters can assist managers and supervisors with actual workplace implementation and application of skills and knowledge gained from the presentation.

Posttraining evaluation is the presenter's most crucial follow-up task. To measure training success, presenters determine the degrees to which learners have accomplished training objectives. This determination is based on a comparison of work levels before and after the training. Pretraining assessment consists of determining the difference between expected and actual performance. If, for example, that difference is 10 percent, the presenter will want the posttraining to be significantly lower, say 0 to 4 percent, indicating little or no difference between the expected and actual performance. The best result, of course, would be a negative value indication that learners have exceeded the expected performance.

Knowing how to deliver your presentation in a more productive manner is a skill that anyone can learn. In today's corporate environment, flatter structures and more emphasis on teamwork mean communications skills are essential for all employees. Making use of the above suggestions for planning, delivery, and follow-up should result in winning presentations. All you need are forethought, practice, and follow-through in order to be successful.

References & Resources

Articles

Brody, Marjorie. "Visual, Vocal and Verbal Cues Can Make You More Effective." *Presentations,* October 1997, p. 34.

Brown, David A. "Delivering Power Presentations." *Security Management,* March 1997, pp. 29-30.

Bryant, Sue. "Speak for Yourself." *Marketing,* October 31, 1996, pp. 29-30.

Carey, James F. "Speak Out, Stand Out." *Journal of Management Consulting,* May 1997, pp. 39-44.

Daley, Kevin, and Irene Kim. "Don't Shy Away from Presentations." *Chemical Engineering,* November 1997, pp. 155-158.

Dervarics, Charles. "On Target: On Your Mark. Get Set. Present!" *Technical & Skills Training,* July 1995, pp. 6-8.

Harris, Richard M. "Practically Perfect Presentations." *Training & Development,* July 1994, pp. 55-57.

Luke, Robert A. Jr. "Managing Bunny Trails." *Training & Development,* January 1994, pp. 19-21.

Malouf, Doug. "The Seven Deadly Sins of Speakers." *Training & Development,* November 1995, pp. 13-15.

Smith, Terry C. "Listen Up." *Technical & Skills Training,* August/September 1994, pp. 21-23.

Warman, Wendy. "Six-Step Guarantee for Powerful Presentations." *Technical & Skills Training,* July 1977, p. 5.

Books

Bartel, C. *Instructional Analysis and Material Development.* Chicago: American Technical Society, 1976.

Bender, Peter U. *Secrets of Power Presentations.* Buffalo, New York: Firefly Books, 1995.

Broadwell, M.M. *The Supervisor and On-the-Job Training.* (4th edition). Reading, Massachusetts: Addison-Wesley, 1994.

Denham, Wendy, and Elizabeth Sansom. *Presentation Skills Training.* New York: McGraw Hill, 1997.

Draves, William A. *Energizing the Learning Environment.* Manhattan, Kansas: Learning Resources Network, 1995.

———. *The Successful Presenter.* Manhattan, Kansas: Learning Resources Network, 1994.

Finch, C.R., and J.R. Crunkilton. *Curriculum Development in Vocational and Technical Education.* (4th edition). Boston: Allyn and Bacon, 1992.

Gilbert, Frederick. *PowerSpeaking.* Redwood City, California: Frederick Gilbert Associates, 1996.

Jeary, Tony. *Inspire Any Audience.* Dallas: Trophy Publishing, 1996.

Jeffries, J.R., and J.D. Bates. *The Executive's Guide to Meetings, Conferences, & Audiovisual Presentations.* New York: McGraw-Hill, 1983 (out of print).

Laird, D. *Approaches to Training and Development.* (2d edition). Reading, Massachusetts: Addison-Wesley, 1985.

Lauffer, A. *Doing Continuing Education and Staff Development.* New York: McGraw-Hill, 1978 (out of print).

Krathwohl, David, and B.S. Bloom. *A Taxonomy of Educational Objectives. Handbook I: Cognitive Domain.* London: Longman, 1984.

Miller, H., and J.R. Verduin. *The Adult Educator.* Houston: Gulf Publishing, 1979 (out of print).

Mills, H.R. *Teaching and Training.* New York: John Wiley & Sons, 1977 (out of print).

Nadler, L. (ed.). *The Handbook of Human Resource Development.* New York: John Wiley & Sons, 1984.

Pike, Robert W. *High Impact Presentations.* West Des Moines, Iowa: American Media Publishing, 1995.

Sullivan, R.L., and J.L. Wircenski. *Technical Presentation Workbook.* New York: ASME Press, 1996.

Van Ments, M. *The Effective Use of Role-Play.* London: Kogan Page, 1983.

Verduin, J.R. Jr., et al. *Adults Teaching Adults.* Austin, Texas: Learning Concepts, 1977 (out of print).

Wilder, Claudyne. *The Presentation Kit: 10 Steps for Selling Your Ideas.* New York: John Wiley & Sons, 1994.

Info-lines

Cramer, Jerome. "Succeed in Facilities Planning." No. 8504.

Plattner, Francis. "Improve Your Communications and Speaking Skills." No. 9409 (revised 1997).

Preziosi, Robert. "Icebreakers." No. 8911 (revised 1999).

Presentation Planner

Here is a checklist to help you work on presentation planning, delivery, and follow up. **Directions:** Complete the checklist by checking yes or no next to each item. Note that "no" answers may indicate weaknesses in your process. Record possible solutions and ways to improve your presentation in the section for comments.

Planning

	Yes	No	Comments

Audience Profile

1. Determined number of participants and planned to accommodate that number.

2. Took into account participants' reasons for attending the presentation.

3. Reviewed audience background and experience and considered this information in planning of presentation.

4. Planned to include preferred learning styles of participants.

5. Identified participants' unique learning needs.

Topic Research

1. Established goals and objectives.

2. Reviewed presentation content for accuracy, relevance, and comprehensiveness.

3. Selected appropriate instructional strategies.

4. Allotted sufficient time for the presentation.

5. Developed instructional plans to accomplish stated goals and objectives.

Facilities Planning

1. Meeting room was comfortable. Temperature, lighting, were adequate.

2. Tables and chairs were arranged to suit participants' needs.

3. Training materials and name cards were clearly printed and ready in time for the presentation.

4. Participants used name tags.

5. All audiovisual equipment was checked and working in good order.

6. Writing boards and flipcharts were available.

7. Break-out rooms were available.

8. Meals and breaks were scheduled and refreshments were arranged for.

Facilities Planning *(continued)*	Yes	No	Comments

9. Information and bulletin boards were up to date.

10. As participants arrived for the training, presenter greeted them at the door.

Delivery

Verbal and Nonverbal Communications

1. Dressed appropriately.

2. Had satisfactory voice projection, pitch, tone, and volume.

3. Introduced presentation effectively; captured audience attention and interest in the rest of the presentation.

4. Maintained eye contact.

5. Used body language to express confidence and enhance presentation.

6. Used facial expressions effectively; engaged participants in discussions and invited them to contribute ideas and comments.

7. Moved around the room and gestured to emphasize and reinforce key points of the presentation.

8. Showed sincere enthusiasm.

9. Used gestures that were not distracting.

10. Communicated on a personal level.

11. Emphasized key points and used relevant examples.

12. Used effective visual materials.

13. Made logical, smooth transitions between topics.

14. Provided a comprehensive, easy-to-follow summary.

15. Gave clear directions for all activities.

Questioning and Reinforcement

1. Asked key questions.

2. Directed questions to the entire group.

3. Presenter targeted questions to individuals.

4. Addressed individuals by name.

5. Walked toward individuals when addressing them.

6. Offered participants praise and reinforcement.

Job Aid

Questioning and Reinforcement *(continued)*	Yes	No	Comments
7. Asked questions on a variety of levels.			
8. Increased participation and interaction by directing participants' questions to others in the group.			
9. Repeated or restated participants' responses for the benefit of the group.			

Humor

1. Used humor effectively. Jokes and stories illustrated key points.

2. Used humor that was acceptable to the group and never offensive.

3. Laughed with individuals, never at them.

4. Used topic-related cartoons, drawings, and illustrations to reinforce training points.

Follow-Up

During Training

1. Greeted participants as they gathered to attend the presentation.

2. Stood at the door and welcomed each participant individually.

3. Was available during breaks to answer participants' questions.

4. Was available after the presentation to answer additional questions and discuss concerns.

Instructional Feedback

1. Provided clear oral and written instructions for all assignments and activities.

2. Returned participant work promptly.

3. Returned participant assignments and other materials with positive written and oral comments.

4. Used a progress chart to map participant progress and illustrate their rate of achievement.

5. Displayed exemplary participant works as reference materials for the rest of the group.

In the Workplace

1. Arranged or conducted on-the-job training or coaching.

2. Assisted supervisors and managers with implementing the training.

10 Great Games and How to Use Them

Issue 8411

10 Great Games and How to Use Them

Editorial Staff for 8411

Editor
Madelyn R. Callahan

Revised 1999

Editor
Cat Sharpe

Contributing Editor
Ann Bruen

Production Design
Anne Morgan

Selecting and Designing Games

Trainers have long believed in the adage "live and learn." Not surprisingly, they have always known that experience is often the best teacher. Experiential learning in the form of trainer-conducted games is frequently more effective than traditional classroom methods in increasing learning and retention. Research shows that adults learn more effectively by doing—by using their new knowledge and skills—than by passively listening or reading.

One study concluded that within one year, adults are likely to forget 50 percent of what they have learned through exclusively passive methods. Another study indicated that approximately half of one day's learning may be lost during the ensuing 24 hours. In two weeks, an additional 25 percent may be lost.

Games frequently provide the basis for successful training programs. They aid in program preparation, instruction, and evaluation. Their strongest feature is the element of fun that relaxes, motivates, and involves every participant from the outset, making learning enjoyable and productive. Games also use the five basic senses, particularly sight, sound, and touch, making for a more comprehensive and effective learning experience.

Strictly speaking, games are competitive activities governed by rules that define players' actions and determine outcomes. For the purposes of this discussion, we will employ a broad definition of *games* that includes the formalized, competitive activities and various exercises, activities, or demonstrations (also known as structured experiences or participative group exercises).

Other experiential exercises, such as simulation, role play, and simulation games, are addressed in other *Info-line*s. These exercises represent a number of either very simple or extremely sophisticated and complex activities. Role play and simulation exercises use real-life situations and applications. Simulation games are both reality based and competitive.

Simple games appeal to a large number of trainers for the following reasons:

■ *Versatility*
Game components can be interchanged easily to create a new focus or an entirely new game, and many different versions of a game can be built on one model.

■ *Cost Effectiveness*
Resource materials for these games are easy to produce and obtain. Some games require no materials at all, and most games involve little more than paper and pencils, which every training budget can afford.

■ *Transfer of Learning*
Learning proceeds from group interaction, with the instructor serving as a guide or resource rather than a detached lecturer or presenter. The instructor facilitates the learning and is an active integral part of the training process.

This issue of *Info-line* will acquaint you with various types of games, their special uses and features, as well as when to use and how to implement them. It will discuss the effective designs and uses of the four most widely used games:

- icebreakers
- competitive games
- exercises
- puzzles

Effective games can have significant impact on your audience. They can sharpen your training session so that your group will comprehend the materials on several levels—cognitive, affective, and empathetic. Such meaningful experiences will increase participation and learning. To accomplish this, be sure to carry out each phase of the game properly and completely.

Start by choosing a room that will accommodate your group comfortably. Check the noise level inside and outside the building. Prepare the seating arrangements in advance, and test acoustics and audiovisual equipment.

Designing Games

Find out as much as you can about your audience, facility, and available resources. Become familiar with a variety of games—their content, time limits, themes, style, format, and required supporting materials. Then decide how you would like to use the game: to identify, examine, critique, or discuss a problem; to develop skills such as empathetic listening, communication, problem solving, decision making, or management; or to start up, conclude, or refresh a program.

Organize your activity by establishing clear and specific objectives. You can proceed on a logical course once you know where you are going. Design resource materials to fit the content, and compile a list of materials for every phase of the game: instruments, forms, information sheets, background reading, diagrams, charts, and props, such as matchsticks, toothpicks, cards, blocks.

Consider the participants' level of interactive training experience to determine how they may respond to particular games. Plan in sequence; each phase of an activity should enhance the next one. Ask another trainer's opinion of your design, and pilot your design by using a test group.

Build into the design ways to gather data: listeners, observers, or questionnaires, for example. Always be certain that games are adaptable to the needs of participants with physical limitations. Determine physical constraints of the game, particularly those that involve movement.

Design Hints

To design games that will enhance your training sessions, follow these tips for success:

- Use a flowchart to plan your steps, and time each step.

- Choose a basic structure—introduction, stages, conclusions—and then add detailed content.

- Prepare all handouts in advance and have them ready.

- Plan for the worst; have back-up activities in case your group is too slow, too quick, or too familiar with your first-choice game.

- Make sure that participants are always actively engaged and challenged.

- Schedule sufficient time for breaks and discussions to alleviate tension.

- Play the game before you use it to make sure you are prepared to administer it properly.

- Be flexible; your game is a learning experience that should evolve naturally.

Conducting Games

Clarify expectations at the beginning of your session and make sure that trainees understand the objectives and game rules. Misunderstanding can lead to resistance and disruptions. Make a contract with the group, agreeing on expectations, roles, responsibilities, and norms. Then make a checklist of participants' expectations; post them and refer to them during the game.

Intervene only when necessary; encourage participants to be assertive and not to rely on you to defend or protect them. Give support and be willing to accept it from the group. Ask for feedback and respond to it (see *Giving and Receiving Feedback* opposite). Be sensitive to whether trainees are comfortable with open or experimental activities. Pick up cues from their behavior and comments. Be prepared to handle participant needs as they arise (see the *The Inevitable Gremlins* on the following page).

Experiment with and learn from your experiences as a facilitator. Maintain good listening skills and a respectful attitude toward trainees by keeping eye contact, repeating for clarity, and answering questions objectively. Be spontaneous and flexible. Whatever the outcome of the game, turn it into a learning experience. Reassure participants that mistakes are part of learning and that they will not be penalized for failures. Finally, close your activities properly by helping participants resolve problems and apply their learning.

The Don'ts of Game Presentation

Guard against these common mistakes made by trainers:

- using excessively difficult or threatening games

- distancing yourself from trainees (share breaks and meals with them)

- using the same techniques repeatedly

- giving long explanations

- changing the game to appease a few people in the group

- becoming more concerned with the game than the learning goals

Facilitating Games

Experts agree that this is the most important step of the learning process. This is the point at which participants examine their experience systematically. Facilitation methods may include a combination of discussion, observer's reports, instrumentation (questionnaires and surveys), and feedback and analysis. Without your planning and guidance, trainees cannot learn adequately. To ensure success, you should do the following things:

- Choose your role in the presentation. Will you act as leader, participant, or observer?

- Decide how trainees will participate: individually, in small groups, or as an entire group?

- Give participants a focus. Should you focus on specific behaviors, attitudes, or problems?

- Decide when to intervene *during* the activity in addition to providing wrap-up procedures.

- Provide supplies such as paper, pencils, markers, flipcharts, forms, and graphs.

Giving and Receiving Feedback

Games, like any learning situation, benefit greatly from constructive feedback. The following considerations will help you improve your group's productivity and participation:

- Establish a climate for testing new behaviors, taking risks, sharing information, and exploring alternatives.

- Establish feedback norms for listening, asking questions, and describing behaviors.

- Listen to and try to understand others' points of view without personal bias.

- Ask questions to get a thorough understanding of the problem. Show your interest with open-ended questions that invite comprehensive rather than yes-or-no answers.

- Be specific. Focus feedback on participants' behavior rather than on their qualities.

- Focus feedback on observations rather than inferences, on what you can see or hear rather than interpretations and conclusions. If you share interpretations and conclusions (it is sometimes valuable to do this), identify them as such.

- Describe the particular behaviors exhibited *during the game.* Do not be concerned with general or known behaviors associated with group members.

- Specify strengths first, then offer concrete suggestions for improving other areas. For example, say, "You are very articulate and observant, but you are most effective when you focus directly on particular discussion themes."

- Ask for a reaction to your suggestion. The trainee may not accept or may want to modify your suggestion.

- Try to close your discussions with agreements, particularly during the processing of competitive games. If you have listened to one another and clarified your ideas, you should be able to agree on specific changes and plans for improvement.

The Inevitable Gremlins

Every trainer must confront the dreaded gremlins of training sessions: the clowns, the hecklers, the disagreeable know-it-alls who manage to disrupt at least 10 minutes of your presentation. If it has not happened already, it is bound to sooner than you think. Take a look at the following pointers; they may make your life easier some day.

- Listen to the disruptive participants and let them know you are interested in their opinions.

- Give them responsibilities by asking them to be observers and to record others' viewpoints. Disruptive behavior is often an attempt to be heard; tell your dissidents that you welcome their *positive* contributions.

- Ask questions to find out what the problem participant really feels and needs.

- If personal problems cause the behavior, speak to the participant privately. Disrupters may become more cooperative once they have talked through problems.

- Reward cooperation and serious contributions.

- Never argue. Restate hostile questions in mild language and direct your answers to the group rather than the heckler. Remain calm and patient. If you lose your temper, your audience may decide to support the heckler.

- Rephrase superficial or hostile questions as statements so that the questioner must take a position.

- Form groups of two to five participants so the disrupter will no longer influence the entire group.

- Use processing time to discuss the activity or program in progress and to emphasize expectations and norms. The discussion will undoubtedly include the problem of disruptive behavior.

- Turn the disrupter over to the group. If a participant wants to argue with you, ask for responses from the group.

- Tell persistent arguers that you would like to hear more of their opinions during a break or after the exercise.

- Ask the disrupter to compare theirs and other members' ideas and to restate others' ideas. This will force the disrupter to listen to and understand other perspectives.

- Compliment the opinions of your talkative participants, but make it a point to solicit the input of less vocal members.

- Deal with class clowns by asking them to explain their remarks in objective terms so that everyone can comprehend their statements.

- Control sidetracking by asking the disrupter and the group to relate off-subject comments to discussion themes.

Facilitating Hints

There are a number of guidelines that are specific to facilitating games. Assess actual learning and determine the degree of goal accomplishment; then examine the reasons for similarities and differences in these two areas. Share discoveries about the learning process as well as personal discoveries, and analyze impressions of how the group worked together. Identify strengths and areas for improvement.

Decide how to apply the training to jobs. Examine personal and job-related changes and make specific plans to implement the changes. Finally, suggest ways to improve the game.

Icebreakers

Whatever the facilitator does at the beginning of a presentation sets the tone for the rest of the training. Thus there is a need for some sort of activity that will get your participants warmed up—an icebreaker.

Icebreakers present program materials in a more interesting way than introductory lectures by instantly involving the entire group; participants become acquainted by sharing personal attitudes, values, and concerns. Nonthreatening activities relax participants and reduce anxiety, encouraging spontaneity even among timid and shy trainees.

Icebreakers establish the pace and tone of the program and help build enthusiasm. They motivate the group quickly with activities that involve physical and emotional energy. In addition, they orient participants to the group's resources and give the group a sense of identity, helping to build trust. Finally, they establish the identity of the trainer as a facilitator rather than a lecturer. For examples of icebreakers, see *What's My Line* at right and *Roles of a Good Trainee* on the next page.

Icebreakers acquaint participants with one another and put them at ease (trainees are more receptive when they are ready to learn). These nonthreatening warm-up activities make a smooth start by introducing and focusing the program. They let participants know that *they* are responsible for their learning and that the trainer's job is to facilitate the learning. They also show participants what kind of trainer you are—demonstrative or reserved, conventional or innovative, program or participant oriented.

15 Icebreaker Tips

To properly set the stage for your training program, follow these icebreaker guidelines:

1. Develop an environment conducive to group interaction by providing a common experience or helping the group share experiences.

2. Never *insist* that participants share personal data.

3. If a trainee is using too much time during a personal statement, intervene tactfully and put the group back on course.

4. Determine the length of your opening activities by estimating the duration of the program (a four-hour session would require only six or seven minutes of icebreakers).

5. Consider your group's expectations when determining the level of activity and involvement of your icebreakers.

What's My Line?

Objective

To illustrate the importance of first impressions and stereotyping.

Procedure

This is a variation of the self-introduction game, using name, job, and favorite hobby. Instead of introducing themselves, however, participants are asked to introduce the person on their right, using strictly guesswork—that is, no clues are exchanged.

After a brief observation of the person on their right, ask participants to introduce him or her with a first name, job, and favorite hobby that they "think" he or she has, giving brief reasons for their guesses.

The person being guessed will then respond with the correct information before proceeding with his or her own introduction. Continue around the circle until everyone has been introduced. (If participants have done the first part of this exercise in a small group, have them return to a large group setting, positioning themselves so that the same person is still on their right. Participants will then introduce the person on their right to the larger group.)

Discussion Questions

1. How accurate are first impressions? What do we base them on?

2. Have you ever opted not to meet someone, based on your first impressions?

3. What are stereotypes? Why do we make them?

4. Do you now feel more comfortable with this group than when you arrived?

5. Do you know more about the people here than when you first arrived?

Materials Required

None.

Approximate Time Required

20–30 minutes.

Jacqueline V. Markus, Department of Communication, Arizona State University, Tempe, AZ

Roles of a Good Trainee

Objective

To create a constructive climate for discussion in a training session.

Procedure

In many groups of entry-level trainees, the participants have previously attended few, if any, formal training programs. Therefore, it is often helpful to establish clear norms for what constitutes acceptable (productive) trainee behavior.

One way to accomplish this quickly, with a certainty of hitting the "right" rules, is to present (orally, by handout, or by overhead transparency) a set of predeveloped guidelines for behaviors that trainees would ideally engage in or avoid. This approach has the advantage of clarity, but has the potential danger of creating a limiting, rule-filled environment. Presented in a positive manner, however, with the use of a handout such as the following example (especially when it is "spiced up" with some humorous illustrations), this exercise can have considerable success.

Example:

Roles of a Trainer (Facilitator)

1. Challenges thinking.

2. Creates lists.

3. Summarizes.

4. Shares ideas.

5. Provides handouts.

6. Serves as a model.

7. Raises questions.

8. Guides discussion.

9. Restates ideas.

10. Provides constructive criticism.

Alternative Procedures

1. Engage the group (early in the session) in a discussion of the productive and nonproductive behaviors they have seen (or can think of) on the part of seminar participants. This has the value of involving them in the creation of their own norms for their behavior.

2. Prepare printed tent cards with participants' names on the front and five rules of appropriate seminar behavior on the back. While the name faces outward to the trainer and other trainees, the rules are visually present to the trainee at all times as a constant reminder.

Materials Required

Possible handout, transparency, or tent cards.

Approximate Time Required

5–10 minutes.

From Games Trainers Play, *by E.E. Scannell and J.W. Newstrom. Copyright 1980 by McGraw-Hill Book Company, New York. Used with permission. All rights reserved.*

6. Select activities that will be appealing to specific kinds of groups. For instance, machine operators might not be as receptive to activities involving fantasies or imagination as would therapists.

7. Consider the background of your group and temper innovative activities with the knowledge of their cultural preferences.

8. Choose opening activities that are appropriate for the particular program. Employee motivation programs, for example, may use more flexible activities than management development programs.

9. Use icebreakers that involve physical energy to stimulate your group.

10. Use icebreakers as an opportunity for *you* to become acquainted with your group.

11. Use them to indicate what will be expected of the group and what the group can expect of the program.

12. Use them to show how you intend to participate in the program.

13. Choose icebreakers that will establish an environment for discussion.

14. Use icebreakers you are comfortable with. Some experiential activities may take time and participants' attention away from the specific subject matter. If you prefer more conventional methods that give you more control, use them.

15. Avoid using icebreakers for very large groups in which they will lose their intensity.

Competitive Games

Turning games into competitions helps to break up the routine of your training session. Participants can have fun and learn at the same time.

Competitive games are active, experiential forms of learning; that is, participants learn from their own actions rather than from what others tell them. This active involvement is motivational—most trainees respond to competition and the incentive to win. In addition, games appeal to learners of differing abilities, because everyone has the opportunity for involvement, and the valuable experience gained from games makes everyone a winner. Moreover, games provide a safe atmosphere for taking risks, away from real-world penalties for mistakes.

Games help trainees retain information and encourage unself-conscious behavior that can be analyzed in discussions. Games are social as well as educational tools, providing participants information about their own behavior in relation to others. For examples of competitive games, see *The Number Game* and *Archeological Game* on the following pages.

Games energize participants and promote interaction. They engage participants' interest and attention and provide them with a common experience. Games reinforce learning and training by demonstration. Among the skills they develop are strategic and critical thinking, communication, negotiation, problem solving, and decision making. Competitive games can inject energy into a low point of the program after lunch or at the end of the day, or they can be used to recap important points and close a presentation.

15 Competitive Game Tips

To use competitive games to best advantage, follow these guidelines:

1. Keep games in line with learning objectives.

2. Be familiar with your game. Trainees cannot be enthusiastic if they are interrupted constantly with corrections of game instructions.

3. Prepare by playing the game several times with friends.

The Number Game

Objective

To allow participants to discover (or reinforce) some principles of adult learning through hands-on activity.

Procedure

Distribute eight copies of "The Number Game" to each participant. Ask them to place a blank sheet of paper over the numbers so they cannot see the placement of the numbers. Tell them this is a simple hand-eye coordination exercise in which they are to work as fast as they can within a given time period. Then tell the participants: "Remove the blank sheet of paper. With pen or pencil, draw a line from No. 1 to No. 2, to No. 3, and so forth, until I say 'Stop.' OK? Go!"

Allow 60 seconds, and then say: "Stop. Please circle the highest number you reached and jot down the number '1' in the upper right-hand corner."

Repeat this procedure seven more times, each time allowing 60 seconds. Make sure each sheet is numbered in sequence.

Discussion Questions

1. In all candor, how did you feel when you were going through the exercise? (*Note:* Responses will be "nervous," "frustrated," "upset," "mad," and so forth.)

2. "Practice makes perfect." If this is really true, we all should have shown a consistent increase in the number attained with each attempt. Is that true for each of you? If not, why?

3. Did anyone have an increase every time?

4. Many of us experienced a slight decline, or "learning plateau." What might cause this?

5. If our trainees are likely to experience these plateaus, how can we be more understanding of these situations and adapt to them?

Materials Required

A quantity of "The Number Game" sheets (4 per person, printed on both sides).

Approximate Time Required

15 minutes.

From Games Trainers Play, *by E.E. Scannell and J.W. Newstrom. Copyright 1980 by McGraw-Hill Book Company, New York. Used with permission. All rights reserved.*

Archeological Game

Objective

To point up how our screening mechanism filters out unwanted data, details, minutiae. This is important so we can get through the day and get our tasks accomplished without being sidetracked by trivia bombardment.

Note: This objective is *not* given to participants, since this perceptual phenomenon is what they will learn from the game.

Procedure

Give the participants the following instructions:

1. "You are to function as archeologists. This means you are interested in reconstructing a given culture based on artifacts you discover.

2. The culture you are concerned with is the United States in the year 7000.

3. You are in a 'dig' and come up with a small, flat, round object. It has a man's face on it; the man has a beard. The object is a U.S. penny and has this year's date on it.

4. *Without* reaching for a penny from your pocket or purse, come up with as many characteristics of the U.S. coin and culture at that date as you can. This is what archeologists do all the time. You will have to rely on your memory to recall the data on the penny. You are in competition with the other teams. You have five minutes for the task."

At the five-minute mark, call time and ask participants to total their cultural characteristics. (The totals typically run in the "teens.") Get a verbal report from the team with the highest number of characteristics, and list its data on a flipchart. Anticipate items such as these:

- bilingual (English and Latin)
- architecture (if Lincoln Memorial is on rear)
- system of writing
- appearance conscious (Lincoln's beard)
- liberty loving (liberty)
- metallurgy
- calendar
- coinage system

- hero worship (Lincoln)
- a federal government ("E Pluribus Unum")
- religion ("In God We Trust")
- mining
- sewing skills or tailoring (Lincoln's shirt and coat)
- cloth production
- dress conscious (coat, tie)
- system of numbers
- agriculture (if a "wheat" penny)
- patriarchal society

Also anticipate friendly rivalry—the losing team will deny the validity of certain cultural traits listed by the winning team. Add (new) items from the other teams to your flipchart list.

Discussion

To process the game, ask participants what was learned. Some possible responses from the groups (list on a flipchart) are: importance of teamwork (several heads are better than one); a group leader is not necessary; importance of background or perception (different groups see different things).

At this point, add: "I'd like to pick up on the perception aspect. Was the task difficult to do, relying solely on memory?" [Participants respond "Yes."] "Why was it difficult to remember what is on an object that you handle *daily?*" [Pause at this point, for this is *the* profound question of the game.] Some possible participant answers are: "We don't pay attention to it. It's not important information. We take it for granted."

At this point, say: "Yes, we overlook the detail, the trivia, because we have a mechanism in our heads (phenomenon of perceptual choice or selective attention) that screens out the unimportant. This is a tremendously helpful device because it allows us to get through the day without getting bogged down by the innumerable stimuli that bombard us constantly—trees, signs, houses, stores, cars, clothing, colors. But at the same time, our screening mechanism may work the other way. It may screen out data we *should be cognizant of*—for example, to call old Harry to our meeting. We forget him, and he gets mad at us. So our screening device works for good and for less than good. We must be aware of this perceptual process and try to keep it from overlooking the important stimuli, which also are out there."

4. Organize all game materials and keep extra supplies of paper, pencils, and other items that are used up quickly or are easily misplaced.

5. If you are using handouts, know when to distribute them for greatest impact and least disruption.

6. Choose comfortable and workable seating and space arrangements.

7. Play the game at the time when participants will benefit most—during the introduction, instruction, or conclusion of your program.

8. Do not over-explain the game; introduce it briefly. If you use a written statement, make sure it is clear and precise.

9. Take questions only after you have completed your explanation. This will also give you time to ease into the game.

10. Choose a method of forming groups that best suits your particular game. If your objective is to build trust, random selection would produce groups of unacquainted individuals. Groups of two or three are ideal for sharing personal data. Groups of people who are wearing one or more of the same colors may also agree on other topics and work well as a team.

11. Refrain from intervening in the game frequently. Participants are playing the game to learn from their interaction with one another.

12. Avoid the role of trainer as authority figure or expert.

13. Assess learning and outcomes without appearing as a strict "evaluator."

14. Remind participants of the time five to 10 minutes before the game is scheduled to end.

15. Allow sufficient time for the entire activity when you plan your program schedule. Games that must be continued later lose momentum, and participants may lose interest before the outcomes.

Exercises

Exercises are structured learning experiences that help to enhance the training atmosphere. They are versatile instruments that can be used in a variety of ways.

Exercises accommodate a wide range of formats and purposes—short or long, simple or complex. They are conducted by the trainer, the group, or both. Exercises can be oriented either toward individuals or groups (of any size). Some exercises involve physical movement while others focus on discussion or writing, but they do not all require supporting materials. They can be made into games by adding competition.

Numerous sources for exercises exist—publishers, colleagues, or training programs—but they also can be created by trainers to suit specific needs, or they can use input from the group members themselves or from supervisors. For examples of exercises, see *Hand to Chin Exercise, One- and Two-Way Communication, What Do People Want from Their Jobs?* and *The Lemon Exchange.*

Exercises can be used to open or close a presentation, to illustrate specific learning goals, or to reinforce learning. They put participants at ease and maintain high participant involvement. In addition, exercises generate information for analyzing a particular problem or behavior and facilitate general and personal learning.

16 Exercise Tips

To make sure that you use exercises to their fullest advantage, follow these guidelines:

1. Select exercises that will fulfill your learning objectives best. Then consider the element of fun.

2. Organize all resource materials and equipment in advance.

3. Make sure the group understands instructions. Hand out written instructions if necessary.

4. Be straightforward.

5. Use relevant practical content that trainees can apply to their personal or job-related goals.

6. Use realistic time frames.

7. Choose the most effective time during the program to use your exercise. If you use it too early in the program, participants may miss the point; too late, and they may be less attentive.

8. Avoid covering too much material. If participants appear overwhelmed, edit extraneous material without causing breaks or long pauses in the activity.

9. Determine when to intervene *during* the exercise, particularly for the longer, more complex exercises.

10. Remind the group of the learning objectives throughout the activity.

11. Clarify your role in the learning process so trainees will know how you can assist them.

12. Show trainees that you identify with the group and are interested in learning with them. Sometimes this may include participating in the exercise.

13. If the exercise is long and multifaceted, use a summary sheet to help reinforce the training.

14. Use facilitation procedures that are appropriate for your group.

15. If you use observers, prepare them adequately with background information.

16. Avoid serious conflicts, too much emphasis on fun, or the generation of too much data. These problems will inhibit discussion and facilitation.

Hand to Chin Exercise

Objective

To illustrate that actions may speak louder than words.

Procedure

As you demonstrate, ask the group to extend their right arms parallel to the floor. Say, "Now, make a circle with your thumb and forefinger." [Demonstrate the action as you speak.] Then continue, "Now, very firmly bring your hand to your chin." [*Note:* As you say, "Bring your hand to your chin," bring your hand to your *cheek,* not your chin.] Pause. [Most of the group will have done what you have, that is, brought their hands to their cheeks.] Look around, but say nothing. After 5–10 seconds, a few in the group will realize their error and move their hands to their chins. After a few more seconds, more people will join in the laughter, and your point can then be verbally reinforced—a trainer's actions may speak louder than words.

Discussion Questions

1. Did you ever hear the saying, "Don't do as I do; do as I say"? Do we practice this as trainers?

2. We all know actions speak louder than words. How can we use this knowledge in our jobs to help ensure better understanding?

3. Communication is always a scapegoat for performance problems. What other barriers to effective communication does this exercise suggest?

Materials Required

None.

Approximate Time Required

5 minutes.

One- and Two-Way Communication

Objective

To demonstrate the many problems of misunderstanding that can occur in a one-way communication.

Procedure

Prepare a diagram similar to the one shown here. Ask a volunteer to assist in this demonstration. Explain to the group that the volunteer is going to describe something to them, and their task is to simply follow instructions in sketching out the illustration.

Give the volunteer the figure. Have the volunteer turn his or her back to the audience so no eye contact is possible. The volunteer can use only verbal communication (no gestures, hand signals). Furthermore, no questions are allowed on the part of the group. In brief, only one-way communication is allowed. When the exercise is completed, project the correct figure on the overhead projector and ask participants to judge whether their drawings are at all similar to it.

Discussion Questions

1. How many of us got confused and just quit listening? Why?

2. Why was the one-way communication so difficult to follow?

3. Even two-way communication cannot ensure complete understanding. How can we make our communication efforts more effective?

One-Way Communication Diagram

(*Note:* If time permits, this activity can be immediately followed with another volunteer using a comparable illustration but allowing for full and free two-way communication.)

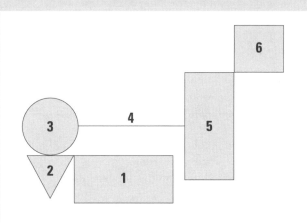

Materials Required

Diagram, as shown.

Approximate Time Required

10–20 minutes.

What Do People Want from Their Jobs?

Objective

To give participants an opportunity to discuss what factors motivate employees.

Procedure

Distribute copies of the form, "What Do People Want from Their Jobs?" Divide the group into subgroups of three to five people each. Ask each person to indicate which of the 10 items listed is thought to be of *most* importance in contributing to employee morale. Weight the items from 1 through 10, assigning 10 to the most important item, 9 for the next, and so forth, in a reverse order so that all 10 numbers are used.

Have each group total the individual weights within their group. Rank the 10 items under the column marked "Group."

Advise the group that this same scale has been given to thousands of workers around the country. In comparing rankings of both employees and supervisors, the typical supervisory group is ranked in the order shown under "Factors."

When employees are given the same exercise, however, and asked what affects their morale the most, their answers tend to follow this pattern [mark in the "Employees" column]:

1. Full appreciation of work done

2. Feeling of being in on things

3. Help on personal problems

4. Job security

5. High wages

6. Interesting work

7. Promotion in the company

8. Personal loyalty of supervisor

9. Good working conditions

10. Tactful discipline

Note that the top three items marked by the employees are the last three thought to be important for them by their supervisors.

Discussion Questions

1. In comparing your group's ratings with those of other groups ("Employees" column), what factors might account for differences of opinion?

2. Why might supervisory evaluations ("Supervisors" column) be so different from their employees ("Employees" column)?

3. If this form were to be used in your department or office, how similar would the results be?

Materials Required

Copies of the form "What Do People Want from Their Jobs?"

Approximate Time Required

20 minutes.

What Do People Want from Their Jobs?

Individual	Group	Factors	Supervisors	Employees
		High Wages		
		Job Security		
		Promotion in the Company		
		Good Working Conditions		
		Interesting Work		
		Personal Loyalty of Supervisor		
		Tactful Discipline		
		Full Appreciation of Work Done		
		Help on Personal Problems		
		Feeling of Being in on Things		

From Games Trainers Play, *by E.E. Scannell and J.W. Newstrom. Copyright 1980 by McGraw-Hill, New York. Used with permission. All rights reserved.*

The Lemon Exchange

Objective

To vividly illustrate the importance of individual differences, the need for astute observational skills, and sensitivity to personal characteristics.

Procedure

Bring an adequate supply of lemons (or almost any fruit).

1. Distribute one to each member of the group. Direct each person to examine his or her lemon carefully by rolling it, squeezing it, and so forth. Ask them to *get to know their lemon* (always good for a few laughs). Tell them to pick a name for it. Encourage them to identify in their minds the strengths and weaknesses of their lemon.

2. Collect all the lemons and mix them up in front of the group.

3. Spread out all the lemons on a table and ask participants to come forward and select their original lemon. If conflicts develop over their choices, assist the parties in reconciling their differences, or simply note the failure to agree and use that as a basis for later discussion. (*Note:* In smaller groups of up to 25 people, the vast majority successfully identify their own lemons.)

Discussion Questions

1. How many are very sure they reclaimed their original lemon? How do you know?

2. What parallels are there between differentiating many lemons and differentiating many people? What differences are there?

3. Why can't we get to know people just as rapidly as we did our lemons? What role does the skin play (for lemons and for people)?

4. What human behavior does this bring to light?

Materials Required

A sufficient quantity of lemons (or other appropriate substitute).

Approximate Time Required

20–30 minutes.

From Games Trainers Play, *by E.E. Scannell and J.W. Newstrom.*
Copyright 1980 by McGraw-Hill, New York.
Used with permission. All rights reserved.

Puzzles

Puzzles are another valuable means of enhancing your learning environment. Like icebreakers, competitive games, and exercises, they encourage active participation.

Puzzles are versatile in form and use, and can be used as either solo or group games. They can be solved orally; visually—with handouts, charts, or blackboards; or physically—with blocks, straws, or sticks. Puzzles are more comfortable ways of exploring ability than stressful, inhibiting exams. They encourage imaginative solutions to problems without the pressure to "be creative." By illustrating alternatives, puzzles point out the value of investigating possibilities in areas such as career planning, taking risks, and assessing the potential of others.

Puzzles illustrate that effective approaches to problem solving use personal touch as well as logical thought. Participants can see themselves improve as they become better at solving the puzzles. This builds confidence and helps develop skills for planning strategies. Puzzles also let people know how they compare with others. For an example, see *Cake Cutting Puzzle,* opposite.

Puzzles involve everyone in an activity and engage the participants' curiosity and imagination. By providing variety and novelty, they show that learning can be exciting and interesting. Puzzles reinforce learning by explaining subject matter or by introducing and demonstrating the importance of both creative and logical approaches to problem solving. They also can be used to break the ice and put participants at ease.

12 Puzzle Tips

To use puzzles effectively, follow these guidelines:

1. De-emphasize the idea that "brain teasers," word games, crossword puzzles, and other puzzles require superior cognitive skills. Less confident participants may avoid puzzles that reveal shortcomings.

2. Use moderately difficult puzzles to stimulate your audience. Extremely difficult puzzles will frustrate and alienate trainees.

Cake Cutting Puzzle

Procedure

Draw an aerial view of a cake on the flipchart as shown in figure 1. Tell the group: "A woman had baked a cake for her party to be attended by eight guests. Her (and your) task is to produce eight pieces of cake with only three cuts of the knife."

Figure 1. Can you produce eight pieces of cake with only three cuts of the knife?

Bird's eye view

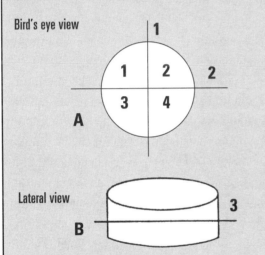

Lateral view

Figure 2. Lateral Cut Method: (A) Right angle intersecting cuts produce four pieces; (B) a lateral cut produces eight pieces.

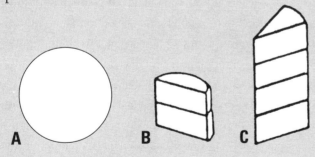

Figure 3. Stacking Method: (A) A vertical cut down the middle produces two pieces; (B) stacking the two pieces and cutting them vertically produces four pieces; (C) a final stacking and cutting of the pieces produces eight pieces.

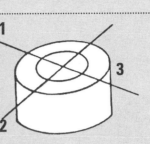

Figure 4. Center Cut Method: Two vertical cuts and then a center circular cut are made to produce eight pieces.

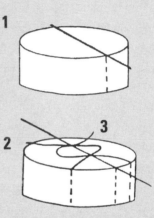

Figure 5. Disgustingly Sneaky Method: Two curved lines and a center straight cut produce eight unequal pieces.

Note: No one said the pieces had to be equal or the cuts made via a straight line. Remember, this is her party with her guests, and she can cut the cake any way she wishes.

Discussion

Ask: "What does the puzzle tell us?" Some answers are: "There may be more options than we think; let's stretch our imaginations and we can produce solutions that are varied and unique."

The puzzle may be used to stimulate thinking about problem solving, creating approaches, and alternative seeking.

From The Winning Trainer *by J.E. Eitington.*
Copyright 1984 by Gulf Publishing, Houston, TX.
Used with permission. All rights reserved.

3. Choose a straightforward puzzle. Some puzzles distance the activity from its purpose.

4. Explain objectives clearly and succinctly at the beginning so that these can be reinforced throughout the activity and the entire training program.

5. Always have a back-up puzzle in case too many trainees are familiar with your first choice.

6. Encourage trainees to approach the puzzles with the intention of taking risks and exceeding their self-imposed limitations.

7. Select a puzzle with a variety of solutions so that the activity is open to creative approaches.

8. Challenge your trainees to find new approaches and options.

9. Make them aware of the valuable uses of right-brain, creative thinking, but point out that there are times when logical left-brain thinking is more appropriate.

10. Keep a large stock of supplies. Participants often make several attempts and many mistakes before they solve puzzles.

11. Always budget enough time to integrate the experience into the training. Most puzzles are representative and must be interpreted at the conclusion.

12. Use puzzles simply for fun, as a change of pace, or to relax or stimulate participants. Puzzles offer a refreshing break from learning, enabling participants to resume their training with renewed energy.

Playing Those Mind Games

Researcher David Meier conducted a study that focused on the use of *mental imagery*—"the guided, self-controlled or spontaneous imagining of any thing or situation that can be seen, touched, smelled, heard, tasted, or experienced in any way." Through his research, he concluded that learning tools using fantasy and the imagination improve retention and recall.

Meier also described a mental imagery training technique, known as *guided imagery,* by which trainers use mental imagery to help trainees do the following:

● develop management skills

● set goals

● reduce stress

● increase confidence and assertiveness

● improve memory, communication, and problem-solving skills

● augment conventional training

These techniques provide experiential activities that are guided by a facilitator and carried out with a partner or by the entire group. For an example of how to use mental imagery, see Meier's professional development game opposite.

Development Through Mental Imagery

This game can be played with groups of any size. Its purpose is to help people identify their unique talents and strengths and discover how best to use them in their professional lives. The group leader can use the following script as a guide, varying it with experience to fit the needs of each specific group. The total time for this procedure is approximately 45 minutes.

■ *Introduction*

In just 45 minutes you will have a better understanding of what your unique talents and strengths are, and you will have a wealth of ideas of how best to use them to achieve higher levels of professional success and satisfaction. You will gain insight and a positive new sense of direction in your career. And you will come out of this experience with a set of guidelines for developing and enriching your professional life over the next year or so. This insight and direction will not come from me, but from you. I will provide the form, but you will provide 100 percent of the content. You will probably find the form to be fun. We will use mental imagery followed by reflection and analysis. In the first imagery session, we will ask you to vividly review in your mind three peak experiences of your life and to become aware of the unique strengths and talents you exhibited in those experiences. Then, after analysis, we will ask you to step into the future and see yourself exhibiting those strengths and talents flawlessly and effortlessly in your professional life. We will ask you to observe what you are doing, and from that, to design your own marching orders for peak performance over the next year.

(*Note:* In the script that follows, the virgule (/) indicates a pause. Most pauses can be for three to five seconds, but follow your intuition when you are in the situation.)

■ *Preparation*

To prepare for the first imagery experience, just get comfortable and relaxed. You can do this easily by breathing a bit more deeply than usual and becoming aware of your breath/ just concentrate on your breath/ just let your whole attention focus on the feeling of the air coming into your body/ notice how pleasurable it is to breathe/ concentrate on the pleasure of breathing/ as you breathe in, feel your whole body being refreshed/ a tingling sensation/ energy/ and each time you exhale, let go/ relax/ inhale and receive pleasure and new energy/ exhale and relax/ becoming more filled with quiet energy/ becoming more deeply relaxed with every breath/ continue doing this for a moment, closing your eyes and getting ready to enter the rich world of your deep inner mind.

■ *First Imagery Session (five minutes)*

Return in your imagination now to a peak experience of your life. Relive a time when your unique strengths and talents shone without obstruction—a time when you were filled with energy and an easy flowing personal power—a time when you were free, open, fulfilled, fully alive, fully

yourself in all your strength/ relive this situation now/ how old are you?/ where are you?/ what are you doing, saying, feeling?/ be totally back there now/ and observe what strengths you are manifesting and how this feels/ take a moment to relive this experience fully now, with total recall and total awareness/// (pause for about one minute).

Now move away from this scene and pick a second time and place in your past that was a peak experience—a time when you were filled with energy and an easy flowing personal power/ (continue as above).

Now move away from this scene and pick a third and final time and place in your life that was a peak experience for you—a time when you were filled with energy and an easy flowing personal power/ (continue as above).

■ *Analysis*

We will bring the imagery session to a close now and ask that when you are ready, you return to this time and place, open your eyes gradually, and get ready to reflect on the experiences you have just had.

Divide a piece of paper sideways into three columns. In each column, record your deepest impressions of each of your three imagery experiences. Use words, pictures, or a combination of both. Just capture in any way you can some of the most important elements of each experience. Reflect particularly on what each experience has to teach you about your unique talents and strengths. Work quickly and without criticism. We will allow three or four minutes for this.

Now debrief with a partner. Find a partner and share your experience and insight at any level you care to. Most important, help each other find the common thread that runs through your three peak experiences. Help each other determine what all three experiences are saying about your unique talents and strengths. We will take about five minutes for this.

Now by yourself, spend the next two minutes synthesizing everything you have experienced thus far down into its essence. Create an annotated list of what you now perceive to be your main unique strengths and talents.

■ *Second Imagery Session (five minutes)*

You have now identified your unique talents and strengths. We want you to enter the world of your imagination a second time now to experience what it is like to manifest these talents and strengths fully in your professional life over the next year or so. You will enter the future and actually experience yourself exercising these talents and strengths in new and creative ways in your professional life. Out of this experience will come some rich and valuable insights regarding how you can direct your professional life for the maximum benefit both to you and to the organization and people you serve.

Your deeper mind already knows what you can do and must do to fully manifest your unique strengths and talents in your professional life. Through an imagery experience, you will now discover what that is.

Let's begin by becoming comfortable and deeply relaxed. (Repeat the instructions of the initial preparation session above.)

Now just let yourself become aware of the needs, problems, and opportunities that exist in your organization or your profession for which your unique talents and strengths are a good fit. Project yourself forward now to a situation where you have successfully met one of these needs, problems, or opportunities in a creative and exceptional way. You have shone. You have that feeling of success and fulfillment and deep satisfaction. You have been able to bring some of your unique talent and strength to bear, and it has worked beautifully. Be in that situation now/ feel how good it is to exercise your unique talents fully, to be fully alive, confident, successful, satisfied/ imagine yourself in that situation now/ what does it feel like?/ what do you see and hear around you?/ what is it that you have done?/ how have you done it?/ what were the steps that led up to your high performance, your success?/ see it all very vividly now/ and take a minute or so to observe everything you can about this situation in great detail/// (pause for about one minute).

Move away from this scene now and enter another one that speaks to another need, problem, or opportunity. Create a second situation, experiencing it even more deeply and vividly, where you have successfully exercised your unique strength and talent in your professional life. You have just turned in a truly exceptional performance/ feel the pride and the quiet satisfaction/ where are you now?/ what do you see and hear and feel?/ what, specifically, were you so successful at?/ what did you do?/ how did that come about?/ what were the specific steps that led up to your success and your sense of full satisfaction that you have now?/ experience this fully for a minute or so and observe everything with total awareness/// (pause for about one minute).

■ *Analysis*

We will bring the imagery session to a close now and ask that when you are ready, you return to this time and place, open your eyes gradually, and get ready to reflect on the experiences you have just had.

Now write nonstop for four minutes about your experience. What did you do? How did you do it? What were the steps that led up to your success? What allowed your talents and strengths to be fully exercised? What product, services, or benefits resulted from what you did? Write first on your first episode. Use words, pictures, anything to capture the essence of that experience. I will stop you in two minutes and ask you to go on to your second episode/// (pause for two minutes).

Now go on to your second episode, capturing in words and pictures as quickly as you can the essence of that experience. What strength and talent did you exercise? How did this manifest itself? What did you do and how did you do it? Write nonstop for two minutes/// (pause for two minutes).

Now debrief with your partner for five minutes, each of you sharing your experience at any level you care to.

(*Note:* At this point, distribute a handout to the participants that is a blank piece of paper with the following written on top: **Specific things I will do in the next year to exercise my talents to the fullest and be exceptionally successful and fulfilled in my work.**)

For the final exercise, complete this handout in any way that is most meaningful and useful to you. Be specific. What do you plan to do? How do you plan to do it? Mention specific people, places, dates, products, services, outcomes—whatever is most appropriate to your situation. You will be creating your job description, your marching orders, your professional development plan, for the next year or so. Be as detailed as you can, and use additional paper if you need it. We will take about 10 minutes to complete this final exercise.

■ *Close*

(*Note:* There are a number of options for closing this session, depending on the nature of the group and the amount of time remaining. Participants could have a final five-minute debriefing with a partner—preferably a different one than they had been working with. Or participants could share their main goals with the entire group for further feedback, suggestions, and refinement.)

Then, with a sense of how your unique strengths can be used to best advantage, go out and do it.

Contributed by David Meier

References & Resources

Articles

Abbott, Katherine. "Games That Work with Techies." *Inside Technology Training,* September 1998, p. 24.

Berry, Bart A. "Getting Training Started on the Right Foot." *Training & Development,* February 1994, pp. 19-22.

Boyd, Susan. "Ten Ways to Break the Ice Before and During Class." *Technical Training,* May/June 1998, pp. 6-7.

Duffy, Joseph R. "Creative Management: Does It Work?" *Quality Digest,* July 1991, pp. 58-67.

Ensher, Ellen A., and Jeanne Hartley. "The Employee Relations Game." *Training & Development,* December 1992, pp. 21-23.

Gunsch, Dawn. "Games Augment Diversity Training." *Personnel Journal,* June 1993, pp. 78-83.

Ireland, Karin. "The Ethics Game." *Personnel Journal,* March 1991, pp. 72-75.

Kirk, James J. "Playing Games Productively." *Training & Development,* August 1997, pp. 11-12.

Mattimore, Bryan W. "Imagine That!" *Training & Development,* July 1994, pp. 28-32.

McIlvaine, Andrew R. "Work Ethics." *Human Resource Executive,* August 1998, pp. 30-34.

Phoon, Annie. "Memory Massage: Review Games That Enhance Retention." *Technical & Skills Training,* January 1997, p. 4.

Thiagarajan, Sivasailam. "A Game for Cooperative Learning." *Training & Development,* May 1992, pp. 35-41.

West, Karen L. "Effective Training for a Revolving Door." *Training & Development,* September 1996, pp. 50-52.

Books

Baridon, Andrea, and David R. Eyler. *Sexual Harassment Awareness Training: 60 Practical Activities for Trainers.* New York: McGraw-Hill, 1996.

Boyan, Lee, and Rosalind Enright. *High-Performance Sales Training: 64 Interactive Projects.* New York: AMACOM, 1992.

Consalvo, Carmine M. *Outdoor Games for Trainers.* Brookfield, VT: Gower, 1995.

Eitington, Julius E. *The Winning Trainer.* Houston: Gulf Publishing, 1984.

Elgood, Chris. *Handbook of Management Games.* (5th edition). Aldershot, Hampshire, UK: Gower Press, 1993.

Engel, Herbert M. *Handbook of Creative Learning Exercises.* Amherst, MA: HRD Press, 1994.

Kirby, Andy. *Encyclopedia of Games for Trainers.* Amherst, MA: HRD Press, 1992.

Kirk, James J., and Lynne D. Kirk. *Training Games for Career Development.* New York: McGraw-Hill, 1995.

Newstrom, John W., and Edward E. Scannell. *Still More Games Trainers Play: Experiential Learning Exercises.* New York: McGraw-Hill, 1991.

Nilson, Carolyn D. *Games That Drive Change.* New York: McGraw-Hill, 1995.

———. *More Team Games for Trainers.* New York: McGraw-Hill, 1998.

———. *Team Games for Trainers.* New York: McGraw-Hill, 1993.

Scannell, Edward E., and John W. Newstrom. *Even More Games Trainers Play.* New York: McGraw-Hill, 1994.

———. *Games Trainers Play.* New York: McGraw-Hill, 1980.

Sikes, Sam. *Feeding the Zircon Gorilla.* Tulsa, OK: Learning Unlimited, 1995.

Thiagarajan, Sivasailam, and Raja Thiagarajan. *Each Teach: Harnessing the Power of Team Learning.* Amherst, MA: HRD Press, 1995.

———. *Interactive Lectures: Add Participation to Your Presentation.* Amherst, MA: HRD Press, 1995.

———. *Take Five: A Participatory Strategy for Better Brainstorming.* Amherst, MA: HRD Press, 1995.

Ukens, Lorraine L. *Getting Together: Icebreakers and Group Energizers.* San Francisco: Jossey-Bass, 1996.

———. *Working Together: 55 Team Games.* San Francisco: Jossey-Bass, 1996.

Info-lines

Darraugh, Barbara (ed.). "More Great Games." No. 9106.

Preziosi, Robert. "Icebreakers." No. 8911 (revised 1999).

Game Selection Checklist

The appropriate game can make your presentation or training session one of the most memorable and productive experiences of your trainees' careers—but before you select a particular game, know the answers to the following questions:

☐ What is your purpose for using the game? What should it communicate to the group?

_____

_____

☐ What is the game's central focus? How does it serve your learning goals for the group?

_____

_____

☐ How large is your training group? What are their backgrounds? Are they familiar with the training material? With each other?

_____

_____

☐ Is the game adaptable to the needs of your training program? Can you use it to introduce, demonstrate, or reinforce the training?

_____

_____

☐ How "playable" is the game? Try it. How is it organized? Does it work according to its instructions? Is it fun?

_____

_____

☐ Do you have the resources and facilities for the game?

_____

_____

☐ Is this game the best way to achieve your objectives?

_____

_____

Simulation and Role Play

Issue 8412

Simulation and Role Play

CONTRIBUTING AUTHOR:

Marilyn Buckner, Ph.D.
National Training Systems, Inc.
P.O. Box 8436
Atlanta, GA 31106
Tel.: 404.875.1953
Fax: 404.875.0947

Editorial Staff for 8412

Editor
Madelyn R. Callahan

Revised 1999

Editor
Cat Sharpe

Contributing Editor
Ann Bruen

Production Design
Anne Morgan

Learning by Playing

We begin learning by pretending. Play is an essential learning experience in our development, for in our childhood imaginations, the real world exists for us with all its possibilities, but none of its risks. As adults, too, we learn well by incorporating the tools of these early learning experiences. Simulation and role play enable us to create a manageable version of our world where we can practice behaviors and correct our mistakes. Creating models of real-life situations prepares us to function more effectively in the real world.

A *simulation* is an intensive, interactive experience in which the content and roles assumed by participants are designed to reflect what people encounter in specific environments. In essence, a simulation is a simplified and contrived situation that contains enough illusion of reality to induce real-world-like responses by those participating in the exercise.

While simulations often have rules "for play," possess room for alternative strategic tactics, and can be fun, they are not, by definition, games. While games generally focus on one intent (that of winning), simulations stress the complex, real-life situations and array of goals that organizations attempt to implement on a daily basis. In addition, the simulated environment should offer opportunities for action and reflection that are not always inherent in a "pure play" environment.

In role playing, participants act out a particular situation or problem before the rest of the group. These activities can help accomplish a wide variety of training objectives, ranging from providing information to changing attitudes. For example, participants can work out handling a complaining customer or practice effective sales techniques.

As organizations respond to rapidly changing economic and technological environments, the need for effective time- and cost-efficient training becomes critical. This issue of *Info-line* will explain how to maximize the benefits of simulation with special attention to simulation games and role play.

Simulation

Simulations are not a new idea (see *A Brief History of Simulations* on the next page). The simulation (experiential learning method) creates an environment that requires participants to be involved in some type of personally meaningful activity, leading to a real sense of personal accomplishment or failure for the results obtained.

An understanding of how people learn is essential to the development of proper simulations. Employers tend to ask employees and potential employees for information that falls only within certain parameters—the "knowledge" category. They do this 80 to 90 percent of the time. While these kinds of questions are not bad, per se, using the same method for garnering our answers can be. Utilizing a higher order of questions requires more "brain power" and, therefore, a more elaborate and comprehensive mode of operational thought.

Luckily, there exist a variety of documented learning models that involve a number of avenues by which to pursue the quest for better employee and organization performance. One model suggests four states that are necessary for effecting behavioral, attitudinal, and knowledge change: concrete experience; observation and reflection; formation of abstract concepts and generalizations; and testing implications of concepts in new situations. Others suggest that learning should be integrative, focusing on learning from differences in content, point of view, and style.

Perhaps one of the best-known models is presented in detail in *Bloom's Taxonomy* (see sidebar for details). Bloom's Taxonomy requires participants to become involved in activities that enable them to apply prior knowledge and theory to the learning experience. When considering a simulation for company use, examine how each of Bloom's components fits with *your* objectives.

A Brief History of Simulations

Simulations have been used for education and development since ancient times. Wei-Hai originated the first war game simulations in China about 3000 BC. These games bore a vague similarity to the early 17th-century warfare game, chess. Soon these parlor exercises became "serious," as observed in the development of other elaborate war games in Germany during the 17th and 18th centuries.

Further development of these games took place during modern times, when many military officers trained with war games in the 1930s and 1940s came home to use their military training in managing civilian businesses. Some of the business game/war game evolution can be traced to the 1950s, when a number of games were developed for organizations to use when they needed to provide training in decision making without the risk of delegating real responsibilities to novices.

Based on a new theory of education, which revolved around the learner instead of the instructor, the successes of war games and operations research techniques, and the development of high-speed computers, propelled the business gaming movement into the nation's business schools and corporate training and development operations. Today, numerous business games are in existence, and thousands of business executives have played them.

Adapted from "The Role of Management Games and Simulations in Education and Research," by Bernard Keys and Joseph Wolfe, Journal of Management, *volume 16, number 2 (1990).*

Simulations are based on the premise that effective training requires a balance of three essential factors:

Content: the dissemination of new ideas, principles, or concepts.

Experience: the opportunity to apply content in an experiential environment.

Feedback: on actions taken and the relationship between performance and the subsequent result.

The two most important steps to take before designing or implementing any simulation are:

1. Review your objectives (identify organization issues that need addressing).

2. Determine group needs.

Once you have reviewed your organization's issues and expectations, set your goals and give some thought to how you are going to achieve them. Before undertaking the time (which varies) and the expense (which also varies) to implement any simulation, however, you also should be aware of the following: Do you need to train better managers? Link organizational goals? Are your employees team-oriented? And, are all teams consciously aware that they are on the same side—making the most of the organization? For further ideas about linking goals within the organization, see the sidebar *Integrating Leadership Skills*.

Remember, there are variations within the audience. Simulations need to be tailored to your participants: Are they executive, middle management, or supervisory? Those models of behaviors promoting improved performance within *each organizational level* should be fully examined prior to making a simulation choice. What problem-solving and interpersonal behavior techniques are required for different job titles? For example, an improvement in executive performance (where the focus is more on organizational issues) may require a distinctly different simulation than one that is targeting a group of managers (whose jobs tend to focus on managing groups). Still another simulation would be appropriate for a group of supervisors, whose focus is most likely on individual issues.

The decision regarding what simulation to use should also be based on the whole picture of the current organization. What methods have been used before to improve or fix the current state of the organization? Have executive interviews taken place, asking what they would like their employees to do differently? Sometimes organizations will use a focus group to identify target individuals and ask them directly what skills they think they need to learn and how the learning experience should be positioned. Others have used more quantitative methods such as training needs analysis to gather data on specific issues. For further information on these topics, see the following *Info-lines*: No. 8502, "Be a Better Needs Analyst"; No. 9401, "Needs Assessment by Focus Group"; No. 9408, "Strategic Needs Analysis"; No. 9611, "Conducting a Mini Needs Assessment"; and No. 9713, "The Role of the Performance Needs Analyst."

Timing

Many of the popular simulations take two or three days to complete. In this fast-paced society, not many organizations have that kind of time to spare. The challenge for those designing a simulation is to find ways to collapse the learning experience into a more feasible time frame—perhaps, one or one-and-a-half days.

The Culture of Simulations

As one might imagine, not every simulation is suited to every organization. Often enough, however, a simulation can (and should be) adaptable to a variety of corporate climates and types of industry. Nonetheless, this does not necessarily translate when one is moving from one hemisphere to another, or even between different corporate cultures within the same country.

The rules of business conduct are not immutable. What is appropriate in Austin, Texas, may be deemed entirely inappropriate in Hokkaido,

Bloom's Taxonomy

In 1956, Benjamin Bloom headed a group of educational psychologists who developed a classification of levels of intellectual behavior important in learning. When you are choosing or designing simulations for your organization, take into account the following question categories as defined by Bloom:

Knowledge:
- remembering
- memorizing
- recognizing
- recalling identification
- recall of information (who, what, when, where, how?)

Comprehension:
- interpreting
- translating from one medium to another
- describing in one's own words
- organization and selection of facts and ideas

Application:
- problem solving
- applying information to produce some result
- use of facts, rules, and principles (How is…an example of…? How is…related to…? Why is…significant?)

Analysis:
- subdividing something to show how it is put together
- finding the underlying structure of a communication
- identifying motives

Synthesis (putting together):
- putting many parts together to make a new whole
- a professional activity referred to as design
- an open-ended process with more than one correct answer
- engineering design of a new product or process

Evaluation (judging):
- making a judgment about a solution, design, report, material
- may involve internal (best models) or external (environmental, legal, economic, sociological) criteria
- selection among designs for implementation
- evaluation of old systems for upgrade

Integrating Leadership Skills

Research shows that executive programs appear to be leading the trend in the use of simulations. Therefore, the introduction of leadership change skills, a primary goal of a leadership simulation, can serve to reinforce all other organizational goals. Here is a list of subgoals to consider when you want to link and integrate leadership skills with other goals within the organization:

● To increase insight into individual development plans for training, promotions.

● To diagnose and develop leadership abilities.

● To develop strategy behaviors not currently present in the organization (for example, teams, process redesign).

● To increase knowledge of the key success factors of a business, and how these relate to the environment.

● To reveal the characteristics of an organization's existing culture for greater understanding, or to change it.

● To introduce new managers to the dynamics of the management process.

● To illustrate concepts such as agenda setting, networking, and influencing upward.

● To understand and appreciate the benefits of teamwork and collaboration in the problem-solving process.

● To understand the linkages between performance and organizational outcomes.

● To diagnose the skills of managers.

● To learn how to think more strategically.

Japan. What one does, wears, or says may be fine in advertising, but entirely misconstrued in the more structured world of banking. In simulations, much like the real world, people behave according to their cultures and values. Since each simulation is a little "world" composed at will, consider carefully the culture you are dealing with before choosing your simulation.

Designing Simulations

When designing your simulation, first select and define your themes and goals. Then begin the design process by choosing techniques, identifying your scoring and feedback procedures, and finally, defining your debrief process (see the *Designing Simulations Model* opposite).

Choosing a Simulation

The choice of a simulation involves clearly defining one's goals. Determine the key issues within the organization. What is the context? Is there a major cultural change? A total organizational transformation needed in order to become a smoothly run organization? A need to learn a new skill? Does the organization want to introduce new leadership behaviors for a new culture and, therefore, make the leadership goals more participative? Or should the leadership model be limited to that of a strategic planning focus?

Decide if the simulation should be assessment oriented—that is, focused on giving feedback to the employees on their leadership skills. Or should it be more developmental in its approach, focusing on teaching the skills in a risk-free environment? Remember to link the simulation to a 360-degree feedback process so that employees can validate their skills sets against another objective source of feedback. (For more information, see *Info-line* No. 9508, "How to Build and Use a 360-Degree Feedback System.")

Finally, decide which model to use—a situational leadership model or a change leadership model. The situational leadership model concentrates heavily on the supervisory skills of balancing task and relationship behaviors, while on the whole, the change leadership model focuses more on the organization and change within it.

Useful Techniques

There are a number of commonly used techniques to choose from, depending on the goals you have established for your simulation.

■ *In-Basket Exercises*

Similar to what can be found on every manager's desk, the in-basket holds massive amounts of information identifying problems or decisions that need to be made.

■ *Role Play Situations*

In contrast to the in-baskets, which attempt to uncover analytical and decision-making skills, role plays are most effective for illustrating participants' interpersonal skills. They are particularly useful in leadership simulations.

■ *Small Group Discussions*

Key to complex simulation design, this technique enables group members to learn from what they have just experienced. The simulation can include such areas as analyzing strategic, financial, and marketing situations, or discussing the restructuring of the organization.

■ *The "Wildcard"*

These are random events thrown into the simulation to see how people will react and respond to an "abnormal" state of affairs. A wildcard can be anything from a sudden loss of capital, normally counted upon, to a seemingly sudden threat of a hostile takeover or loss of a key employee.

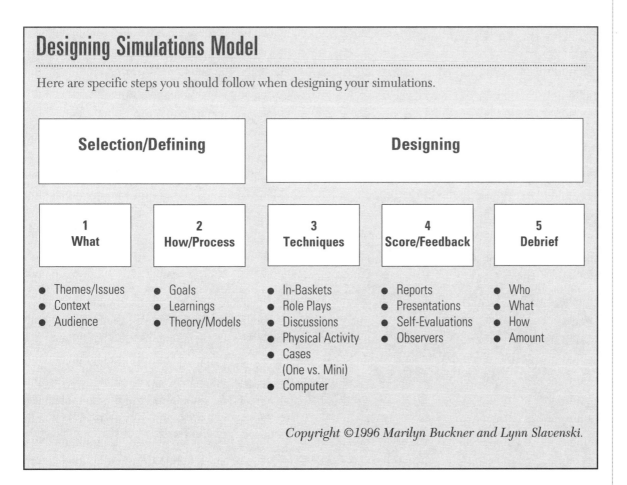

Designing Simulations Model

Here are specific steps you should follow when designing your simulations.

Selection/Defining		Designing		
1 **What**	**2** **How/Process**	**3** **Techniques**	**4** **Score/Feedback**	**5** **Debrief**
• Themes/Issues • Context • Audience	• Goals • Learnings • Theory/Models	• In-Baskets • Role Plays • Discussions • Physical Activity • Cases (One vs. Mini) • Computer	• Reports • Presentations • Self-Evaluations • Observers	• Who • What • How • Amount

Copyright ©1996 Marilyn Buckner and Lynn Slavenski.

Scoring and Feedback Procedures

If you are using an assessment approach to simulation design, choose some method of testing to provide feedback. This method of scoring is simplest when judging financial or quantitative models, in which you can ask multiple-choice questions. When dealing with qualitative or leadership simulations, however, use a scoring of possible right answers, similar to the grading of essays by a college professor. When using presentations, have other teams score their content and delivery. The important thing is to have individuals self-score by giving them "typical" right answers and having them compare their own answers. This provides them with a checklist of events, which they can use when returning to their workplace.

If you are using a purely developmental approach to simulation design, you probably would not need a scoring component, and a debrief discussion would suffice.

Debriefing

Debriefing the participants of a simulation helps reinforce the original goals and can ensure that participants focus on implementing their new knowledge in a variety of real-life situations. Furthermore, the debrief provides trainers with a measurement of their effectiveness in teaching these new concepts, thereby offering opportunities for future improvement in the design, practice, and outcome of simulation implementation.

As debriefing may very well be one of the most important components of a successful simulation, a multistage approach is recommended, with each stage identified by a specific question. While there are several effective approaches you can take (ranging from asking participants to discuss their experiences with one another, to administering a carefully construction questionnaire), the main component of the debrief will consist of these key questions:

- What happened?
- Why did it happen?
- How will you apply this in the future?

When considering the "how" of the debrief, decide whether it will be more effective or convenient to perform it in small or large groups. If your simulation is of a fairly complex nature, is delivered to a large group, or has used more than one facilitator, then the small group approach may be best.

Review both the content of the simulation and its outcomes. Were the rules of the simulation explained well enough that the participants "got" its meaning? For example, if your simulation was supposed to serve the purpose of team building, did its design fully promote that aspect, or was it so competitive that the participants became overwhelmed with the need to win?

The "how" component of the debrief can and should consist of a variety of approaches. While the final outcome of the simulated environment itself may seem of extreme importance to the participants (whose focus may have been more on competition amongst themselves than on the teamwork that needs to occur for an organization to run at optimum efficiency), the facilitator's role should encourage participants to review the simulation as an entire, ongoing process, rather than a series of discrete events occurring in a vacuum. Participants should be coached to reflect on *how* outcomes occurred, examining the roles they play in determining those outcomes.

Consider carefully how much time to devote to the debrief. Often, it is one of the most neglected aspects of the process. Remember that whatever the amount of time you choose to spend, the action or reflection process of the simulation is absolutely essential.

Drawbacks

One obvious shortcoming of using a simulation is that although a good simulation is similar to, it is not the same as, reality. Like all knowledge, the simulation model is culture conditioned and contextual, so the value depends on the context in which it is used. One must be ever-vigilant in using the simulation *critically,* not as a pure representation of reality. The experience of a simulation may be best used as inspiration for the *critical examination* of one's own business. A simulation is only as good as the thought and follow-up devoted to it.

The amount of resources required to conduct simulations is another possible drawback. They take longer and demand more of participants than other teaching techniques. The potentially positive outcomes of utilizing simulations can far outweigh their possible drawbacks, however, as long as those who are implementing the simulation approach it in an organized and well-considered manner.

Multimedia Simulations

Noting that content, experience, and feedback are essential components of successful simulations, and that they must occur in a relatively specific milieu, many multimedia producers are creating programs that mirror a simulation for accessing the abundant, sophisticated (but sometimes hidden) business intelligence. Although most simulations are delivered via CD-ROM, Internet delivery or some combination of CD-ROMs and the Internet or intranet are becoming popular. For an overview of the organizational and learner benefits of these kinds of simulations, see *Benefits of Multimedia Training* at right.

Benefits of Multimedia Training

For the Organization	For the Learner
Reduces training delivery time by 30 to 50 percent.	Reduces learning time up to 50 percent.
Increases productivity through cross-training, efficient retraining, less time away from job.	Increases retention by 25 to 50 percent.
Reduces training costs; once break-even point is reached, training is free.	Evaluates existing knowledge to avoid unnecessary training.
Ensures every trainee reaches a level of mastery.	Provides individualized, self-paced instruction.
Reduces the need for a dedicated training facility.	Allows flexible time, place, and privacy for training.
Requires fewer trainers and subject matter experts.	Provides unlimited practice and remediation.
Delivers standardized, consistent instruction.	Delivers consistent, nonjudgmental instruction.
Relates directly to job skills and performance through customized course materials.	Relates directly to job skills and performance through customized course materials.

Courtesy of Electronic Learning Facilitators, Inc., as printed in Training & Development, *August 1998.*

Successful Simulations

Here are 10 secrets for creating successful training simulations. They represent lessons learned from hard-fought struggles to understand the elusive, often perverse human dynamics at work in simulation training. Taken in sequence, they can supply relatively safe passage through the tricky terrain of simulation design.

1. Don't Confuse Replication with Simulation.

The temptation in designing a simulation is to make a small-scale replica of some full-blown reality. But in "soft skills" training, the job of the designer is to look past the details to the essence of reality.

2. Choose the Right Subject to Simulate.

Some subjects lend themselves better to simulation training than others. A topic is more apt to be suitable for simulation if it embodies at least one of the following characteristics:

- Seeing the world through others people's eyes. The simulation can illuminate the threat posed by a competitor.

- Performing tasks simultaneously. In the real world, skills are often needed in clumps; a simulation can create an environment in which several tasks are completed at the same time.

- Performing under pressure. Simulations can create environments full of genuine but nonthreatening pressure, affording trainees opportunities to practice their skills under duress.

- Developing systems thinking. A simulation can put people inside a system, whereby they see firsthand how change to one component affects the others.

- Recognizing cognitive dissonance. Holding contradictory attitudes or beliefs without being aware of it is known as *cognitive dissonance*. Simulations can reveal these contradictions.

3. Develop a Design Plan.

In preparing to design a simulation, you must make two key planning decisions: design it alone (or use a design team); or employ a structured creative process (fly by the seat of your pants). Whatever you decide, you will need to fill the following positions:

- Principal designer, who has firsthand knowledge of training simulations (and, for a team, the commitment to lead).

- Subject matter expert, who has a thorough understanding of the subject to be simulated.

- Administrator, who sets and maintains the design schedule, oversees acquisition or production of materials, and schedules tests.

- Client or representative, who provides a reality check as the project develops (in an oversight capacity only).

A well-defined creative program should make use of these suggestions: avoid premature closure of ideas; get outside a problem and look at it from different angles; and give your subconscious a chance to work on the problem.

4. Ensure Trainees Take Responsibility for Actions.

Whenever trainees disavow responsibility for their behavior during the simulation, their motivation to learn from the experience evaporates. When you design your simulation, watch out for these guaranteed responsibility evaders:

- Pretending. Design all roles in simulation so trainees must be themselves.

- Using competition for its own sake. If competition is not a factor in the real-world situation you are simulating, leave it out.

- Giving inappropriate value to chance. Limit chance to events that actually occur randomly in the real world.

5. Use Symbols to Deal with Emotional Ideas.

Occasionally a simulation focuses on an emotionally charged issue that threatens to overpower the learning experience. Avoid participants' assuming stereotypical roles by assigning each group names that represent an abstract concept—for example, Circles, Squares, and Triangles, with the Squares having power over the other groups.

6. Don't Play Games with Trainees.

If the odds are going to be stacked in favor of one group, have the facilitator reveal that at the start, so that trainees don't feel manipulated. Do not trivialize the experience by using cute names like the "Yell and Holler Telephone Company" or "Caught in the Act Security Services."

7. Use Nontrainees to Add Realism.

When appropriate, using people who have no stake in the outcome of the simulation can add real-world authenticity to the training experience.

8. Develop an Appropriate Assessment Model.

Quantitative models for assessing trainee performance may be appropriate for quantitative simulations—those dealing with financial or other formulaic disciplines—but for most qualitative simulations they are not suitable.

9. Alpha Test Your Simulation.

Alpha testing is a design technique for evaluating the basic assumptions of the simulation, its overall structure, and the logic of its progression. If problems surface, be prepared to reinvent the whole simulation if necessary.

10. Set Your Own Standards for Success.

When you spell out the purpose and goals of your simulation at the beginning of the design process, you are defining standards by which to judge its ultimate success. Don't lose sight of those standards as your project nears completion.

Adapted from "10 Secrets of Successful Simulations," by R. Garry Shirts, Training, *October 1992.*

When deciding whether or not to use multimedia simulations, trainers need to address the following issues:

Content: Does the material lend itself to media presentation; does it need frequent revision?

Audience: Where are the learners; how well do they read; are they comfortable with computers?

Environment: Is there access to computers; what kind of computers; are they part of a local area network?

Implementation: Will learners have time to study; how will progress be measured and recorded; is there enough hardware available?

Multimedia products attempt to simulate a variety of real-world situations so convincingly that trainees make the same choices they would in actual situations. They also experience the real-world consequences of their decisions, through the use of unexpected e-mails, phone calls, organizational charts, memos, and actual interactions with persons represented in videos. A multimedia approach alone, however, is limited in simulating interpersonal situations that occur in a business climate. The nuances of human interaction skills and sensitivities are impossible to render adequately with video alone. Therefore, although multimedia simulations are useful in many areas, they lack the group interactions that live simulations offer.

Role Plays

Role play activities can help you accomplish a wide variety of training objectives. To get your point across with impact, make the right choices in selecting and carrying out the role play.

Always start with ideal physical surroundings. Choose a room that is large enough to accommodate multiple role playing comfortably (single role plays work well in any size room). The room should measure at least 25, but no more than 50 square feet per person. Avoid a room with stationary seating, like some classrooms or an auditorium. You will need an open space with movable furniture.

Avoid noisy locations that are open to distraction. No one should be able to enter the room, observe through the windows, or eavesdrop on the sessions. Restrict telephone or visitor interruptions. Try to find a location with adjacent breakout rooms, or use available partitions, blackboards, or large plants for privacy.

You can use role plays to accomplish many training goals, such as:

● maximize participation and stimulate thinking

● promote learning through imitation, observation, feedback, analysis, and conceptualization

● inform and train participants, evaluate their performance, and improve their skills

● test and practice new behaviors participants can use in their jobs

● develop skills for implementing solutions and decisions

● develop interpersonal and practical skills in areas such as counseling, interviewing, customer relations, effective selling, and conflict management

● experience and understand a variety of problem situations from others' points of view and learn how to empathize with persons being discriminated against

● generate feedback that will give participants insight into their behavior, help them understand how others view them, and encourage them to be sensitive to others

Types of Role Plays

The trainer has a variety of role-play techniques to choose from.

■ *Single Role Plays*
Volunteer players act out one role at a time before the group. For example, one participant plays a customer relations manager and another plays the role of complaining customer. The manager must demonstrate the most effective way of easing the customer's anger and handling their complaint.

Single role plays have the advantage of allowing the group to share the experience and, under the direction of the trainer, analyze different facets of human behavior and problem solving. But only one person is able to practice skills, and players may be embarrassed to perform in front of the group. Poor performance may invite negative criticism that can be difficult for the trainer to handle. Thus, single role plays should be used only after multiple role plays, or when the group has become comfortable and members trust one another.

■ *Role Rotation*
Volunteers take turns playing the same role. Using the example above, one person plays the role of the customer relations manager and another the angry customer. After one player finishes handling the complaint problem, the other takes over the role of manager and demonstrates his or her approach to the problem.

Because the role passes from one participant to another, players are not embarrassed as in single role plays. Role rotation also provides the advantage of a range of problem-solving techniques and promotes further analysis and discussion. In a large group, however, it can be too time consuming and runs the risk of losing the training focus.

■ *Multiple Role Plays*

Small teams perform role plays simultaneously. Everyone has a chance to participate in a non-threatening format that reduces anxiety and embarrassment (see *Curing the Spotlight Syndrome* at right). Teams generate a broad variety of ideas and conclusions from the same data, and then discuss their outcomes, providing a variety of approaches to problem solving.

Multiple role plays have some disadvantages, however. Processing discussions may be limited; teams may be interested in discussing their individual outcomes but not those of other teams whom they have not observed. In addition, teams may be distracted by the other activity, and trainers may have scheduling difficulties because teams will begin and conclude enactments at varying times.

■ *Spontaneous Role Plays*

Without a planned structure or script, players improvise problem situations, agreeing on what to portray and assisting each other in developing roles and the situation as the exercise progresses. In this instance, trainers have more interaction with their players and help them develop feeling and insight during the enactment, but they must be skilled directors and work well with improvisations.

Deep involvement in the role play and analysis help trainees better understand the underlying reasons for various behaviors, but the involvement of only a few players leaves the rest of the group in the role of observers. In addition, players may feel anxious about performing in front of the group.

Other Scenarios

A number of additional role-play situations can be used effectively.

Soliloquy. A role player is given a script and describes his or her character in detail while the group observes. Players discuss their feelings and obtain support and useful feedback from the group.

Curing the Spotlight Syndrome

Anxiety can inhibit learning for the shy individual forced to the center of attention in a role play. Here are some ways to eliminate stage fright.

■ *Before*

Choose a quite, private setting for your role play activity. Introduce the activity by informing the group that each person will be playing a role during the session. Follow this with a comprehensive orientation of the activity that includes specific purposes, methods, and feedback guidelines. Explain that the role-playing environment is safe, without real-world consequences for mistakes.

■ *During*

Establish a supportive atmosphere that will encourage participation; use multiple role plays before single or rotational role plays. Allow participants to develop their own experiences for the role plays and processing guidelines. Choose role plays that could produce favorable experiences on the *first* try. Never start by appointing participants; ask for volunteers. Don't use role players who will be inhibited by each other's presence, for example, a boss and subordinate. If possible, rehearse, so the acting will be appropriate and natural.

■ *After*

Read aloud the rules for conducting discussion of single role plays. Establish feedback guidelines to ensure that comments will emphasize the positive aspects of the performance. Use *nondirective* or open-ended discussion methods that let trainees determine the course of the discussion and give them more opportunities to participate.

■ *Tips*

Use role plays late in the program when trainees are more comfortable with one another and more confident about taking risks. Use role play planning sheets before beginning the activity and self-evaluation sheets after it ends.

Reversal. Two role players switch roles and take on each other's characters. This method is useful for helping players understand another's point of view, and for illustrating how each character is perceived by the other and how that perception affects behavior.

Doubling. This is a variation of the soliloquy, in which one player responds to the other as their "inner voice," conscience, or auxiliary ego, articulating those silent thoughts and feelings the other cannot express without difficulty. This method is useful for helping players focus and clarify issues.

Mirror. One player reflects or mirrors another's role. This scenario can be used to engage players who resist demonstrating their ideas and helps them communicate without negative feedback.

Empty Chair. A player speaks openly to an empty chair that represents a person with whom he or she is experiencing communication problems. This technique gives trainees practice in overcoming difficulties addressing the person without worrying about their reaction.

Designing Role Plays

Design your role plays in three parts: preparation, enactment, and analysis. **Prepare** trainees by explaining role play objectives and reading role descriptions. Start **enactments** without dramatic buildup, and focus on learning desired skills and behaviors. **Analyze** participants' success with applying the new behaviors, not their acting ability. Permit trainees to demonstrate their alternative interpretations of roles.

Begin by writing simple role plays, using short sentences and a job-related vocabulary; then build up to complex ones. Define clear purposes and training objectives through the use of surveys, interviews, and questionnaires regarding training needs. Identify goals and problems related to these objectives, and design component roles and situations accordingly. Prepare instructions well in advance so that you can test them to ensure that participants will understand what they are to do and why. Design a discussion format of key issues.

Design Tips

- To ensure involvement, ask participants to discuss their problems handling specific situations and include these concerns in the role play scripts.

- Choose problems around which you can build a conflict situation easily, and focus on behaviors that require only two or three characters.

- Define role play characters by giving each one a name, age, personality, reputation, job title, strengths, weaknesses, and a perspective on the problem.

- Use gender-neutral names, so that any male or female participant can play the roles.

- Make the role play flexible. Characters and situations must not be so defined that players feel locked into the activity and unable to exercise their creativity.

- Don't pose too many conflicts, or problems that are beyond the players' control.

- Write cases that invite creative solutions; participants should be able to handle the problem in a variety of ways.

How to Conduct Role Plays

Arrange chairs in a circle so trainees can see one another easily. Solicit volunteers to play roles and describe the situation to the rest of the group. Distribute written role descriptions clearly explaining the characters' identity, feelings, motives, and situations, and allow sufficient time for players to adjust to their roles. Tell participants what to focus on and explain that they are portraying their *characters'* emotions, not their own.

Begin by stating the identity of the characters and briefly describing the initial actions. Intervene during a single role play only when the actor is having difficulty with the burden of illustrating the desired skill. Never intervene in multiple role play. In this case, role players and observers learn by finding their own solutions.

Enactment Tips

● Choose players who have the appropriate experience and technical backgrounds for their roles.

● To ensure productive learning experiences, control players' sidetracking, overacting, or irrelevant behaviors.

● Discourage participants from portraying their personal problems, and avoid using situations that may embarrass players.

● Be prepared to handle emotional problems or difficulties that may affect participants.

● If you are planning to videotape role plays, obtain consent from the group beforehand. Use a fixed camera to avoid distracting and inhibiting the players.

● Consult with players only in *private* showings of the tape, permitting them to critique their performances before the group analysis.

Follow up role plays with analysis so players can learn how others perceive their solutions to problems. Focus analysis on training objectives—for example, sharpening decision-making skills or communication skills. Have the players discuss their behaviors, reasons for acting as they did, and feelings about other role players' behaviors. Use printed sheets for observation, listing questions regarding verbal responses, nonverbal behavior, and players' interpretations of one another's behaviors and expressions. Following are some tips to help you:

● Never rush through a follow-up discussion.

● Aim to have trainees understand that there can be a variety of solutions to a problem.

● Have the individual or groups of players explain the reasons for their outcomes, and then open up a group discussion.

● Use a set of prepared questions that focus on behavioral issues or skills development—stressing techniques for effective performance—and ask participants how they can apply what they have learned to their jobs.

● Summarize the learning in printed handouts or present it orally.

Putting It All Together

Remember that simulations and role plays don't just happen. They are versatile teaching tools applicable to a variety of educational objectives, but they must be planned and carried out with care. Used properly, they can bring realism to concepts that have been learned in a more formal manner. Moreover, they can be a good technique for encouraging class camaraderie, measuring participant understanding, and stimulating trainees' interest in further inquiry.

References & Resources

Articles

Alexander, George, and Ron Lawrence. "Creating a Process Improvement Situation." *Journal for Quality and Participation,* October/November 1996, pp. 18-24.

Balli, Sandra J. "Oh No… Not Role Play Again!" *Training & Development,* February 1995, pp. 14-15.

Eline, Leanne. "A Virtual Reality Check for Manufacturers." *Technical Training,* January/February 1998, pp. 10-14.

Garhart, Casey. "Simulations: How Real Is Real Enough?" *Journal of Interactive Instruction Development,* Fall 1991, pp. 15-18.

Keys, Bernard, and Joseph Wolfe. "The Role of Management Games and Simulations in Education and Research." *Journal of Management,* volume 16, number 2 (1990), pp. 307-336.

Lierman, Bruce. "How to Develop a Training Simulation." *Training & Development,* February 1994, pp. 50-52.

Mattoon, Joseph S. "Modeling and Simulation: A Rationale for Implementing New Training Technologies." *Educational Technology,* July/August 1996, pp. 17-26.

McAteer, Peter F. "Simulations: Learning Tools for the 1990s." *Training & Development,* October 1991, pp. 19-22.

McBride, Mary, and Mike Uretsky. "Global Strategy: Making It Happen Through Simulation." *National Productivity Review,* Spring 1991, pp. 245-252.

Morag, Meir. "Free-Play Simulation in CBT." *Technical & Skills Training,* October 1995, pp. 20-23.

Parzinger, Thomas M. "A Valuable Training and Development Tool." *Bankers Magazine,* May/June 1992, pp. 75-80.

Reintzell, John F. "When Training Saves Lives." *Training & Development,* January 1997, pp. 41-42.

Salopek, Jennifer J. "Workstation Meets Playstation." *Training & Development,* August 1998, pp. 26-35.

Shirts, R. Garry. "10 Secrets of Successful Simulations." *Training,* October 1992, pp. 79-83.

Slack, Kim. "Training for the Real Thing." *Training & Development,* May 1993, pp. 79-89.

Smith, Vernita C. "Live It, Learn It." *Human Resource Executive,* June 1997, pp. 38-41.

Solomon, Charlene M. "Simulation Training Builds Teams Through Experience." *Personnel Journal,* June 1993, pp. 100-108.

Storts, Carol. "The Case for Industrial Simulation." *Technical & Skills Training,* November/December 1996, pp. 20-23.

Wager, Walter W., et al. "Simulations: Selection and Development." *Performance Improvement Quarterly,* volume 5, number 2 (1992), pp. 47-64.

Wook, Choi. "Designing Effective Scenarios for Computer-Based Instructional Simulations: Classification of Essential Features." *Educational Technology,* September/October 1997, pp. 13-21.

References & Resources

Books

Eitington, J. *The Winning Trainer.* Houston: Gulf, 1984.

Fripp, John. *Learning Through Simulations.* London: McGraw-Hill, 1993.

Jones, Ken. *Simulations: A Handbook for Teachers and Trainers.* London: Kogan Page, 1995.

Laird, D. "Tips on Using Role Plays." In *The Training & Development Sourcebook.* Ed. by L.S. Baird, et al. Amherst, MA: HRD Press, 1983.

Randall, J.S. "Methods of Teaching." In *The Training & Development Sourcebook.* Ed. by L.S. Baird, et al. Amherst, MA: HRD Press, 1983.

Shaw, M.E., et al. *Role Playing: A Practical Manual for Group Facilitators.* San Diego: University Associates, 1980.

Info-lines

Austin, Mary. "Needs Assessment by Focus Group." No. 9401 (revised 1998).

Callahan, Madelyn R. (ed.). "Be a Better Needs Analyst." No. 8502 (revised 1998).

Gupta, Kavita. "Conducting a Mini Needs Assessment." No. 9611 (revised 1998).

Kirrane, Diane. "The Role of the Performance Needs Analyst." No. 9713.

Shaver, Warren J. "How to Build and Use a 360-Degree Feedback System." No. 9508 (revised 1998).

Sparhawk, Sally. "Strategic Needs Analysis." No. 9408 (revised 1999).

Job Aid

Selecting a Simulation

The fit of a simulation to your organization is key. The following checklist can help you in finding the simulation that is right for you.

☐ The type of business context (for example, manufacturing, services, global or domestic, government, public or private sector).

☐ The organizational structure (for example, functional, product or matrix, team-based, decentralized, or cross-functional).

☐ Turbulent versus stable environment.

☐ The number of corporate versus divisional problem situations.

☐ The amount of individual versus group actions required.

☐ How much and what type of feedback required.

☐ The type of culture the participants have come from (for example, authority-based versus group consensus-based cultures).

☐ The mixture of individuals from different hierarchical levels.

☐ The amount of reading participants are required to prepare.

☐ The need for an "assessment of skills" approach without prior information versus a "development" approach, which provides information before the simulation to increase success in the exercise.

☐ Decide how important "playful" versus "serious" is.

☐ Length of time available.

☐ Decide if "physical-handling or movement" simulations are needed versus "knowledge based."

The material appearing on this page is not covered by copyright and may be reproduced at will.

Job-Oriented Software Training

Issue 9810

AUTHORS:

Susan Boyd
Susan Boyd Associates
270 Mather Road
Jenkintown, PA 19046-3129
Tel: 215.886.2669
Fax: 215.886.7931
E-mail: susan@susan-boyd.com
Web: www.susan-boyd.com

Debra Exner
Exner & Associates
724 Foxdale Road
Wilmington, DE 19803
Tel: 302.478.5919
Fax: 302.478.5992
E-mail: exner@compuserve.com

Editor
Cat Sharpe

Associate Editor
Sabrina E. Hicks

Production Design
Anne Morgan

ASTD Internal Consultant
Phil Anderson

Job-Oriented Software Training

Job-Oriented Training

The computer revolution that began in the 1960s, snowballed in the 1980s, and reached new frontiers in the 1990s, continues to evolve at an accelerated rate. To keep up with the process of change, computer trainers need to understand that employees no longer value training that is software specific: what employees want is training that is job specific.

Why should trainers move toward teaching computer skills that are job specific? Because the computer training audience has changed over the last 15 years. In the 1980s, trainers trained the *pioneers*—a hardy breed of early computer users who were exploring the new world of personal computing. These people absorbed all the content presented to them because they had the motivation and aptitude to figure out how to use the software.

As a result, most of the training materials focused on the software, not the job. Trainers felt comfortable learning the software, but they had no real idea or understanding of how their trainees would use it on the job. They taught how to use menus and commands, not how to accomplish specific job tasks. Trainers believed that if you teach the software well enough, learners easily and independently cross the gap from knowing the software to knowing how to use the software on the job.

No longer considered pioneers, members of the late 1990s' audience are instead the *settlers*—persons responsible for harvesting the crops of the "new (computer) world" before the weather changes. The settlers have one enemy in common: time. There is not enough time to learn new techniques (and no reason to learn them) if settlers cannot put them to use immediately. Technology for the sake of technology does not excite them. Technology is simply a tool to get work done; therefore, they want and need training that focuses only on how to use the software to complete a job task.

Settlers have neither the time nor the incentive to find ways to cross the gap between training and their job. Trainers must build the bridge for them by understanding how their audience uses computer skills on the job and designing the software training within the scope of that job.

What Does "Training for the Job" Mean?

Between learning software capabilities and knowing how to use the software for specific job tasks exists a large gap. Training for the job means bridging this gap by not **teaching** the software but by actually **using** the software during training classes on real-life practice job tasks. What trainers need is a method of developing and delivering training that focuses on job tasks and is flexible enough to keep pace with the rapid rate of change in the computer software industry.

This method needs to strike a balance between content and comprehension. When focusing on content, the main goal is to cover topics and finish the course manual. The content approach ensures only one thing: the trainer has presented the material. You cannot assume that your trainees have learned just because you covered the pages in the manual. Trainers who use this approach forget that the purpose of training is not to just cover the material; the purpose is to help learners understand the material.

Trainers who have comprehension as their objective consider mastery of the important topics the goal. To do this, trainers know that students must learn, practice, and apply the software skills to fewer topics. Using job-oriented computer-based training (CBT) ensures that participants learn skills applicable to their job by covering fewer topics with more practice time and focusing on the *need-to-know*. The *nice-to-know* must be identified and addressed through other training and other resources.

This *Info-line* defines a job-oriented approach to training and discusses its benefits. The components of the job-oriented training program and the activities involved in the planning, delivery, and follow-up of training are identified. In addition, suggestions are listed to adapt this approach for diverse groups, and sample forms and checklists are included to illustrate training models.

Benefits of the Need-to-Know Approach

The main benefit of this approach is a more immediate application of the skills. Learners leave class knowing how to use the specific parts of the software that are essential for performing their job tasks. Because trainers have not sacrificed practice time for content, learners use the software in class on the real, practical applications they use on the job. This teaching method leads to learner buy-in during class and increases learner participation. Because learners are more involved in the learning process, they know that the software contains more features than a trainer can cover in class; thus, they are more likely to seek and use other resources (such as manuals, CBT, software on-line help, quick reference cards, macros, templates, and so forth).

With the job-oriented approach, training becomes an essential step in implementing new software programs, rather than an optional off-to-the-side activity. Training is elevated to this status because managers see a direct return on their training investment and are willing to commit their staffs to training. Both management and employees view time in the training class as a productive use of resources because the skills learned apply directly and immediately to the job. This applicable knowledge decreases the downtime that often occurs as employees try to figure out on their own how to get a job done using the new software program.

When to Use Need-to-Know Approach

The job-oriented approach is not appropriate for an organization that has requested a class covering every feature or command in a software package. However, when an organization requests software training that relates to employees' real-world applications, this is the perfect time to implement the job-oriented approach. Trainers should teach these skills and allow time for practice (and not just in the first hour of the course, but integrated throughout as employees progress through the applications).

An easy way to implement this method is to teach a software command and then ask learners to get into teams and list three ways to use this skill. This exercise allows trainers to gather information with a minimum of invested time and helps them perform the following tasks:

- develop job-specific reference cards
- design more practice exercises
- pre-screen participants more
- redesign popular or most problematic courses

Obviously, implementing this approach is easiest when you are designing training for a new system and a fairly homogenous group (that is, homogenous in job function). For example, you can use this approach to develop training for over 500 pharmaceutical sales representatives who are learning a new sales automation system, as well as for 300 customer service representatives learning Windows NT to access their mainframe credit check application systems. You could also design a customized Windows 95 word processing course for over 600 reporters and editors of a large newspaper.

Tools for Job-Oriented Training

The job-oriented approach contains the following general components.

■ *Creation of a Team*
Trainers cannot design training in a vacuum, and often management sponsoring the training project is too far removed from the real world of the learners. Ask for one or two subject matter experts (SMEs) to be on the project team to act as representatives of the learners. Having employee representation ensures that training is job-focused and encourages learner buy-in from the start.

■ *Definition of Training Project Goals*
For new system implementations, training is only one part of the overall plan, and often the systems staff or business units present training solutions without an in-depth training knowledge or experience. Management may ask for a two-day course covering only certain topics, but, typically, they have not performed a needs assessment or analysis. If the training department takes on this project without either conducting a needs assessment or defining the goals and scope, they just become an order taker, instead of a consultant and partner in meeting company goals. (For

more information on needs assessment, consult *Info-lines* No. 9713, "Role of Performance Needs Analyst," and No. 9808, "Task Analysis.")

■ *User-Centered Design*

Job tasks should determine the logical sequence and integration of how trainers teach skills, not the menu order. Skills are identified in the following categories:

Mission critical—skills that must be presented, practiced, and reinforced in class.

Nice-to-know—skills that could be presented later or simply introduced in class, perhaps by using a team approach or having learners participate in a scavenger hunt (that is, searching on-line help, reference cards, or software manuals to learn a skill on their own or with the team).

Not-essential-now—skills are not addressed at all but could be part of another course.

In addition to a sequential design, trainers ensure that training does not include skills that the employee will not use back on the job. Often trainers are asked to teach something the learners will never need to know how to do again. For example, a systems staff will frequently request that at the start of a new class trainers teach novice personal computer users how to set up a new network ID and password—a complex procedure. The systems staff does not have the resources to set up the 350 new user IDs on the network; thus, it would ease their workload if employees learned how to do it themselves.

This request, which involves mapping network drives and obscure system commands the user will never use again, can take up to 30 minutes of valuable training time. This procedure does not belong in a training class. Instead, recommend that the systems staff hire a temporary to set up the network IDs, and provide a list of class participants on a weekly basis so the temporary can set up IDs as needed for training. Trainers must be willing to take a stand when asked to include tasks that do not belong in the training course.

Planning for Training

What can trainers do before, during, and after class to bridge the gap between the job tasks and using the software? The trainer's job before class is to better understand the job needs, the learners, and how learner's will actually use the software tools. With this information, trainers can design the training program and materials accordingly. The following sections introduce some pre-class tasks for trainers.

Assess On-the-Job Needs

Interview typical users of the new system to better understand their job and how they currently perform the job tasks. Review their work samples, and identify the following:

- features of the current system that learners use most

- users' biggest frustrations with the current software

- users' expectations of what the new system will provide

Review your results with the system design staff to see how the new system will meet the job demands. If the new system will not address all the users' concerns, identify which features are being implemented now and what later development phases are planned. (See *Job Task Review* sidebar for sample form.)

Trainers should conduct a pilot (typically one to three classes) for all major projects to test and enhance the training before presenting to learners. A pilot allows trainers to refine and revise course materials, ensuring that the training meets the job needs.

If there is time between a pilot program and a major roll-out, go back and meet with specific learners to see how they are actually using the software, what tips and tricks they have discovered, and what gaps may be in the training or software.

Job Task Review

Below is a sample interview form used by Susan Boyd Associates and Exner & Associates to identify the job skills and system needs of pharmaceutical sales representatives.

Name: _____

Department: _____ Date: _____

1. Describe the activities in a typical sales rep's day.

2. How do you envision using the laptop? (daily after calls, during calls, weekly?)

3. What is your most onerous paperwork task?

4. What paper reports do you receive that are most valuable for your daily activities?

5. What typical data searches do you envision doing on the new system?

6. Have you ever used a computerized sales automation system before? What were your experiences?

7. How many new contracts do you typically work with? How many typically expire around the same month?

8. What are typical comments you might enter for a contract?

9. When adding a product to a contract, what would be a good example of products to use, price requested (typical percent of discount), competitor's price, and annual usage?

10. What types of individuals do you typically see for individual accounts? (doctors? pharmacists?)

11. What departments, job titles, or staff do you typically work with on your hospital accounts?

12. What type of information do you currently record manually about your accounts?

13. What are some examples of notes you would enter for an account visit?

14. What do you hope to accomplish with the new system?

15. What do you hope the training class will accomplish? What do you hope the class will not be like?

Shadow Typical Participants

The best way to understand someone's job is to watch him or her do it. Trainers should meet and shadow a representative from the department that is to receive the training. Learn how the employees do their job and how they would do it with the new software. Look for and ask what job tasks would be easier or harder with the new software to better orient your training.

For example, when training sales representatives on a new system, trainers need to spend a day with several representatives in the field to observe how they prepare for a sales call and enter data after a call. This approach works with everyone from office personnel to reporters to customer service representatives. The information gained helps make the course sequence and exercises more real world oriented. (This also gives you an opportunity to make contacts in the field and build credibility as trainers and course designers.)

Use Content Experts

Use content experts as a sounding board when developing the training outline, exercises, and materials. These individuals are knowledgeable about the job tasks and expert in the use of the present software system. Content experts may be the people who you were able to shadow and interview earlier, or they may be a manager or part of the project team. Through phone calls and e-mail, you can direct questions to these individuals to help keep the course focused on meeting job needs. Have content experts review your materials and exercises to ensure that they reflect how the job is done and contain information relevant to the job.

If trainers do not use the input of content experts, the exercises may come across as impractical training scenarios rather then the real-world examples that are useful for the learner. For example, if you are responsible for training a newspaper staff, take real stories from the paper and use as stories to write and edit. In making the edits, however, you may inadvertently use a style that was not in sync with their standards if you do not take advantage of the content experts' expertise.

Design Realistic Task-Oriented Exercises

Arrange the training outline so that you teach software commands and features in a job-related sequence, rather than a command-by-command approach. All tasks should mirror real-life activities, and you should only cover the essential ones in class. For example, in a sales training class, you can have a training database already created with records containing realistic information. Content experts and systems staff can help create this database, thus allowing the sales representatives to use the database to plan and record sales calls with meaningful data and realistic sales notes.

Build-In Independent Practice

During class, you will want to assess if the learners have mastered the skills, so allow them time to complete—independently—short practice exercises using the software. Create hands-on practice exercises that are job-focused and designed to allow the learner to use the skills and concepts presented in the lesson, as well as integrate those concepts from prior lessons. When designing the class agenda, trainers should schedule the independent exercises after each lesson to provide learners time to practice all the job tasks they have learned to date, before new material is introduced.

Develop Job Aids

Learners have found that job aids, such as *quick reference cards,* are one of the most valuable tools back on the job. Class participants use them long after they complete the training. Quick reference cards contain examples and step-by-step instruction not only on how to do common job tasks but also the tasks that may be performed more infrequently (such as, changing a password).

You can create cards in many formats, based on project needs, but one form that is particularly successful is to print the cards on color card stock and then clip them in the top corner with a binder ring so that cards may easily be added or updated. (See *Sample Quick Reference Card* sidebar.) Providing learners with a form they can use throughout class helps them organize their hints and allows for easy reference later. Because learners write down the

Follow-Up Survey for Pilot Class Participants

After conducting a training session for the initial pilot, follow-up with a survey to determine how participants are using the system and what materials and examples you need to develop to make the training more job specific. Below is an example of a typical follow-up survey.

Name: _____

Department: _____

Date: _____

1. How often do you enter data or review information in the XYZ system?

   - daily
   - several times a week
   - once a week
   - occasionally

2. What topics do you think should be included in quick reference cards for the new XYZ users?

3. What parts of the system did you find most challenging to learn or use on the job?

4. What parts of the XYZ system do you use most frequently on the job? Describe your use of the functions.

5. What parts of the XYZ system do you use only occasionally on the job? Describe why.

6. Do you copy XYZ data to other programs such as Word, PowerPoint, or Excel? If so, please explain what data is copied and how it is used.

7. How useful do you feel the training was to prepare you for using the system back on the job?

8. What suggestions do you have regarding the training of the new XYZ users?

9. How often have you called the help desk in the last two weeks? What problems did you discuss?

10. Should these problems be added or addressed more in-depth in the training class?

Sample Quick Reference Card for Creating and Running Reports

Below is a sample quick reference card that illustrates how useful these cards can be to participants once they have completed the class. The *Report* function selects accounts based on whether or not they meet a particular criteria.

Step 1: Opening a Report
- Open the XYZ system.
- Select *Format* → *Report*.
- Click the *Create* button.

Step 2: Selecting Columns
- To remove columns, in the *Columns* tab, select the column you want to remove and then click on the *Delete* button on the toolbar. (The *Delete* button looks like a brush-stroked "X.")
- If you want to put a deleted column back on the end of the list, double-click on the desired column.

Step 3: Selecting Conditions
- Click on the *Conditions* tab.
- Double-click on the columns on which you want to build a condition. Make the appropriate selections for the column (for example, Sale date >= 1/1/98 AND <=3/31/985 to select accounts with a sale date in the first quarter of 1998).
- Click *OK*.

Step 4: Saving, Running, Printing a Report
- Enter a name for the report and click *OK* to save.
- Click on the name of the report to select it, and click *OK* button to run the report.
- Wait a few seconds until the results of the report appear. (Hour glass appears.)
- Click on *Tool* → *Print* menu to print.

Step 5: Modifying a Report
- To modify an existing report, select the report name and click the *Properties* button in the dialog box.
- Make the desired changes and click *OK*.

---

commands and how to use them, their retention rate of the topics increases. Having learners create their own job aids or "cheat sheets" is also valuable. (For more information on job aids, consult *Info-line* No. 9711, "Create Effective Job Aids.")

Develop Help Tools

During your review of job tasks, work samples, and the new software system, you may notice that certain procedures have to be done by everyone in the same format, such as the following examples:

- formatting letters on company letterhead
- creating mailing labels from address list
- completing an expense form

These tasks can be automated with macros and templates and should be created before the training begins to become part of the software setup. During class, trainers show learners how to use these electronic performance support system (EPSS) tools rather than teaching the many indi-

vidual commands necessary to create their own format. Use of the EPSS tools shortens the learning curve and also ensures consistency in completing company-wide tasks and forms. (For more information on EPSS, consult *Info-line* No. 9806, "EPSS and Your Organization.")

Trainers should automate tasks that are requirements for everyone. Although trainers have less time to teach, they can effectively get learners using macros and templates rather than wasting valuable time teaching how to set up spreadsheets or creating the margins for a letter (both of which can be taken care of by a template).

Sometimes trainers are asked to teach tasks that should have been automated from the start. For example, on a sales automation training project, the help desk may report that users were not using important system utilities (for example, backup, virus check, and scan disk). Because the past training efforts did not cover these topics, only mentioned them in passing, this should not have been a surprise. A good idea would be for future trainers to suggest the placement of an icon on the desktop itself for these activities and set automatic times for these activities to occur. Trainers could also then develop a short reference card to explain the following:

- why these desktop utilities exist
- how they work
- how often they run automatically

During class, trainers could explain why these programs were important, rather than how to find them buried under the Program → Accessories → System Tools menus.

Pre-Screen Learners

You need to assess learners by obtaining information on their background, experiences, present skill levels, and planned use of the software. Use this information to adapt the materials, as well as to group the learners if classes are taught by levels (such as, novice, intermediate, and experienced). A pre-screening form is useful in gathering pertinent information.

A pre-screening form introduces the added benefit of involving learners before the class has begun. This allows trainers to market the training and manage the learners' expectations regarding the software and the course objectives.

If classes are formed with mixed levels of learners, such as when an entire department or district is being trained, trainers use the pre-screening information to assign seats within that class. It makes good training sense to place a novice learner next to an intermediate learner and within easy access to the trainer. Assigned seats based on the pre-screening information help prevent the novice learners from sitting in the back where the trainer cannot easily assist them.

Send pre-screening forms through e-mail with incentives for returning the completed form (for example, if a prospective class member returns your form by the deadline, he or she is eligible to win a gift certificate.) You can give managers incentives as well. Managers whose entire staff complete their forms by a specific date are eligible to win dinner certificates, tickets, and so forth. The best pre-assessment is to list skills and ask for frequency rat-

ings. Trainers then use this information to assign the course level. (See *Pre-Class Assessment Survey* sidebar on the following page.)

Another way to pre-assess learners is to ask managers to rank their staff. Some clients prefer that trainers use this assessment method rather than sending forms directly to the learner. An unfortunate occurrence with this method is that trainers and learners often find that a manager's assessment is incorrect: the manager places the learner in a higher or lower level class than he or she would have personally selected. By dealing directly with learners, trainers can manage their expectations and solicit their involvement in the learning process.

Conducting the Training

The following activities are essential to delivering quality training that meets job needs.

Present Day-in-the-Life Approach

Based on information gathered during the planning phase, trainers should teach the course topics in a logical job sequence and integrate skills throughout. Because this approach mirrors the job activities, learners better comprehend and retain the concepts. For example, in a sales automation training program, trainers could begin by using the system for pre-call planning activities. This activity involves the data that the sales representatives review before scheduling and making new calls. After representatives learn and practice all parts of the system that pertain to pre-call planning, progress into recording a sales call, the next logical activity that happens as part of their day.

Compare New to Old

Whether they are moving from a manual system to a computerized one or from one software program to a new software program, the *way* learners do their job may remain basically the same. Point out and ask learners to identify ways the new system is the same as the old. This comparison allows learners to reach a new comfort level with the software program—even though their screens have changed, they recognize that the basic concepts of their job have not. Identifying the differences between the programs

Pre-Class Assessment Survey

Below is a sample pre-class assessment survey that was used for a sales automation course. Customize this form to accommodate your course topic and specific software program.

Name: _____ Department: _____ Date: _____

1. Overall, how frequently do you use your computer?   several times a week   once a week   occasionally

2. Indicate your level of usage of the following software programs: (check appropriate box)

Software	Daily	Weekly	Occasionally	Never
Word Processing				
Spreadsheet				
Presentation				
E-mail				
PC Program Manager				

3. Rate your skill in each of the following areas: (check appropriate box)

Software	High Skill Level (do not need help)	Medium Skill Level (occasionally need help)	Low Skill Level (need more teaching/review)	Never Use Skill
Creating, editing, printing letters				
Creating spreadsheets with formulas, graphs, and charts				
Reading, sending, filing e-mail				
Viewing file lists, copying and deleting files in program manager				

4. Have you ever used a sales force automation program?   yes   no

   If yes, please circle the answer that describes how you use it:

   profiling   call   contract   expense   other
   physicians/staff   planning/history management   reporting

and the added benefits of the new program is important in establishing learner buy-in of the new system. Training is a key part of that process.

Equating old terms with new ones is important because this allows learners to fit the new term in their knowledge bank. In many classes, writing feature-by-feature comparisons of the terms and functions of the old and new systems helps to distinguish added features from old features with new names.

Provide Practice and Review

Learners need many opportunities to practice and use the commands and concepts that trainers teach. The best way to see if learners have truly mastered the skills is to write independent practice exercises in a real-life job scenario. Trainers should never sacrifice comprehension for the sake of covering more content. Mistakes are the most important part of the practice exercises. Typically, learners make very few mistakes when following along with the trainer because they are told what to do at each step. Valuable mistakes happen during the independent practice exercises, and these mistakes become learning opportunities for the learner and the rest of the class.

Review activities (such as those listed in the *Review Activities* sidebar on the next page) provide a way to reinforce learning and ensure that learners comprehend the topics before covering new material.

Use Reference Materials in Class

If learners do not use training manuals, reference cards, on-line help, or user guides in class, they will not use them back on the job. The trainer's goal is to develop independent learners who can do the tasks outside of the classroom; thus, teaching them how to use all the resources available must be an important element of the training.

Many of the review activities in the sidebar involve using the resource materials as part of a game or team assignment. Whenever you introduce or conclude a topic, ask learners to check where that topic is covered in the resource materials. This way, learners develop confidence in finding and using information and know that they do not need to take extensive notes or try to remember all the commands.

Encourage learners to personalize their reference materials by providing highlighters and Post-it Notes® for them to mark sections that pertain to their job tasks. For example, a reference card can hold over 50 word processing commands and seem overwhelming to read. For anxiety control, have learners highlight the top 10 commands they need to use on a regular basis. Highlighting these commands enables them to quickly locate each command on the reference card.

Develop Independent Learners

Your expectations of your learners need to increase, both in and out of class. Adult learners are responsible for their own learning: trainers cannot make learning happen. They can only guide and facilitate the process. Learners need to be active participants.

Being active means asking questions, answering questions, using the resource materials, making mistakes, and learning from their mistakes. It also means communicating with the trainer throughout class—not just on the evaluation form. When learners need more assistance or are having problems with the pace and instructional method, they have to let the trainer know.

Identify Why and How to Use the Software

During class, having learners identify why and how they will use the software commands back on the job is essential. If they see no application of the skills, learners will not retain the skills. You can assign them to work in teams of three or four to identify ways of applying the training. This exercise also provides a learning process for the trainer because learners understand their jobs better than any outsider.

Assess Comfort Level During Class

Trainers cannot wait until the end of class to find out if the training met the learners' needs. By then, there is nothing a trainer can do about it for that class; he or she can only make adjustments and enhancements for future classes. Using a variety of ways to have learners evaluate the class throughout the sessions allows trainers to make the necessary changes to enhance training—*now*.

Review Activities

The following review activities offer a varied approach to reinforcing and practicing the skills learned in training.

■ *Independent Practice Exercises*

These exercises are hands-on practice activities that are job-focused and designed to allow learners to use the skills and concepts presented in the preceding lesson. Design these exercises in two parts: Part One covers the essential commands and features, and an optional Part Two allows for additional concepts and practice.

■ *Walk-Through Procedures*

Ask volunteers to do a step-by-step walk-through on how to complete a specific procedure or job task using the software. The volunteer can review this process for the whole class, or you can set up partners and ask one partner to guide the other through all the steps. Typically this takes less than five minutes for each procedure or job task.

■ *Stump the Class*

Create teams of three or four people, and give each team three index cards. Have participants write a review question and answer on each card to test the class's knowledge of the topics covered so far. Allow 10 minutes for the teams to review all their training materials and come up with the questions. The trainer collects the cards and tosses a ball randomly. The person who catches the ball may answer the question, confer with the team, or toss the ball to someone else. Once the question has been answered correctly, the person who has the ball tosses it to someone else, and the process continues until all the questions have been answered.

■ *Help Scavenger Hunt*

This review activity places learners in teams to answer a list of questions using the help resources available. This includes the on-line help facility, user manuals, and reference cards. Learners learn to be independent because they become more familiar with the help resources. Assign a time frame of 10-15 minutes for this activity.

■ *What Have You Learned So Far*

Teams list all the skills, concepts, and topics they have learned so far in the course. The team with the most items will win a small prize. Encourage learners to go back to their notes, training manuals, user guides, reference cards, on-line help, and the software screens and menus to come up with their list. Allow only 5-10 minutes for this exercise so that learners have to work quickly. Reward the team with the most items and then have everyone stand. Do a ball toss, and ask each person to state one thing that he or she knows how to do. As each person answers, have him or her throw the ball, then sit down. The only rule is that you cannot repeat what someone else has already stated.

Learners can use e-mail or index cards to identify their comfort level with the topics and pace and to identify topics they wish to review or cover in more detail. (See *Comfort Level Assessment* sidebar for an example form.)

A good idea for measuring learner comfort level is to paste a stoplight symbol on each computer or desk and, periodically, before a break, ask the learners to move the pointer to the following colors to indicate their comfort level:

- Red—stop, need to go back before covering the next topic

- Yellow—slow down, do a quick review or exercise

- Green—go ahead, pace and topics are fine

Evaluate the Class

Have a simple evaluation form that can be easily completed and summarized. Trainers can use many survey software programs to create and compile the data into meaningful information, or they can use a spreadsheet program to record the scores.

The *Class Evaluation Form* sidebar that follows shows a form trainers can use and then easily summarize. Stress to learners that the comment area is the most valuable section of the form, and ask that they really think about their comments for this section. Trainers should hand out and explain evaluation forms early on so learners understand its layout and importance. A good time to ask participants to complete the form is during the last break—rather than waiting until the end of class as learners rush out the door.

An instructor evaluation of the class is also an important tool that is typically overlooked. This evaluation provides a way for the instructor to communicate any problems with the course materials, participants, equipment, and so forth that management may need to address before the next class. The instructor also indicates if the individual learners met the pre-requisites and mastered the course objectives. What the trainer recommends as a next step is also part of this evaluation.

Follow-Up After Training

The learning process does not stop because class is over. Training is an on-going process. Trainers should perform the following activities after the class has ended.

■ *Follow-Up With Learners and Managers*
Investigate to see if learners are using the training and what additional training they need. Get out of the classroom and talk to managers to ascertain if training addressed the job needs and what other needs training could meet. Observe which skills the participants use and do not use and develop a way for training to encourage learners to use all taught skills. You can use e-mail and phone interviews to gather this information. (See the *Follow-Up Training Form* sidebar for a sample follow-up evaluation form.)

■ *Review Help Desk Statistics*
Within the first two weeks after class, track help desk calls immediately and note patterns in topics or callers. If help desk calls or surveys show people are not using a skill or that they are having problems with a skill, this is a sign that the trainer needs to readdress how he or she teaches this issue. It is not that a skill was not taught—calls to the help desk prove that it was not *learned*.

■ *Fine-Tune, Enhance Materials and Exercises*
You should compile feedback from the trainers, course evaluations, follow-up evaluations, interviews, and help desk reports, and address areas of concerns. You need to determine if there are better ways to teach a specific skill. Is a reference card needed? Are procedural changes needed? Are topics to be added or dropped?

■ *Send E-mail From Graduates*
If you are doing a series of classes, ask past graduates to e-mail you their thoughts about what they learned that proved to be most valuable and what tips or tricks they have found useful. Compile these, and e-mail them to the next class so that they can see how the training is really used back on the job. Messages from their peers are invaluable in showing new learners that the training is useful and applicable.

■ *Make Training an On-Going Process*
Use e-mail to send tips of the week and questions and answers to common help desk calls. Identify other resources that can provide additional training and support (such as Web sites, CBT/Internet training, other classes, and publications).

Comfort Level Assessment

Below is a sample form that you can use during class to identify the learner's comfort level with the topics. Participants could also relay this information on index cards or through e-mail.

Name: _____

1. What topics have you mastered so far?

2. What topics need more explanation and practice?

3. What is your overall comfort level with the topics?

   - very comfortable
   - somewhat comfortable
   - feel lost

4. What is your overall comfort level with the pace?

   - pace is just right
   - pace is too fast
   - pace is too slow

5. What can the **trainer** do to enhance your learning?

6. What can **you** do to enhance your learning?

Class Evaluation Form

The following sample is a one-page evaluation form that you can easily use to summarize events once the class is over. It includes a rating checklist and open-ended questions.

Name: _____ Date: _____ Instructor: _____

To ensure that this course meets training goals and objectives, please evaluate the following areas of the course.

Rating Scale:
5	4	3	2	1
strongly agree	agree	uncertain	disagree	strongly disagree

	5	4	3	2	1
The course content and exercises met my learning goals.					
The instructor was knowledgeable about the system and presented the information in a clear, concise manner.					
The course exercises were job-oriented and helped reinforce the learning.					
The course pace and schedule were appropriate to my training needs.					
The course pace and schedule were appropriate to the overall class needs.					
The facilitators were patient and helpful in providing assistance.					
I would recommend this type of training program.					
I think I have mastered the basics of the system and can begin using it on my job.					

What I liked best about the workshop was _____

_____

_____ .

For future courses, I would suggest the following enhancements or improvements: _____

_____

_____ .

Overall, I feel the workshop was _____

_____

_____ .

Adapting Approach

While it would be most beneficial to radically redesign and refocus all courses to meet the job need, often the most important or challenging courses are the only ones to get this type of specific attention. These courses typically have the highest attendance or the most problems, or they are courses for new projects. What can trainers do about the "other" courses? The following text describes some ideas to try.

■ *Create Job Modules*
People have less and less time for training these days. Offer shorter, targeted courses. Use creative titles to market the course, such as the following:

- Mail Merge: Sending Personalized Letters to Hundreds of Unknown People

- Using the Excel Expense Report

- Where, Oh Where, Has My Print Job Gone?

These titles are more focused and descriptive than titles using ambiguous words like "Introductory," "Intermediate," or "Advanced."

■ *Assess Learners at Start of Class*
If pre-screening is not possible, do the next best thing: in-class screening. When the participants arrive at class, find out their background and learning goals. Have a short questionnaire, and ask them to pick a skill rating from one to five that identifies their skill level or ask each learner to review the objectives posted around the room and mark their top three objectives.

■ *Pick Top Objectives*
When time is limited and learner needs are diverse, you may need to be flexible and first focus on the top objectives that most learners have selected from the previous task. Set a time to address other topics so that people can leave if they do not have a job need for that topic. This works best when teaching at more advanced course levels because training typically covers a number of diverse topics that are not integrated with each other.

■ *Prioritize*
Within every course and every lesson, there are topics that are mission critical and topics that are nice-to-know, but not essential. Know where to skim or skip based on the learners' needs and experience levels.

■ *Bring Real Work*
Allow some free time for learners to work on real work instead of completing an exercise. Tell them this ahead of time, and provide guidance as to the complexity of the document.

■ *Create Teams*
No computer user is an island. Most employees rely on their peers to help them solve problems. Create teams of three or four people. Let the teams choose a name and compete in review activities. Teams foster a sense of ownership in mastering, using, and applying the skills. The team members also build their own network of support contacts that can continue on after class.

The job-oriented training approach works for all kinds of training:

- instructor led
- CBT
- multimedia training
- Web-based training

If you start bridging the gap now, you will be ready for wherever the next phase of evolution in computer training will take us—to cyberspace and beyond!

Follow-Up Training Form

The purpose of the follow-up training form is to identify how learners use the training skills back on the job. This feedback is important because trainers can use it to identify course enhancements and needs for future training sessions.

Name: _____ Department: _____ Date: _____

1. Are you using the software and skills you learned in the training course?   yes   no

   If no, please explain why not:

2. Listed below are the topics that the trainer covered in class. Use the following codes to describe how often you use these topics and at what skill level.

Frequency of Use: 3-daily   2-weekly   1-occasionally   0-never use

Mastery Level: 3-mastered   2-can do with help   1-have problems using   0-never use

Topic	Frequency of Use	Mastery Level
Logging into specific program.		
Changing passwords.		
Moving and sizing windows.		
Viewing multiple windows on same screen.		
Opening multiple applications and switching between opened applications.		
Copying between applications.		
Changing screen colors.		
Changing screen colors and screen saver.		

3. Now that you have completed the course and used the software back on the job, what enhancements would you suggest to improve the training class?

4. How has the personal computer impacted your job? Discuss any advantages or improvements still needed. Identify any future training needs.

References & Resources

Articles

Barron. Tom. "CBT Recycling: An Interview With Barry Raybould." *Technical & Skills Training.* February/March 1997, pp. 17-19.

Cavalier, James C., and James D. Klein. "Effects of Cooperative Versus Individual Learning and Orienting Activities During Computer-Based Instruction." *Educational Technology Research & Development.* Vol. 46, No. 1 1998, pp. 5-17.

Davis, Clare. "Retrofitting Instructor-Led Training to CBT." *CBT Solutions.* March/April 1996, pp. 19-24.

Densford, Lynn E. "Major Public-Private Effort Launch to Standardize Computer-Based Training." *Corporate University Review.* November/December 1997.

Keith, Philip A. "Off-The-Shelf CBT: Where Do We Go From Here?" *CBT Solutions.* January/February 1997, pp. 85-88.

Kemske, Floyd. "The CBT Software Market." *CBT Solutions.* May/June 1997, pp. 54-62.

———. "The Shift is Real." *CBT Solutions.* January/February 1998, pp. 8-25.

———. "Technology, Politics, and Metadata: Part 2 of Our Authoring Roundtable." *CBT Solutions.* March/April 1998, pp. 12-22, 30, 56.

McCord, Ron. "CD-ROM vs. Internet to Deliver Training." *Multimedia & Internet Training Newsletter.* March 1998, pp. 6-7.

McKim, Pat. "Where We Stand With Interoperability." *CBT Solutions.* July/August 1997, pp. 28-32.

Neitzka, Kim. "Alive and Well: CBT on the Mainframe." *CBT Solutions.* March/April 1998, pp. 40-43.

Paul, Lauren Gibbons. "The Right Formula for Training." *Datamation.* September 1997, pp. 96-101.

Piper, Travis. "It'll Cost How Much?" *CBT Solutions.* January/February 1997, pp. 76-79.

Pisik, Ginger Brill. "Is This Course Instructionally Sound? A Guide to Evaluating Online Training Courses." *Educational Technology.* July/August 1997, pp. 50-51.

Sevilla, Christine, and Timothy Wells. "Dynamic Learning and Performance Improvement." *Performance Improvement.* May/June 1997, pp. 26-28.

Thornburg, Linda. "Investment in Training Technology Yields Good Returns." *HRMagazine.* January 1998, pp. 37-41.

Tongue, Ken. "One Man's Journey to Digital Metering." *CBT Solutions.* March/April 1997, pp. 21-24.

Weinschenk, Susan. "Performance Specifications as Change Agents." *Technical Training.* October 1997, pp. 12-14.

Weiss-Morris, Loretta. "Just-in-Time Training: How One Company Blends LAN-based CBTs With Instructor-Led Classes." *CBT Solutions.* March/April 1996, pp. 1, 5-11.

Books

Brandon, Bill (ed.). *The Computer Trainer's Personal Training Guide.* Que Education & Training, 1996.

Broad, Dr. Mary, and John W. Newstromz. *Transfer of Training: Action-Packed Strategies to Ensure High Payoff From Training Investments.* Perseus Press, 1992.

Clothier, Paul. *The Complete Computer Trainer.* Computing McGraw Hill, 1996.

Eitington, Julius E. *The Winning Trainer: Winning Ways to Involve People in Learning.* Gulf Publishing Co., 1996.

Lee, William W., and Robert A. Mamone. *The Computer Based Training Handbook: Assessment, Design, Development, Evaluation.* Educational Technology Publications, 1995.

Mosher, Bob. *Training for Results: Teaching Adults to be Independent, Assertive Learners.* Logical Operations, 1996.

Robinson, Dana Gaines, and James C. Robinson. *Training for Impact: How to Link Training to Business Needs and Measure the Results.* San Francisco: Jossey-Bass Publishers, 1989.

Schank, Rober. *Virtual Learning: A Revolutionary Approach to Building a Highly Skilled Workforce.* New York: McGraw-Hill, 1997.

Silberman, Mel, et al. *Active Training: A Handbook of Techniques, Designs, Case Examples, and Tips.* San Francisco: Jossey-Bass Publishers, 1997.

Info-lines

Kirrane, Diane. "The Role of the Performance Needs Analyst." No. 9713.

Raybould, Barry. "EPSS and Your Organization." No. 9806.

Russell, Susan. "Create Effective Job Aids." No. 9711.

Waagen, Alice K. "Task Analysis." No. 9808.

Wynn, Pardner. "Delivering Quick-Response IBT/CBT Training." No. 9701.

Checklist for Job-Oriented Training

As you prepare to conduct training that is job specific, use the following checklist to help you organize your planning and development efforts.

Recognize the Need

☐ Realize that there is less time for training and that a software's shelf-life decreases as the rate of change accelerates.

☐ Recognize that learners have changed from *pioneers* to *settlers*.

☐ Remember the impact of downsizing—less staff to do more work.

Automate Common and Standard Tasks

☐ Create macros and templates for company- and department-wide tasks.

☐ Investigate electronic performance support systems (EPSSs).

Identify Job Functions in Relation to Software

☐ Identify key departments you want to work with and obtain their sponsorship.

☐ Review work samples and job tasks.

☐ Prioritize job tasks in relation to software functions.

Customize and Tailor Curriculum

☐ Pilot approach with most popular course or most troublesome course.

☐ Build a mix of mediums: classroom, multimedia, videos, software tip books, and so forth.

☐ Plan for shorter, targeted specialty courses versus "Introductory," "Intermediate," and "Advanced."

Customize Materials

☐ Develop quick reference cards that could also be tailored to a department.

☐ Create tip and trick sheets.

☐ Create customized exercises.

Customize Training Approach

☐ Teach how to use the macros and templates.

☐ Integrate on-line help and software "coaches" along with teaching.

☐ Get learners to prioritize topics based on job tasks and to bring in work samples.

Get Manager Buy-In

☐ Identify the process and benefits.

☐ Get their commitment to earn a return on their training investment.

☐ Ask them to discuss objectives with their staff before and after the course.

Get Learner Buy-In

☐ Communicate course objectives, benefits, and prerequisite skills.

☐ Identify the process, benefits, and learner's role before, during, and after training.

☐ Ask learners to discuss the course with their manager before and after the training.

Follow-Up and Evaluate the Results

☐ Conduct in-class assessments on comfort level and applicability to the job.

☐ Track help desk questions and make enhancements to course or materials.

☐ Conduct interviews with learners and managers to see how skills are used on the job.

Develop Independent Learners

☐ Teach learners how and when to call the help desk.

☐ Have learners use reference manuals during class.

☐ Conduct "scavenger hunts" during class using on-line help to find answers to common questions.

On-the-Job Training

Issue 9708

On-the-Job Training

AUTHOR:

Charles I. Levine, Ph.D.
President, Instructional Design
Associates
P.O. Box 457
Sharon, MA 02067-0457
Tel. 781.784.5994
Fax. 781.784.2578

Dr. Levine, a nationally respected and active educator on the subject of OJT, has over 25 years experience as a trainer and consultant. He has held key management and training positions with Raytheon, Honeywell, and The University of Wisconsin. His clients include Toyota Motor Corporation, Michigan Bell, Illinois Bell, and Heinz, Inc.

Editor
Cat Sharpe

Associate Editor
Patrick McHugh

Designer
Steven M. Blackwood

Copy Editor
Kay Larson

ASTD Internal Consultant
Dr. Walter Gray

On-the-Job Training

On-the-job training (OJT) is one of the oldest forms of training; it was born when the first parent took his or her child aside and said, "Let me show you how to do that." OJT at its most fundamental level can be defined as two people working closely together so one person can learn from the other. Whether the person teaching is called trainer, mentor, or guide, the function is the same—to teach the student so that he or she can correctly and safely perform a task. OJT's strengths are in its flexibility and portability, all the while remaining an informal and human form of training.

There is no company, factory, or home business in the world where one person—the so-called expert—has not helped a fellow employee learn a new skill. This *Info-line* covers the essentials of OJT and just how you and your organization can best employ and enjoy OJT's far-reaching benefits. The concepts and advice presented apply to any organization, ranging from manufacturing to services and from government to education. Whenever and where ever employees need training in specific work-related tasks, OJT is the training method you'll want to consider.

Everyone has their own definition of what OJT means. Essentially, it is a just-in-time training delivery system that dispenses training to employees as and when they need it. An OJT system can be as small or as large as the needs and resources of an organization allow.

Whether they know it or not, all companies have OJT systems in place. There is always someone standing next to another worker who says the magic OJT words, "Let me show you how to do that," and then teaches the other how to run a machine or perform a task. This is called *unstructured OJT* because it occurs haphazardly—the employee-trainer (a.k.a. expert) teaches the tasks as he or she knows and remembers them. Because of time or other pressures, important steps may be forgotten or simply skipped. As an unstructured system, no criteria are established for the quality of training, nor are records of the training maintained.

Building a Structured OJT System

In response to quality, ISO 9000 (see "ISO 9000 and OJT" on the next page), and budget constraints, companies have been "organizing" the OJT process. Specific employees are designated OJT trainers, checklists of required skills are used to ensure that all employees receive the same training, and the training effort is tracked and recorded. Because an organizational structure supports the training, this is called *structured OJT*. Structured OJT is more efficient than unstructured OJT and in some reports, companies relate a 60 to 80 percent decrease in training time.

Most companies want to implement a structured OJT system, but few achieve this goal. What typically happens is that the already existing, but unstructured OJT system, also begins to fail. In unstructured OJT, all the training time is casual—untracked and therefore invisible. It never appears on a budget or time sheet. Structured OJT, on the other hand, makes this time visible and in many companies visibility is risky. Once training time becomes real, supervisors often move to eliminate or convert it into production time, since they, of course, are measured by production output. This explains how many organizations simply botch an existing unstructured OJT system when moving to a structured one.

Before making the transition, beware of the fact that structured OJT only exists with the assistance, support, and understanding of management and production supervisors. Training takes time; if supervisors do not allow enough time for preparation and training, they will thwart any structured OJT effort. If you cannot gain internal support from the organization's managers and supervisors, don't waste time trying to implement structured OJT. Instead, work to strengthen the existing training process.

Similar to quality programs and true ISO 9000 programs, a structured OJT system will change your production operation: training assumes new importance—trainers are included when developing new production processes and are given time to carry out proper training. As with any system, trainers still need to be flexible when dealing with production and customer needs.

When to Use OJT

The use of OJT as a training method is determined by the following:

- safety considerations
- size of the training unit
- geographic distribution of the trainees

When safety is a major issue, some companies use simulators or spare machinery for OJT training. Though simulators are expensive, they allow trainees to experience potentially catastrophic circumstances without any danger to themselves or the facility. If you are going to use simulators or spare machinery for OJT training, be sure to have scripted scenarios so the training is useful, realistic, and consistent. In some companies, regulatory statutes require the use of simulators within the boundaries of a very structured OJT system.

ISO 9000 and OJT

ISO 9000 is a set of generic standards that provide quality management guidance and identify system elements necessary to assure quality. Each company decides how to implement the standards to meet its own and its customers' needs. Basically, the ISO 9000 standards require a company to document procedures, follow those procedures, review the process, and then change them when necessary.

Under ISO registration, training checklists and any other OJT documentation should become controlled documents that cannot be changed without appropriate approval. Trainers must become part of the procedure development and sign-off process, thus establishing a link from the OJT system to quality and engineering. As OJT systems grow, they become further intertwined into normal daily operations of the company. Wherever new employees need to learn specific skills or procedures in order to succeed on the job, the OJT concept is applicable.

For example, a company implementing an OJT system under mandate from their ISO 9000 registrar might devote more resources to the system due to requests from production supervisors. It is a fact of life that problems that threaten to close a facility or cause it to loose its certification will receive more attention than those having less impact. For more information on quality systems, see *Info-lines* No. 8805, "Training for Quality" and No. 9111, "Fundamentals of Quality."

If group interaction, interpersonal skills, or other personal communication objectives are part of the training, classroom instruction is probably the best delivery medium. OJT instruction cannot fulfill interpersonal skills objectives since **OJT, by definition, is one-on-one training.** If the trainer has the requisite skills in specific training techniques and there are sufficient controls in place over the training methods, OJT can be used for conceptual training in areas such as quality and customer satisfaction. In this scenario, trainers act as role models and instruct students through skills and behavior training. If a large number of employees need to be trained or if the potential trainees are geographically dispersed, other methods of training should be used.

OJT has one major drawback—it assumes that trainees are capable of learning and have the background skills, such as math and reading, necessary to perform the task. If prerequisite skills are not present, the OJT training will fail. Trainers should be educated to recognize these deficits and respond appropriately.

From Unstructured to Structured OJT

Building on the example of unstructured OJT where two people stand together and one person informally teaches the other, we can begin to construct a more structured system.

The next phase in the growth of an OJT system is to train the trainers in methods and techniques. Most OJT trainers have never been shown how to adapt to various student learning styles or how to most effectively present materials. This is one of the most critical and important steps in the growth of OJT within a company. Untrained trainers will surely cause an OJT system to fail.

Until now, we have been dealing with casual trainers, that is, employees who work in a production area and train when there is spare time. As the OJT system continues to grow, some companies will "bite the head count bullet" and assign full-time trainers to the OJT system. These trainers may have the responsibility to train new personnel, retrain existing employees who are changing jobs, or recertify staff on their current jobs. Full-time trainers do not need to be experts in all tasks; they may delegate some training tasks to part-time trainers who are experts in specific skill areas, but it is the full-time trainers' responsibility to ensure that all checklists are completed. At this time the company may assign an employee as an OJT system coordinator to track and record employee training progress.

Components of an OJT System

There are a number of components to an OJT system. Every OJT system contains all of the components, but the intensity of each varies significantly depending on the type of implementation.

Management Support

Management controls all of the resources you need and without their support you have little chance of success. This includes attention to the details of OJT training, review of tracking reports, support with supervisors and production managers, and specific allowances for your budget—both in terms of dollars and time. The budget is used for:

- OJT training materials
- computers
- software for tracking students
- training the OJT developers and trainers
- time for the training
- time to work on processes and procedures

It is important to note that management may approve these expenditures, but in the crush of production, may never actually get a chance to spend the money.

Unfortunately, production supervisors (in any type of company, from financial to manufacturing) are caught in the middle between two completely conflicting goals—training and production. If supervisors take people out of production and allow them to go into training, they lose production time and their numbers may be lower than those of other supervisors who do not allow for training time. Supervisors/line managers generally do not want to hear "let me have your workers today and I will give them back to you trained tomorrow." To a supervisor, that means a loss of production today, and he or she may not care about tomorrow.

OJT Myths

Management and supervisors find several basic OJT concepts confusing or hard to understand. Understand and work through these misconceptions before you implement an OJT system, otherwise there will be trouble and confusion later on.

■ *Myth # 1: OJT Is Free*
OJT systems take time, money, people, and energy. When finished, OJT may be as expensive as classroom training, but produces a much higher return on investment for specific skills training.

■ *Myth # 2: Training Time Is Production Time*
Production personnel who participate in OJT cannot produce at full capacity and trainers cannot perform in both positions at the same time.

■ *Myth # 3: OJT Is Simply Part of the Job*
OJT training is work and necessitates trainers who agree to perform the training and tracking activities. Workers should not be "volunteered" to become OJT trainers. OJT structures such as training procedures, lists of tasks, assigned personnel, training materials, and equipment are essential.

■ *Myth # 4: Anyone Can Be an OJT Trainer*
Trainers should be selected carefully and then schooled in OJT training techniques and the use of the OJT materials.

■ *Myth # 5: Once Implemented, OJT Is Forever*
OJT systems require continuous review of OJT checklists, OJT trainer decisions, return on investment, resource allocation, and so forth.

■ *Myth # 6: OJT Changes Organizational Development*
OJT does change the organization and increase communication and force power sharing, but it is implemented *on top* of existing systems, not in place of them.

©1997, I.D.A.

Formal Trainer Support Process

Supervisors are very busy people and are not always known for their problem-solving or people skills. Generally, first-line supervision is the weakest link in the management chain. Trainers need another person, outside their organization, to go to for support, help, and advice on sensitive personnel issues.

Successful systems appoint an OJT-coordinator from a neutral organization (usually HR) who regularly interacts with the trainers. The trainers then work for the production area but have a dotted-line relationship with the support organization. In some systems, the trainers are transferred to the support organization and have a dotted-line relationship with the production organization.

Trainer protection is needed when the trainer does not think an employee is ready to be checked off on a task, but the supervisor insists that they be allowed to work and asks the trainer to check them off anyway. In this case where does the trainer go for help and support? In other cases, when the trainer and the student have a conflict or when the trainer is asked to fix a nontraining problem, who supports the trainer? In extreme cases, the student may actually verbally attack the trainer and accuse him or her of not being a good trainer. Safeguards need to be in place to protect the trainer.

Checklists

To succeed over the long term, OJT must be linked to other plant or company systems. Usually OJT is linked to ISO 9000, pay-for-performance, procedure sign-off, or regulatory or mandated training systems. Linking the OJT system to another company system simply means that the OJT system cannot go away or be mortally wounded without also wounding the linked system. It provides some protection to the funding, time availability, and resource availability for the system and its trainers.

The basis of the linkage to any system is the checklist, which proves that the student is capable of performing a specific task at a specific competency level. OJT systems without checklists cannot be linked to others, and generally are not acceptable as a basis for ISO 9000 registration.

The checklist is the foundation of any OJT system. It lists the tasks that need to be trained along with administrative information such as the student name, training dates, and completion dates. It also has room for the signatures of the trainer and student for each task along with the supervisor signature when the entire checklist is completed. A sample checklist is shown on page 136.

Skills checklists also add structure to the process. With a list of specific skills that need to be taught, fewer tasks slip through the cracks and the employee is "checked off" as each task is successfully performed. While checklists decrease the variation in skills being taught, some will still exist. During training, some trainers will let the students operate the equipment, while others push the student to the side and show the student how to operate the equipment. Some trainers let students explore and make mistakes, while others make the students follow their exact directions step by step.

Important OJT Concepts

There are several important concepts to remember when implementing an OJT system:

■ *OJT Systems Are Not Implemented To Improve Training*
They are implemented to improve productivity, lower scrap, or to meet ISO 9000/quality requirements. The decision to implement an OJT system is a *business decision* not a training decision. Keep this in mind lest you get carried away with the training aspects of the system.

■ *OJT Systems Take Resources From Other Projects*
Energy, time, and personal may be taken away from other projects, including production. Do not attempt to implement a system beyond the needs of your company.

■ *Good OJT Systems Grow*
Build the foundation carefully—checklists, trained trainers, and most importantly, buy-in from all stakeholders. Remember, OJT systems will change your organization and you cannot succeed without acceptance from those you seek to change.

■ *OJT Systems Are Nonexclusionary*
They are about training, helping, and ensuring that every employee has an equal opportunity to complete the tasks on his or her checklist and become a productive employee.

©1997, I.D.A.

Characteristics of Good OJT Systems

The number of variations in OJT systems is staggering: every company designs a slightly different system to solve its OJT training problems. Certain characteristics of OJT training are consistent across every system, however. Before implementing an OJT system, it is vital that you understand these characteristics. Unfortunately, like many concepts, these characteristics are subjective. This list does not comprise the "golden rules of OJT training"—what is successful in one company may prove disastrous in another. OJT systems should generally possess the following characteristics:

Structure

- OJT processes are written and part of your company's operating procedure.

- OJT materials and training guides are fully described and developed.

- Supervisors include performance checklists in performance (or new hire) reviews.

- Trainers are familiar with job and OJT training skills.

Objectives

- Students know what is expected of them on the job.

- Quality and quantity variables are clear and explicit.

- Skills are broken down into manageable segments and recorded in the OJT structure.

Accountability

- Standardized evaluations are established for all major tasks.

- Students are tested on job-related skills as called for in the OJT procedures.

- Skill/task is checked off from a list when performed to trainers' satisfaction.

Preparation

- Trainers are given adequate time to prepare their training, develop aids, and collect materials.

- Training activities, visual aids, and materials are completed ahead of time.

- Training time is scheduled.

Consistency

- Training does not vary by trainer, shift, or time of year.

- All students complete training with the *same* set of core skills.

Humanity

- Trainers are sensitive to learners' needs and can change instructional strategies as required by student, content, and time requirements.

- Students are coached until they can successfully perform the tasks.

- Training is a one-on-one, human-to-human activity.

©1997, I.D.A.

Benchmarking Exercise

The objective of this exercise is to measure your company's current OJT system against an ideal system. It can serve as a convenient discussion tool with management as you explain the process of implementing an OJT system.

Instructions

Listed below are the six basic characteristics of an OJT system (explained on page 137). Think about your company, analyze your current OJT system, and score each characteristic on a scale of 0 to 5 according to the following scale:

0 = this characteristic is totally absent from our OJT system

5 = our company devotes enormous amounts of time, energy, and money to this characteristic.

Scoring

Please note that this is an awareness—not a pass or fail—exercise to show where you stand in relation to other companies and the "perfect" OJT system.

Companies that score below 10, with no one score above three, tend to have disorganized and unstructured OJT systems. Most training is informal and uncontrolled with little management attention given to the OJT training area. Attention may be devoted to a training "problem," but requests for time, money, or personnel are inevitably turned down.

If your score is between 10 and 20, one or more characteristics may be scored highly while others are relatively low. This indicates a system in flux—growing and preparing for additional structure, or shrinking and becoming more informal. A score in this range calls for a more detailed investigation of each of the characteristics and the direction each is taking.

If you score above 20, congratulations! Your company has devoted resources to OJT and received buy-in from managers, supervisors, and workers. This is not an excuse to sit back and relax, however. OJT is ever-changing and you need constant vigilance to maintain your enviable standing.

Characteristics	Score	Comments
1. Structure		
2. Objectives		
3. Accountability		
4. Preparation		
5. Consistency		
6. Humanity		
(MAXIMUM = 30)		

In some companies, the checklists and other OJT documentation are "controlled" and cannot be changed without approval. In good OJT systems trainers are on the sign-off list for procedure changes and know about them far in advance. This gives trainers the chance to contribute to the decision-making process and ensure that procedures are realistic. It also gives them the opportunity to update training materials and evaluations before the change is implemented.

In the case of mandated training or in a pay-for-performance system, the checklist assumes increased importance. In both cases the checklist may become a legal document, either due to an accident or in connection with pay rates. Trainers should never take shortcuts or check off students until they can perform the task to specifications because they could be held responsible for any accidents or pay disputes.

OJT Training Materials

OJT trainers should not train "off the top of their heads." This is dangerous and invites mistakes. In addition to checklists, students should also receive procedures or other job aids. If students can take notes during training, they should be provided with a notebook or other organized method for writing. Students should not take notes on "little pieces of paper." These will quickly get lost and the effort will be wasted.

If students cannot take notes, or get copies of the procedures, they should be posted near the machine or work area. Many companies keep copies of procedure manuals in supervisors' offices, but rarely does anyone use them.

Some companies support trainers by giving them a room complete with computer equipment and printers where they can go to develop the handouts or procedures necessary for the training. For more information on training materials, see *Info-lines* No. 9707, "High Performance Training Manuals" and No. 9711 "Effective Job Aids."

The time, equipment, and resources necessary to develop OJT materials are also vital to trainers. One training scenario might go like this: "Here is a good widget [as the trainer picks up a widget from the line]. Notice how the edges meet and the color is even throughout the part. If the color is not uni-

form or if the edges do not meet, reject the piece." What do you think of that training? Is it sufficient? Will the student learn how to inspect the product properly? The answer is "no" to all of these questions. The student does not know what "uniform" or "edges meet" mean. Do they have to meet exactly, with absolutely no overlap, or is a little overlap OK? The student has not been told these criteria or have a context within which to learn them.

Train-the-Trainer Program

Do not assume that training comes naturally or that anyone can be an OJT trainer; selection and training must be carefully considered and may involve considerable effort and expense. But remember, poor trainers will kill OJT systems and, in the long run, will be more expensive. Good trainers increase acceptance of a program, perform the training faster, and increase the efficiency of the training process.

No one has a fail-safe method for selecting trainers. OJT trainers succeed or fail for several reasons including:

- lack of training skills
- lack of support
- an unstable political situation
- caught between supervisors and management
- blamed for employees' performance
- blamed for lower production numbers

A successful process consists of two parts: select the trainers and then train them.

Step 1: Trainer Selection

■ *Write a Job Description for the Position*
Define training goals, tasks to perform, and available support. Delineate how much time will be devoted to training, materials development, and other responsibilities. Also specify how training will be measured and the process by which trainers will be schooled—the train-the-trainer program.

Writing the job description forces management to think carefully about trainers, how they will be supported, and how they will fit into the organization. Having early answers to these kinds of questions eliminates unnecessary work later in the process when these questions typically are asked.

■ *Select Trainers*

Post the job description and ask if anybody wants to volunteer for the training position. Ask supervisors or others who already perform OJT to recommend well-respected employees (not necessarily the most proficient) for the positions.

■ *Enroll as Many People as Possible*

This may be the most expensive option, but it also produces the best results. Many employees do not want to be trainers because they don't know what the job entails, but people who consider themselves experts may want to be trainers and get upset when

they are not chosen. By sending these experts through train-the-trainer programs, you allow them to decide whether they want to be trainers. This also lets those who are excited about training take the lead.

Step 2: Train-the-Trainer

Companies implement many different types of train-the-trainer programs, some successful and some not. It is important to decide what program objectives should be. Following are the three main objectives of an OJT trainer program:

Sample Checklist

Widget Task Training Checklist

Widget Inspection

Student Name: _____ Employee No. _____

Date Started: _____ Date Completed: _____

Widget Inspection Task

TASK	DATE	TRAINER	EMPLOYEE
1. Use of gloves and glasses			
2. Handling of widget			
3. Calibration of elevator			
4. Inspection product—color striation			
5. Inspection of product—edge alignment			

Completion Signatures

Supervisor _____ Student _____ Trainer_____

Date _____

©1997, I.D.A.

■ *Ensure Trainer Buy-In*

For some trainers this involves a massive change in the way they conduct training. Most OJT trainers use a dump method—that is, they sit next to their student and dump out everything they know. It may be easy to teach specific OJT training techniques to trainers, but getting them to apply them is another task. Changing the behavior of an OJT trainer requires process activities in the train-the-trainer program rather than lecture or skills activities. They should be able to use alternative instructional strategies, checklists, and appropriate evaluation techniques.

■ *Teach Training and Learning Styles*

This enables trainers to know something about themselves and their style of training. Many have been training for years but have never learned about training styles or students' learning styles. These introspective activities help trainers understand how their style impacts students' learning and also find ways to fine tune their training behavior. For more information, see *Info-line*s No. 9604, "How to Accommodate Different Learning Styles"; No. 8804, "Training and Learning Styles"; No. 9608, "Do's and Don'ts for the New Trainer"; No. 8808, "Basic Training for Trainers"; and No. 9003, "How to Train Managers to Train."

■ *Teach One-on-One Training Techniques*

Use specific OJT training skills such as the four-step OJT training model, OJT-oriented instructional strategies, and appropriate evaluation techniques. If these skills are taught without the benefit of the process and behavior adjustment activities, then students will smile, nod, perform the class activities, leave the class, and generally go out on the floor and do what they want. **They do not learn.**

Experience shows that OJT trainers rarely conduct formal classroom group presentations, but rather perform one-on-one training by standing or sitting next to a student. Therefore, they do not need to use overhead projectors, give presentations, or use large group-training techniques. OJT train-the-trainer programs should concentrate on techniques best suited to one-on-one learning.

A word of caution here. The OJT training program described on the following page is a high-process class and contains many introspective activities designed to help students interpret, use, and place in context specific OJT skills. This class is closer to an intervention than to a traditional skills training program because the primary objective is to change the trainers' behaviors.

Most companies either design and run the trainer program in-house, purchase materials for a program to be run by an internal trainer, or bring in an external trainer to conduct the program. If you design and conduct an OJT trainer course with internal talent, make sure the personnel assigned to this task have experience in high-process training activities or organizational interventions. Typically, these employees have designed and trained management, supervisory, or career development classes and are comfortable in the role of facilitator. This class can not be taught as a lecture.

If you purchase an OJT trainer course or contract with an outside trainer, make sure the course meets the requirements discussed above. As an extra check, contact previous clients for references and make sure the contract trainer has conducted similar courses before. Sometimes local colleges offer to teach courses like this, but be prepared for an academic overview of adult learning taught by a person who has never worked in a factory. A little investigation at this point in the project can save enormous amounts of money and keep the OJT project on the right track. See *Info-line* No. 8610, "Find the Right Consultant" for more information on outsourcing training.

Tracking and Report Generation

It is important that an OJT system be able to track and report on its activities. Generally, these reports are statistical, providing numerical data on:

● number of students trained
● checklists completed
● number of training hours
● percentage of successful students
● cost of training (total and per student)
● return on investment of training

Some systems report on training development activities, test or evaluation results, and trainer effectiveness. Some systems also report on certification expiration and notify employees when they need retraining.

The administrator or coordinator who is responsible for the tracking system should also be prepared to produce reports supporting ISO 9000 audits, GMP audits, or annual budget reviews.

When checklists are created, you can decide if the checklist is valid forever or carries an expiration date. When students complete checklists, the expiration dates should be recorded and tracked within the system. In some cases, regulatory requirements will define retraining or recertification time intervals. Both students and trainers should be automatically notified when recertification training is required.

Some systems distribute "smile sheets" so students can evaluate their instructors. These student critiques are no more valid in this environment than in classroom training environments but are useful for detecting trends and highlighting areas for improvement or praise.

Sample Train-the-Trainer Program

This sample OJT trainer program is designed to meet each of the three objectives as well as provide a pleasant experience and some fun along the way. The course typically takes three days, although it can be taught in two if the class is small. A successful program should:

- build training skills and encourage buy-in to the OJT program and use of the OJT materials
- contain high-impact exercises to change trainer behavior from telling to coaching
- include modules on training skills, instructional strategies, practice training activities, and introspective activities

Typical outline for a three-day OJT training program

Day 1	Day 2	Day 3
Introduction/outline	Introspective exercise:	Videotaped OJT coaching sessions— 10 minute coaching sessions that are videotaped, reviewed, and critiqued by the class and instructor
What is OJT training?	• Instructor styles inventory	
Learning curves	• Identifying types of students	
Four-step training model	• Instructional strategies for different types of students	
Lunch	**Lunch**	**Lunch**
Practice training exercise in groups of two	Practice training exercise in groups of three	Class wrap-up
Introspective exercise	Prep time for video coaching teaching sessions	Course critique
		Presentation of certificates

©1997, I.D.A.

Implementation

There are several techniques and procedures you may want to consider before and during the OJT implementation process. Take into account that OJT systems change the production environment and often require supervisors, management, and workers to change how they train and, in some cases, the way supervisors supervise. In hierarchical and authoritarian organizations, OJT systems often intrude on others' turf, and this can be risky, both to the OJT system and to individual career aspirations.

This is not a complete listing of techniques used to implement OJT systems, neither is it a full discussion of the ways in which you can change an organization. For that you will need several books on organization development and the help of several knowledgeable assistants. Think very hard about the effort required to implement the system and the support you really will receive. If you realistically will not receive any management or supervisory support, use the materials at the beginning of this *Info-line* to design a very low-level system, keep your head down, and go with the flow. If you really need help, find assistance within the company at the corporate level or go outside for a good OJT consultant. Think about these issues when making the decision:

■ *What Is Your Motivation?*
Is it your idea? Do you have the political and financial muscle to implement the system by yourself? Is this an assignment? If it is, can you negotiate a realistic effort level for the system?

■ *What Is in It for Them? (WIIFT)*
What will the rest of the people in the plant get for their efforts? People will not buy in to systems without first asking WIIFT and getting meaningful answers. An attempt to implement the system by edict may receive lip service, but as soon as you, the champion of the system, turn away it will be ignored and disappear.

■ *What Problems Does the System Solve?*
What will be better after the OJT system is implemented? You should be able to list specific problems and the ways OJT will solve them. Do not list training—everyone wants training to be better, but very few will expend the effort and resources to do it. Training must also solve a particular problem or help the organization achieve a goal. Problems should be specific and solutions should be directly connected to the OJT system. This forms a foundation for the WIIFT needed to implement the system.

After you answer these questions, you are ready to implement your OJT system. Successful techniques for bringing out the best of a company during the implementation process include:

■ *Hook to Another Project*
You usually cannot lose by hooking up with another project, especially if that project has some urgency about it. Projects like this include ISO 9000, quality, and customer satisfaction. The upside of this association is that you will receive more support and resources than you would if OJT were implemented alone. The downside is that you will have to share resources, power, and may lose some implementation authority. Usually this is a fair trade.

■ *Build on a Crisis*
Every company has its annual or semi-annual crisis. They usually revolve around production, late shipment, or similar "emergencies." If it makes sense, offer OJT as a partial solution. There are two downsides to this: You may end up as the scapegoat if the problem occurs again or, once the emergency is over, all of your support may disappear. The advantage of this strategy is that you—for a limited time—receive resources that may allow you to build a foundation for the system and keep it operating after the "emergency" is over.

■ *Start Small and Build*
Many successful OJT systems begin like this. The implementor recognizes the current support level, designs an appropriate system at that level, and produces a system that is useful to the corporation. Supervisors slowly buy in as they see the usefulness of the system. Problems such as additional staffing are answered over time and the system grows slowly, receives more support, and eventually becomes part of the corporate culture.

This approach does not work in all situations, especially when a fully implemented system is needed immediately. It may not work in situations where another OJT implementation has failed.

■ Wait for the Right Time

Let's say you have read everything so far and feel overwhelmed. You know you do not have much support and have lots of responsibilities besides setting up an OJT program. Sit tight, continue to talk about the program with supervisors and management, find people who will support you and the system, and most importantly, wait for the right time. Just remember, OJT implementation has components of both training and organizational development, and any successful implementor has experience in both of these skills.

Finally implementing an OJT system is a major undertaking and may result in significant changes in your facility or factory. Don't fight the established informal OJT system and insist on starting from scratch. Instead, go with the OJT flow, investigate, improve, and begin to control the informal OJT system. Then harness OJT's considerable energy to help build better projects, customer satisfaction, and a better OJT system that will grow, adapt, and provide better training as time goes on. Good luck on your OJT system.

OJT Training Procedures

The OJT procedure calls out the functions, responsibilities, and interfaces of the OJT system. Located between the trainer, production requirements, and the supervisor, these interfaces are sources of potential conflict and misunderstanding. A complete procedure will govern the activities of the trainers and describe the process for solving misunderstandings.

Specific items that should be covered in the procedure include:

■ Escalation Procedure

What happens if the student fails the checklist—how many times will they be trained and what happens if the student asks for another trainer?

■ Trainer Responsibilities

What specifically are trainers' responsibilities with regard to procedures, development, and training?

■ Supervisor Responsibilities

What are the supervisors' specific responsibilities regarding signing checklists, releasing people from the line for training, and so forth?

■ Checklist Sign-off

Should the supervisor conduct the final evaluation before checklist sign-off, or can the trainer conduct the evaluation? On what basis? Remember that the checklist could become a legal document for pay or regulatory purposes.

■ Organizational Responsibilities

What is the organization required to provide to the trainer and the training process?

■ Procedure Interfaces

Are trainers added to the sign-off list for procedure changes and revisions to production processes? How is this interface implemented?

■ Conflict Resolution

In the event of a conflict between training and production requirements, what procedures are followed to resolve it?

■ Certification Expiration

If the certification for an employee has expired, but production requirements do not allow release from the line for training, should the employee be allowed to work? What are the regulatory and liability issues? Can a temporary waiver be signed? What is the procedure for that?

Within any organization there are many other interfaces to be negotiated and resources to be assigned. Without clear procedures, turf issues will arise and, generally, trainers end up yielding. It is best for everyone concerned to sit down and draw up appropriate procedures during the development of the OJT system. See *Info-lines* No. 9706, "Basics of Instructional Systems Design" and No. 8909, "Coming to Agreement: How to Resolve Conflict" for information on setting up OJT procedures.

©1997, I.D.A.

References & Resources

Articles

Al-Ali, Salahaldeen. "An Assessment of On-the-Job Training Programs in the Ministry of Finance (MOF): A Case Study of Kuwait." *Human Resource Planning,* June 1996, pp. 50-53.

Alexander, Steve. "Training You Can Build On: Fannie Mae's In-house Programs." *Computerworld,* January 15, 1996, p. 77.

Arjas, Bridget Kinsella. "Trainer Needs Company Support." *Graphic Arts Monthly,* August 1992, pp. 74-77.

Barron, Tom. "A Structured Comeback for OJT." *Technical & Skills Training,* April 1997, pp. 14-17.

Benson, George. "Informal Training Takes Off." *Training & Development,* May 1997, pp. 93-94.

Charney, Cy. "Self-Directed Peer Training in Teams." *Journal for Quality and Participation,* October/November 1996, pp. 34-37.

Filipczak, Bob. "Who Owns Your OJT?" *Training,* December 1996, pp. 44-49.

Fisher, Susan E. "Hands-on Training." *PC Week,* February 19, 1996, p. E1.

Grant, Linda. "A School for Success: Motorola's Ambitious Job-Training Program Generates Smart Profits." *U.S. News & World Report,* May 22, 1995, pp. 53-56.

"How to Get More Out of Training Workers on the Job." *Refrigeration News,* December 10, 1993, p. 28.

Hubbard, Andrew S. "Typical Training." *Mortgage Banking,* July 1995, pp. 105-106.

Kupanhy, Lumbidi. "Classification of JIT Techniques and Their Implications." *Industrial Engineering,* February 1995, pp. 62-66.

Levine, Charles. "Unraveling Five Myths of OJT." *Technical & Skills Training,* April 1996, pp. 14-17.

Lynch, Lisa M. "The Role of Off-the-Job vs. On-the Job Training for the Mobility of Women Workers." *American Economic Review,* May 1991, pp. 151-157.

McFarland, Bonnie. "Smart Training Means Getting Managers Involved." *Washington Business Journal,* January 5, 1996, p. 20.

Marsh, P.J. "On-the-Job Learning." *Technical & Skills Training,* August/September 1994, pp. 7-12.

———. "Training Trainers." *Technical & Skills Training,* October 1995, pp. 10-13.

Mont, Michael A. "Training Toll Collectors." *Technical & Skills Training,* April 1995, pp. 25-26.

Moore, Tony. "Training Tips for Managers." *Performance & Instruction,* May/June 1996, pp. 10-11.

Mullaney, Carol Ann, and Linda D. Trask. "Show Them the Ropes." *Technical & Skills Training,* October 1992, pp. 8-11.

Nemec, John. "Supervisor as Clerk Trainer." *Supervision,* January 1996, pp. 11-14.

Phipps, Polly A. "On-the-Job Training and Employee Productivity." *Monthly Labor Review,* March 1996, pp. 23-29.

Schriner, Jim. "Where Are the Quality Workers: Skills Shortages Proves Urgency of New Job-Training Approaches." *Industry Week,* September 2, 1996, p. 52.

Semb, George B. "On-the-Job Training: Prescriptions and Practice." *Performance Improvement Quarterly,* vol. 8, no. 3, (1995), pp. 19-37.

Stevens, Margaret. "A Theoretical Model of On-the-Job Training with Imperfect Competition." *Oxford Economic Papers,* October 1994, pp. 535-561.

Vickers, Margaret. "A New Take on On-the-Job Training." *Vocational Education Journal,* March 1994, pp. 22-23,

Walter, Diane. "A Model for Team-Driven OJT." *Technical & Skills Training,* October 1996, pp. 23-27.

Walter, K. "The MTA Travels Far with Its Future Managers Program." *Personnel Journal,* vol. 74, no. 3, pp. 68-72, 1995.

Yawn, David. "On-the-Job Training: Motorola Veterans Buy Service Center." *Memphis Business Journal,* May 20, 1996, pp. 58-63.

References & Resources

Books

Jacobs, R.L., and M.J. Jones. *Structured On-the-Job Training: Unleashing Expertise in the Workplace.* San Francisco: Berrett-Koehler, 1995.

Lawson, Karen. *Improving On-the-Job Training and Coaching.* Alexandria, Virginia: ASTD Press, 1997.

Rothwell, William J., and H.C. Kazanas. *Improving On-the-Job Training: How to Establish and Operate a Comprehensive OJT Program.* San Francisco: Jossey-Bass, 1994.

Info-lines

Darraugh, Barbara (ed.). "Coaching and Feedback." No. 9006 (revised 1997).

Hodell, Chuck. "Basics of Instructional Systems Development." No. 9706.

Meyer, Kathy. "How to Train Managers to Train." No. 9003 (revised 1997).

Novak, Clare. "High Performance Training Manuals." No. 9707.

O'Neill, Mary. "Do's and Don'ts for the New Trainer." No. 9608 (revised 1998).

Payne, Tamara, and Michael Mobley. "Valuing and Managing Diversity." No. 9305.

Waagen, Alice. "Essentials for Evaluation." No. 9705.

Robinson, Dana Gaines, and James G. Robinson. "Measuring Affective and Behavioral Change." No. 9110 (revised 1997).

OJT Process Steps

As you develop your OJT system, be sure to complete each of these steps:

1. Develop management support and secure resources.

Date completed_____

2. Create a formal trainer support process.

Date completed_____

3. Link your OJT to another system with checklists.

Date completed_____

4. Produce training materials.

Date completed_____

5. Implement a train-the-trainer program.

Date completed_____

6. Select trainers.

Date completed_____

7. Design tracking and report generation procedures.

Date completed_____

8. Develop OJT training procedures.

Date completed_____

9. Implement your system.

Date completed_____

10. Evaluate training.

Date completed_____

Testing for Learning Outcomes

Issue 8907

Testing for Learning Outcomes

AUTHOR:

Deborah Grafinger Hacker
PowerVision Corporation
Senior Instructional Designer
8945 Guilford Road
Columbia, MD 21046-2620
Tel. 410.312.7243
Fax 410.312.9970
E-mail
   dhacker@powervision.com

Deborah Hacker has her master's degree in ISD and bilingual education from the University of Maryland. She has been in instructional design for 14 years —designing, writing, and teaching principals of design, and working in distance education and industry. She is currently at PowerVision Corporation, a company that concentrates on IT and training development.

Revised 1998

Editor
Cat Sharpe

Designer
Steven M. Blackwood

Contributing Editor
Ann Bruen

Testing for Learning Outcomes

Test!
Quiz!
Exam!
Performance Appraisal!
Evaluation!

Do these words make your palms sweat? Increase your heart rate? Keep you awake at night? If so, don't feel alone. Dread of being evaluated is a feeling shared by grade school students and company executives alike. Of course, the company line is that it is for your own good, which is true—provided the evaluation is done right and results are used constructively.

Unfortunately, most of us have had a bad experience somewhere along the way that has made us nervous about tests. Here are just a few typical testing and evaluation nightmares that are responsible for our test phobias.

- After listening to their instructor for an entire course, learners still don't have the slightest idea of what they will be tested on.

- Learners work hard to master complex skills and ideas covered in a particular course, but the evaluation consists of multiple-choice and true-false questions that test their memories for minor details.

- Test questions are written so badly that learners cannot figure out what is being asked.

- The instructor, annoyed with restless learners, punishes the class by giving a surprise pop quiz.

- Learners find trick questions designed so that no one gets a perfect score. (Too many "A" grades make the course seem too easy.)

- An employee evaluation is based on an unrealistic job description; the employee is evaluated on irrelevant job skills, while critical skills are ignored.

If you haven't experienced any of these situations, you are a lucky person and probably have no trouble sleeping the night before you are evaluated. Before you get complacent, however, consider that while *you* may have no problem, you may inadvertently be the cause of someone else's nightmares. If you've ever written a test, chances are you've written a bad test question. The best way to eradicate test phobia is for evaluators themselves to try to understand and adopt good evaluation practices.

Let's look at some of the main testing methods. You've probably experienced most of these methods, but one or two are a bit exotic, not often seen outside special training situations. Written test items can be divided into two major groups: objective items and subjective items.

Objective Tests

Objective test items are those that have only one correct answer. They include the following:

- multiple-choice

- matching columns

- true-false

- fill-in or completion items (when the correct answer is only a word—or its synonym—or phrase)

They are called *objective* items because they can be objectively graded. Anyone with an answer key can grade them with identical results, and the grader doesn't need to make any decisions. Objective questions are used in computerized testing because the correct answers can be easily programmed. See pages 4 and 5 for tips on writing objective test items.

Objective tests have the following advantages and disadvantages:

■ *Time and Effort*
Good objective test items are difficult to write and take a lot of thought. But once they are developed, they can be administered by one person, and are easy to correct. They can even be corrected by a machine or by an assistant unfamiliar with the subject matter.

■ *Cost*
The main expense of using objective tests is in the initial development. But once developed, the test items can be reused with minimal cost.

■ *Relevance*

Objective test items are not appropriate for every learning objective. They are generally suitable when the objective calls for selecting or identifying correct information.

■ *Computer-Based or Online Testing*

Objective test items lend themselves to computer-graded testing. Just make sure that your learning objectives can be properly tested with multiple-choice, matching columns, true-false, or short-answer questions.

While objective tests are economical (after they have been developed), they are sometimes misused because they aren't always the appropriate means for testing learning objectives.

Subjective Tests

An instructor or subject matter expert (SME) must grade each item and decide whether or not it meets the criteria of acceptability. See the sidebar on page 150 for hints on writing good subjective test items.

Subjective test items have many possible answers. Examples of subjective items include the following:

- essay questions (usually several paragraphs or pages)

- short-answer items (requiring a short explanation of a few sentences)

Subjective tests have the following advantages and disadvantages:

■ *Time and Effort*

Subjective test items are easier to write than objective items, but the developer should take care that the questions are clearly written and well organized. The decision-making process of grading is time consuming, as is writing a detailed answer key to ensure that tests are graded using the same criteria.

■ *Cost*

Cost of development is generally low, but grading costs are higher since only instructors or subject matter experts can grade them.

■ *Relevance*

Subjective test items are appropriate when learners are expected to produce the correct information themselves. Subjective questions are suitable for testing a broad range of learning tasks from low-level objectives (for example, reproduction of a memorized definition) to objectives using multiple, high-level skills (such as analyzing a problem, applying complex concepts to find a solution, and organizing an explanation and defense of that solution).

■ *Computer-Based or Online Testing*

While a subjective test item can be administered online it must be graded by humans with adequate expertise in the field to correct the answer. Nevertheless, it may be advantageous to administer online subjective tests to students being tested at a distance.

Oral Tests

Oral test items are usually subjective. Types of oral testing in training include the following:

- panels of subject matter experts who gauge the depths of the learner's knowledge

- walk-throughs, in which the learner walks through a task and explains a procedure or points out locations of components in a plant or on equipment

- talk-throughs, in which the learner explains, step by step, how a particular task is carried out

The use of oral tests has the following advantages and disadvantages:

■ *Time and Effort*

Since the tests usually are administered with one or more instructors (or subject matter experts) and one learner, oral tests are time consuming.

■ *Cost*

The cost factor of the instructor's time makes oral testing expensive.

■ *Relevance*

Oral testing is appropriate whenever a more accurate evaluation of the learner's knowledge can be gained through conversation than from a written test. This includes situations such as the following:

- Learners have problems answering in writing.

- The examiner wants to question learners in depth on their responses.

- The examiner wants to clarify questions or add details at the learner's request.

■ *Computer-based or Online Testing*

While this seems unlikely, Internet software that allows for synchronous video and sound between an instructor and learner would make it possible for oral testing to be administered online at a distance.

Certain advantages exist for the learner in an oral testing situation that do not exist in a written testing environment. For example, if the learner does not understand a question, the instructor can reword it. The instructor may also prompt the learner to give more information by asking further questions. Oral testing is a good way to explore the depths of a learner's knowledge because there is always an opportunity to ask more questions.

Psychomotor Tests

Psychomotor skills are tested through the actual performance of a physical task using real equipment or a simulator. These tests allow the instructor to see if the learner has the physical and intellectual skills to perform given tasks. Any time an objective asks the learner to perform a physical skill, such as measuring, adjusting, operating, or repairing, it should be tested by actual physical performance of that task.

Physical skills should be tested in the same or a similar environment and under conditions similar to those on the job. If a mechanic is being tested on car repairs, he or she should be tested in a garage that has the same equipment used on the job. Sometimes it isn't possible to test in the actual environment because of costs or dangers involved in on-the-job testing. Examples include nuclear plant operations or fire control training. In those cases, tasks may be tested in a shop, laboratory, or simulator.

An instructor or supervisor monitors and rates the learner's performance. In order to ensure that each performer is rated by the same standards, he or she uses checklists that define the standards of acceptable performance. See the sidebar "Steps for Psychomotor Testing" for hints on developing psychomotor checklists.

The use of psychomotor tests has the following advantages and disadvantages:

■ *Time and Effort*

Psychomotor tests are time consuming because the learner and instructor are usually in a one-to-one testing environment.

■ *Cost*

In addition to the cost of the instructor's time, psychomotor tests can be expensive because they usually involve the use of costly equipment or simulators.

■ *Relevance*

Despite the cost, a physical demonstration is the only valid way to test psychomotor skill. For example, some electrical utilities use simulators to train the personnel who buy and sell electricity on the national grid. These people must make quick decisions that will affect the cost of electricity to the consumer.

■ *Computer-Based or Online Testing*

While this seems unlikely, Internet software that allows for synchronous video and sound between an instructor and learner would make it possible for oral testing to be administered online at a distance.

Writing Objective Test Items

There are four types of objective test items: true-false, multiple-choice, matching column, and fill-in or completion.

True-False Test Items

True-false test items often are used because they are:

- easy to write
- easy to correct
- don't take up much class time

True-false testing should be used cautiously. True-false questions should be used only to test knowledge objectives. They are valid only for objectives that ask learners to recognize or identify correct information rather than to state or recall it. The method can be invalid and unreliable because questions are easy to guess (there is a 50 percent chance of being correct), and knowledgeable learners tend to be tricked by them because they are aware of exceptions.

Guidelines for True-False Items

1. Test only one idea at a time. Learners may know the answer to one part of the question, but not the other. Then it is impossible to know what they know and what they do not know. More than one statement in a question also may be confusing.

   Example: *Thomas Edison invented the light bulb and Henry Ford invented the automobile.* This is a weak true-false item because it asks about unrelated events.

2. Avoid ambiguous questions. Words like "seldom," "often," and "possible" tend to confuse.

   Example: *It seldom rains in Greece during the summer.* How often is seldom—once a week? Once a month? Where in Greece? In the mountains? On the islands? In the north?

3. Avoid using "always," "never," and "none." Many learners realize that such definite statements usually are false, so they will guess without really reading the question. Or they may get the question right for the wrong reason.

   Example: *Pure water always boils at 212° C.* The learner may get this item right for the wrong reason. He or she may answer "false" because of the word "always," rather than because water boils at 212° F.

Multiple-Choice Items

Multiple-choice items are most appropriate for knowledge-based objectives in which the learner needs to choose correct information, or simple problem-solving skills where it is appropriate to select a certain solution. Multiple-choice questions are difficult to write. They are commonly used because they are easy to grade and do not use a lot of class time to administer. The problem is that often they are misused and poorly written.

Guidelines for Multiple-Choice Items

1. Put any blanks toward the end of the main part of the question (the stem). This makes it easier for learners to read and understand what is being asked.

2. The stem is usually followed by four or five possible responses. There should be only one correct response; the rest should be distracters—words or phrases meant to distract the learner's attention away from the correct response.

3. Writing good distracters is the most difficult part of constructing good multiple-choice items. All distracters should be believable. One or more obviously wrong distracters makes the correct answer easier to guess.

   Example: *The capital of Maryland is (a) Baltimore (b) Aberdeen (c) Columbia (d) Annapolis.*

   or:

   The capital of Maryland is (a) Miami (b) New York City (c) Kansas City (d) Annapolis.

The first of these items has more plausible distracters. The second item has such poor distracters that the correct answer is obvious to most people. Distracters should agree grammatically with the stem so they don't provide clues to the learner. Distracters should be about the same length as the correct response. A response that is substantially longer than the rest often is the correct one.

The correct responses should be placed in random positions. Test-wise learners know that (c) and (b) are favorite spots for correct responses. It is important not to develop a pattern of correct responses across the test.

Using Multiple-Choice for Math Problems

Multiple-choice items should be used to test calculation objectives only with extreme caution. Test-wise learners often can pass multiple-choice math tests with minimum knowledge because of implausible distracters.

Multiple-choice items should be used to test math problems only if the distracters are very good. One way to construct good distracters is to go through the problems, making different common mistakes for each distracter. Warning: Changing the decimal point is not a difficult-enough distracter to fool all learners (unless it is a common mistake for that particular problem).

Matching Column Items

Matching column items are a lot like multiple-choice items, so many rules of construction are the same. The matching items have directions, the problems, and the distracters.

Example: *Directions: Match the part of a gas combustion engine to the function it performs. Only use answers once.*

Part (problems)	Function (distracters)
____ *1. Alternator*	*a. Cools the engine*
____ *2. Carburetor*	*b. Ignites fuel*
____ *3. Spark plug*	*c. Keeps track of mileage*
____ *4. Radiator*	*d. Mixes oil with gas*
	e. Mixes gas and air
	f. Recharges the battery

Guidelines for Matching Column Items

1. All the problems should be related so the distracters sound reasonable.

2. Distracters should agree grammatically.

3. There should be more responses than problems so the last problem won't automatically match the last response.

4. Responses should be in a logical order, such as alphabetical order, or, if numbers are used, in numerical order.

5. Every item should have directions. If responses can be used more than once, the directions should so indicate.

Fill-In or Completion Items

Fill-in items are generally easy to construct. They cannot be used for information recall, or for short responses to mathematical problems.

Examples: *A univalve is a mollusk with one*

_____.

or:

The area of a square with three-inch sides is_____ square inches.

Guidelines for Fill-In Items

1. The context of the question must be included; the learner should not have to guess what the question is asking.

   Examples: *An alligator is a(n)*

   _____.

   Better: *An alligator is in the phylum*

   _____.

In the first example, the learner can't tell how to answer the question. The instructor would be forced to accept any correct response, such as animal, lizard, reptile, and so forth.

2. The blank should come toward the end of the statement to lessen confusion.

   Examples: *A(n) _____ is a hybrid from a donkey and a horse.*

   Better: *The hybrid offspring of a donkey and a horse is a(n)*
   _____.

3. No grammatical clues should be given. Using "a/ an, a(n), he or she, him or her" will prevent the learner from eliminating items through grammatical clues.

If you use fill-in items in a computer-graded test, you must determine all synonyms and spellings (correct and incorrect if spelling is not an issue) and program your software to accept them. Otherwise you may mark acceptable answers as wrong.

Using Objectives

One of the most important things to remember when developing a test item is that it must match an objective, that is, the statement that defines the following:

- what the learner should know how to do by the end of the course

- conditions under which the task is to be performed

- criteria by which acceptable task performance will be determined (how performance will be evaluated)

It is difficult—if not impossible—to determine what should be tested and how it should be done without linking testing with objectives. Objectives are the heart of education and training. They tell learners the skills and knowledge they will be expected to acquire, and how they will be tested.

Some of the problems learners face when being evaluated are directly related to the absence of objectives. Objectives help course designers and instructors make decisions about evaluating. Proper use of objectives helps to ensure that:

- important skills and information are covered in class

- support materials match the class work and test items

- important skills and knowledge are evaluated

- appropriate types of test items are used

In a systematic approach to course or program development, the objectives and test items are developed together—before the course is even written. This is a good time to develop test items because, in the design and development stage, the course designer can make sure the written objectives are testable before writing the materials to support them.

Selecting Testing Methods

Every objective should be tested, when possible, by performance of the objective. Depending upon whether you are testing for knowledge, skills, or attitude, here are some guidelines to follow.

Knowledge should be tested as the specific objective indicates. If the objective says, for example, to *list* or *state*, then the objective should require that the learner recall and reproduce the information. If the objective says to *identify*, then the learner is only required to select the appropriate answer (as with multiple-choice or completion items).

Intellectual skills such as calculating, analyzing, or using knowledge can be evaluated in a written test (though an oral test might also be appropriate). The test item should require the learner to *perform* the skill, not *describe* how it is done.

A **psychomotor** or physical skill such as calibrating, repairing, or parking can be tested *only* by performance of the skill. The testing situation should be under the same conditions (noise, distractions, equipment used, and so forth) as those encountered on the job. If the objective is to park a fully loaded truck at a loading dock, the dock should meet typical conditions. The truck should be filled with a load of similar weight and volume carried so the truck handling properties will be the same.

Although many training professionals test for **attitude,** it is very difficult to do since any attitude evaluation will be, by definition, subjective. Training and testing for attitude change should be undertaken with care, because any evidence of coercion or use of peer pressure could have serious legal and moral implications touching on the rights of the individual and free will. When appropriate, attitude can best be evaluated through questionnaires or surveys (see the sidebar on surveying attitudes).

Writing Subjective Items

A subjective test should not test the learner's ability to understand complex questions and organize essays *unless* that is clearly a requirement for the course. In order to avoid testing essay *writing* as a hidden skill, write essay questions so they require only a few paragraphs each. It should be made clear—both orally and in writing—that brief answers are expected.

Questions should be short and concise. If one question covers a lot of information, break it up into sections. This helps the learner to understand the question, and the instructor to organize the answer. Look at the following examples of subjective questions for customer sales representatives at a bank. Which one is easier to understand?

Describe the procedure for selling and opening a money market account: how to determine who's a prospective customer, advantages of a money market account over other investments, and rates of interest and paperwork to be completed.

or:

Write short descriptions of the steps for selling a money market account. Include in your answer:

- *determining the customer's needs*

- *introducing the idea of a money market account*

- *describing the advantages of a money market account over other investments*

- *explaining interest rates and how interest accrues*

- *completing the paperwork for the customer*

The second item organizes the learner's response and lets the learner know exactly what the instructor wants.

Follow these steps when writing subjective questions and grading keys:

1. Write a question. Check it for clarity. Compare it with the objective to ensure a match.

2. Write the expected answer.

3. Ask a colleague to read the question, checking it for clarity and writing an answer.

4. Revise the question (if needed), based on the answers written by the instructor (if you are not the instructor) and your colleague.

5. Construct a grading key. The key should include all components of a correct answer, and the point value for each piece of the answer. Make sure that point values assigned to different parts of the answer are weighted according to their importance.

6. The first time you administer the test, ask another instructor to grade copies of some of the questions using the answer key. Compare your results. Ask the other instructor about problems he or she had using the key. If the other instructor's results differ greatly from yours, discuss the differences and determine how the key can be improved.

Evaluating Tests

The two key goals of creating an evaluation instrument are that it must be valid and reliable. Validity is the measure of whether a question tests the intended skills and knowledge. Reliability measures whether an item differentiates between individuals who know the information and those who do not.

Measuring the validity and reliability of test items requires collecting and analyzing test score data. While we are not going to get into determining validity and reliability at this time, we can help you assess whether a test item is likely to be valid and reliable by examining certain characteristics.

Validity

A valid test is one that tests what it is meant to test. In other words, it tests the specific skills and knowledge defined in the objectives. To assess the potential validity of a test item, we need to ask the following questions:

- Does the question test the intended objective, matching the performance described in the verb as well as any predefined conditions and standards?

- Is the material in the question important information or incidental detail?

- Was the material in the test item covered in the training?

If an objective states that the learner must install an Omega model 105 dishwasher, then the only valid test of that skill is for the learner to install that specific brand and model of appliance. It is not a valid test for the learner to install another brand or model of dishwasher. The differences in design between the two models may require other skills and knowledge. It is also not a valid test for the learner to *describe* installation of the dishwasher. That would only test the learner's *knowledge* of how to perform the task, and not the actual *skills* needed for performance.

Sometimes the difference between the objective and the test item can be seen clearly. For example, an objective may state that the learner is to install a dishwasher, while the test item asks the learner to describe how the installation is done. It is easy to see in this case that the objective and test item do not match. Sometimes the difference between

the objective and the test item is so subtle that it is difficult to recognize that an item is invalid. For example, look at the following objective:

List the steps for starting up the engine room boiler, in procedural order.

Now look at this test item:

Number the following steps in procedural order for starting up the engine room boiler.

_____ *Open the choke.*

_____ *Light the burner.*

_____ *Open the fuel line.*

_____ *Check the air intake valve.*

_____ *Check the fuel level.*

The second test item does not really test the knowledge required by the objective. The learner does not need to know the steps for boiler start-up to answer the question correctly. The test item only requires the learner to put the steps in order. It does not tell us if the learner can remember all of the steps without prompting. This may seem like a small difference, but if one of the safety steps is missed, it could cause an accident. In order to ensure that test items are valid, it is a good idea to get a second opinion from a colleague on whether or not test items truly match objectives.

Reliability

A reliable test item is one that consistently measures the learner's ability to perform the objective. A test item that consistently differentiates learners who can do a task from learners who cannot is a reliable item.

To assess the potential reliability of a test item we need to ask the following questions:

- Is the answer to the question common sense?

- Does the question's wording make it easy to guess the correct answer?

- Does the item contain tricks that might fool learners into picking the wrong answer?

Steps for Psychomotor Testing

Here is one possible sequence for developing psychomotor checklists:

1. Analyze an expert performing the task. Determine the critical steps and key decisions that must be made by the learner in order to perform the task correctly. Have a colleague check your results.

2. Set the guidelines for checklist construction. They will be dependent on the types of skills or procedures you are testing and your grading criteria. Checklists can be organized in a number of ways, including:

   Product measure. Arrange the checklist according to the products that are created throughout the test. This measure is most appropriate where product quality is more important than process.

   Performance criteria. These checklists specify a task or procedure at the top and list the areas of applicable criteria below. The examiner has a copy of the procedure and related standards to check against. This type of checklist would be appropriate for procedures that have several applicable criteria (for example, speed, safety, product, technique, and accuracy).

   Sequential order. Set up the checklist of tasks in their sequential order. This type of checklist lends itself to testing procedures or tasks that must be done in sequence.

3. Determine the rating scales to be used. Will there be:

   - a two-point scale (such as yes/no or pass/fail)?

   - a numerical scale grading performance from 1 to 10?

   - a graphic rating scale? (See the example below.)

4. Spell out guidelines for rating learner performance. Remember, there is a certain amount of subjectivity to rating the performance of physical tasks. In order to ensure that all raters will grade by the same criteria, it is necessary to write a set of guidelines and discuss them with raters before the test is administered.

Graphic Rating Scale

Engine starts immediately.   Engine hesitates.   Engine doesn't start.
                                   There are knocks and pings.

Pass   **Fail**

- Are negatives or absolutes used within the question that might lead to misinterpretation?

We know that a test item is *unreliable* if it falls into the following categories:

- It is easy to guess because it fails to separate skilled, knowledgeable learners from those who cannot perform the task.

- It is difficult to understand because some learners who can perform the task will not understand what they are being asked to do.

- It is evaluated differently for different learners, such as in an essay test.

To ensure the reliability of essay tests, it is important to define an acceptable answer before the test is given; and to determine whether or not partial credit will be given and, if so, how many points each part of the answer is worth. Reliability can be affected by the conditions under which a test is given. Learners who are tested in an uncomfortable, noisy room are not likely to perform as well as those tested in a comfortable, quiet environment.

Learners should be given the same amount of time to take the same test with the same tools, materials, and resources. If one learner is allowed to take an open-book test, and another takes the test with no resources, the results will not be consistent because one of the learners had advantages the other did not.

Look at the following objective:

Replace the spark plugs, wires, and distributor cap on a Ford Escort at recommended manufacturer's internals, within 30 minutes, given the necessary tools and manuals.

If some learners are asked to perform this task without the required manuals, it would be an unreliable test. Without the manual to look up the specifications, learners would not have the opportunity to demonstrate their ability to perform the task correctly. Having learners perform this task without a time limit also invalidates the test. It would not show which learners could perform the task in the allotted time and which could not.

Here are some additional steps you can take to help ensure reliability.

- Ask colleagues to review test items. They should be clearly written and easily understood, but not easy to guess.

- Define acceptable answers for essay items before the test is given. Determine how they will be marked. If more than one person will grade the tests, make sure all graders apply the standards in the same way.

- Choose a comfortable, quiet environment for testing learners unless a different setting more closely approximates the actual job conditions.

- Make sure that all learners are taking the test under the same conditions (with the same tools, materials, resources, and time limitations).

Playing Fair

Every time instructors or course designers construct a test item, they should make sure that it is as fair as possible, while giving learners who know the material a chance to prove what they know. *The main point of evaluation is to determine what skills and knowledge a learner possesses.*

■ *Keeping Learners Informed*
Objectives serve the purpose of informing learners what is expected of them. Each session should begin with an introduction addressing objectives to be covered during that session. This way, learners constantly know where they are in the course and what is to be accomplished.

Objectives should also be used for review before testing. Learners should be told which objectives are being covered by the test and how they will be tested. Informed learners are motivated and in control of their learning process. They are more likely to succeed than those who do not know what is expected of them.

■ *Writing Clear, Concise Test Items*
It is difficult to write good test items that are easily understood. One way to ensure good test construction is to have someone else review the test to make sure it is written clearly. The instructor can also ask the reviewer to answer the questions to see if the test yields the expected answers.

Surveying Attitudes

Writing a good attitude survey is as difficult as writing a good test. Here are some steps for developing a good questionnaire adapted from *Handbook of Training Evaluation and Measurement Methods* by Jack Phillips.

1. Determine the information needed. List subjects, skills, or abilities covered. An outline form is helpful for grouping related questions.

2. Select the type of questions. Keep in mind the kind of information to be gathered and how it will be used.

3. Develop the questions. Base them on the type of questions planned and the information needed, keeping them simple and concise.

4. Test the questions. If possible, test the questions on a group of participants in a pilot program. Or test them on a group of employees with skills that approximate those of potential participants. Revise questions as needed. Testing a control group (people not involved in the training program) allows for comparison of responses with those of participants.

5. Develop the complete questionnaire and prepare a data summary. Integrate questions and write clear instructions. Develop a summary sheet for quick tabulation and interpretation.

Types of Questions on Attitude Surveys

Several types of questions can be used in a survey:

Short-answer questions, in which learners explain their thoughts.

Selection or multiple-choice questions, in which learners check off items on a list or pick an answer that best expresses their opinions.

Yes-no questions, in which a learner agrees or disagrees with a statement.

Ranking scales, in which a learner ranks the importance of different ideas or determines their degree of agreement or disagreement with given statements.

Here are some typical examples of these question types.

Short-answer Question
What can you do to transform the workplace into a safer environment?

_____

_____

_____

Selection Questions
What do you think are the three most important qualities of a customer service representative? (May be in multiple-choice format.)

- ☐ Administration skills
- ☐ Communications skills
- ☐ Good rapport with customers
- ☐ Good rapport with service technicians
- ☐ Knowledge of company policy
- ☐ Product knowledge
- ☐ Telephone skills
- ☐ Troubleshooting

Yes-no Questions
Do you think that present company policies on handling toxic materials are sufficient for protecting employees?

☐ Yes   ☐ No

Ranking Scales
The plant technicians are given sufficient opportunities to express their ideas on company policy.

- ☐ Strongly agree
- ☐ Agree
- ☐ Neutral
- ☐ Disagree
- ☐ Strongly disagree

■ *Giving Away the Answers*

Objective test items are notoriously easy to guess by test-wise learners. The following are some of the common clues found in test items:

● grammatical hints—disagreement among the number and tenses in distracters, or use of "a" and "an" instead of "a/an" in the question

● poor distracters—wrong selections in multiple-choice or in matching columns—sensible enough to provide the learner possible choices or to make guessing easy

● word cues—using a key word in a question that is also in the distracter or in the answer, such as asking what piece of equipment transforms current into voltage and writing "transformer" as the answer

■ *Hidden Skills*

Test items should test only the skills and knowledge they were meant to test. But sometimes items test hidden skills. That means that a learner is required to do or know something outside the prerequisites and requirements of the course. For example, asking a bank teller trainee for a well-organized essay on customer service would call for written communications skills unnecessary for the training program and the job.

■ *Good Grading Practices*

Subjective tests should be graded using the same criteria—a difficult challenge. Here are some problems and possible solutions.

There are grading differences among instructors. If a test is standard and given by more than one instructor, or more than one person is grading, learners may be rated differently. A key should be used, detailing the grading criteria. All raters should meet and discuss how these criteria will be applied. Decisions to give partial credit must be uniform. Ensure continuity by having each instructor grade selected questions across the entire test and one person look over all tests at the end of the grading process to standardize marks.

The order in which tests are graded is also an issue. It is difficult to rate performance by consistent criteria. If the initial performances are very good, the grader tends to judge the following ones harder. If initial performances are poor, succeeding ones tend to be judged more leniently. Reviewing all papers a second time helps to ensure equal application of criteria. It is also helpful to grade one question across all learners before moving on to the next. You can shuffle the papers between questions to make sure you grade each test item in a different sequence.

Prejudice based on past performance can also influence an instructor during grading. When a grader rates a learner he or she knows, it is difficult to separate current performance from past performance. Good past performance tends to work favorably for the learner, while poor past performance may unfavorably color the rater's evaluation of current performance. On written tests, names should be covered or numbers assigned.

■ *Trick Questions*

Some instructors try to fool learners by asking them trick questions. Unless an item tests for recognition of a specific tricky situation that is part of the necessary training, trick questions are simply not a fair test of a learner's skills and knowledge. Sometimes an instructor will inadvertently write a trick question. He or she must be open to removing or changing an unfair question when it is pointed out.

Evaluating Test Results

There are two methods of evaluation that you should be familiar with:

1. Norm-referencing—a traditional and familiar means of evaluating learner performance. It is how we frequently were graded in school, but it is not always the best way to evaluate performance.

2. Criterion-referencing—another perspective on evaluation. It compares performance with objective standards.

Norm-Referenced Evaluation

Do you remember back in school when the class did badly on a test but the teacher assured us that it would be "graded on the curve"? Do you remember the importance of class rank for students who wanted to get into certain colleges? Class ranking and grading on the curve are artifacts of norm-referenced evaluation.

Norm-referenced evaluation compares an individual's performance with that of all the others taking a particular test or in the same class. The worse the rest of the population performs, the higher the scores of those in the top 50 percent of the class.

When a large number of people take a standardized test, their marks usually fall within a normal range. This range, when plotted, forms a bell-shaped curve like the one shown here. It shows the performance of most people falling in the middle, with a few doing very well and a few doing very poorly. When scores are marked on a curve, marks are adjusted so that they still form a bell curve, but instead of an "A" starting at 100 percent, it may begin at 75 percent or 80 percent.

This seems like a strange way to evaluate whether or not a learner can perform a task or demonstrate knowledge. If the best mark is an 80 percent, does that mean that none of the learners was able to perform the task completely?

The truth of the matter is that norm-referencing evaluation should not be used to determine who can and who can't perform a task. The purpose of norm-referencing is to identify the best and worst performances by comparing each individual to the rest of the group. It may be used in cases like the following:

- There is room in a training program for five learners. The company wants to give the spots to the best five applicants.

- A scholarship will be given to the top quarter of the class. They need to be identified.

- An organization is offering remedial math and reading courses. Employees who need them most will be admitted into the courses first.

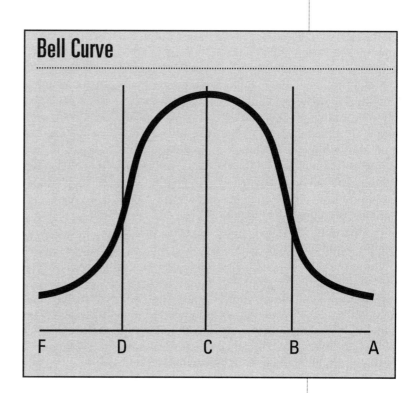

Bell Curve

F   D   C   B   A

Criterion-Referenced Evaluation

Criterion-referencing means that an individual's performance is measured against the standards of the objectives being tested. This type of evaluation should be used in any program in which learners must master particular skills or knowledge before continuing. Criterion-referenced evaluation enables learners to compete against their own performance rather than that of others. In order to reach their goals, they must meet the necessary objectives. Most organizations are interested in whether or not an individual has the skills to perform a particular job. They aren't interested in the individual's ranking among 20 other trainees who may or may not have the necessary skills.

Still, instructors tend to compare learners' performances without knowing whether or not any of them have the skills and knowledge it takes to continue. This is a mistake made in both educational and training environments. Criterion-referenced evaluation is based on meeting the objectives. The most appropriate way of grading a course that uses criterion-referenced evaluation is pass-fail. When learners pass, it means they have mastered all the skills and knowledge needed to perform specific tasks.

References & Resources

Articles

Anonymous. "Testing Buyers' Guide." *Human Resource Executive,* November 1994, pp. 62-66.

Blair, David, and Steve Giles. "Evaluating Test Questions: More Than Meets the Eye." *Technical & Skills Training,* May/June 1996, pp. 23-24.

Jones, Paul E. "Three Levels of Certification Testing." *Performance & Instruction,* October 1994, pp. 22-28.

Lapp, H.J. "Rate Your Testing Program." *Performance & Instruction,* September 1995, pp. 36-38.

Lee, William W., and Robert A. Mamone. "Design Criteria That Make Tests Objective." *Journal of Instruction Delivery Systems,* Summer 1995, pp. 13-17.

Marrelli, Anne F. "Writing Multiple-choice Test Items." *Performance & Instruction,* September 1995, pp. 24-29.

Parshall, Cynthia G. "Practical Issues in Computer-Based Testing." *Journal of Instruction Delivery Systems,* Summer 1995, pp. 13-17.

Reynolds, Angus. "The Basics: Evaluation." *Technical & Skills Training,* August/September 1994, pp. 5-6.

Schriver, Rob. "Testing Employee Performance: A Review of Key Milestones." *Technical & Skills Training,* April 1997, pp. 27-29.

Shrock, Sharon A. "Testing Triage: Maximizing Effectiveness in Assessment With Minimal Investment." *Performance Improvement,* March 1997, pp. 46-50.

Sidick, John T., et al. "Three-Alternative Multiple-choice Tests: An Attractive Option." *Personnel Psychology,* Winter 1994, pp. 829-835.

Stape, Christopher J. "Techniques for Developing Higher-Level Objective Test Questions." *Performance & Instruction,* March 1995, pp. 31-34.

Weekley, Jeff A., and Casey Jones. "Video-Based Situational Testing." *Personnel Psychology,* Spring 1997, pp. 25-49.

Books

Berk, R.A. (ed.). *Criterion-Referenced Measurement: The State of the Art.* Baltimore, Maryland: Johns Hopkins University Press, 1980.

Birnbrauer, Herman (ed.). *The ASTD Handbook for Technical and Skills Training.* Vol. 2. Alexandria, Virginia: American Society for Training & Development, 1986.

Briggs, Leslie J. *Instructional Design: Principles and Application.* Englewood Cliffs, New Jersey: Educational Technology, 1981.

Craig, Robert L. (ed.). *Training and Development Handbook.* New York: McGraw Hill, 1987.

Deming, Basil S. *Evaluating Job-Related Training.* Alexandria, Virginia: American Society for Training & Development, 1982.

Fitch, Brian. *Testing in Employment and Training Programs.* Columbus, Ohio: National Center for Research in Vocational Education, 1983.

Finch, Curtis R., and Robert McGough. *Administering and Supervising Occupational Education.* Englewood Cliffs, New Jersey: Prentice-Hall, 1982.

References & Resources

Books

Gagne, Robert J., and Leslie J. Briggs. *Principles of Instructional Design.* 4th ed. New York: Holt, Rinehart & Winston, 1986.

Heinich, Robert, et al. *Instructional Development and the New Technologies of Instruction.* New York: John Wiley & Sons, 1982.

Kirkpatrick, Donald L. (ed.). *More Evaluating Training Programs.* Alexandria, Virginia: American Society for Training & Development, 1987.

Lutterodt, Sarah A., and Deborah J. Grafinger. *Measurement and Evaluation: Basic Concepts.* Columbia, Maryland: GP Courseware, 1985.

———. *Measurement and Objective Test Items I.* Columbia, Maryland: GP Courseware, 1985.

Mager, Robert F. *Measuring Instructional Results or Got a Match?* Atlanta, Georgia: Center for Effective Performance, 1997.

Morris, Lynn Lyons, et al. *How to Measure Performance and Use Tests.* Newbury Park, California: Sage Publications, 1987.

Tenopyr, Mary L., and Robert L. Craig (eds.). *The ASTD Training and Development Handbook: A Guide to Human Resource Development.* New York: McGraw-Hill, 1996.

Wentling, Tim L. *Evaluating Occupational Education and Training Programs.* 2nd ed. Boston, Massachusetts: Allyn and Bacon, 1980.

Info-lines

Long, Lori. "Surveys From Start to Finish." No. 8612 (revised 1998).

Martelli, Joseph T., and Dennis Mather. "Statistics for HRD Practice." No. 9101.

O'Neill, Mary. "How to Focus an Evaluation." No. 9605.

Robinson, Dana Gaines. "Tracking Operational Results." No. 9112.

Waagen, Alice K. "Essentials for Evaluation." No. 9705.

Job Aid

How to Test a Learning Outcome

Use the following worksheet to make decisions regarding *how* to test and to help in the actual *writing* of the test.

Determine the type of test item to be used:

1. Look at the objective. What type of objective is it (knowledge, skills, or attitude)?

_____

2. What are the best ways of testing this type of objective?

_____

_____

_____

_____

_____

3. List any constraints on testing. (Is there a time limit? Are there enough instructors to administer or grade the test? Is the equipment available?)

_____

_____

_____

_____

_____

4. How will any of the constraints affect your choice of test item types?

_____

5. What type of testing will you use?

_____

How to Facilitate

Issue 9406

How to Facilitate

Editorial Staff for 9406

Editor
Barbara Darraugh

Consultant
Don Aaron Carr

Revised 1999

Editor
Cat Sharpe

Contributing Editor
Ann Bruen

Production Design
Anne Morgan

How to Facilitate

Getting Teams to Work

The EXITS Publishing Company was experiencing difficulties in maintaining inventory on the rapidly increasing sales of a popular how-to book series. The organization wrote, published, marketed, and filled orders, handling all aspects in-house. As a result, this product required input and actions from many different units in the organization:

- *customer service*
- *fulfillment*
- *editing and design*
- *product management*
- *accounting*
- *computer services*

Although product sales were growing, the product manager frequently heard complaints about the handling of the product from the other area managers. Customer service and fulfillment often ran out of stock and became frustrated when clients ordered an unavailable issue. Accounting had difficulties with the computer reports it received. And the product manager often had to intervene in the process to soothe ruffled feathers and order emergency restocking of the product.

After several years, the organization instituted total quality management and decided to form a quality team to address what was considered to be an inventory problem. Through its total quality management mechanism, the organization brought together managers in each of the departments to discuss the problem. Each of the managers—Sara from customer service, Dan from fulfillment, Paula from accounting, Tom from computer services, and George, the product manager—were very enthusiastic about finally having a forum in which to address a problem that affected them all and that they had been unable to solve individually. They were hopeful that with the tools taught to them during their quality training, easy solutions to their problems would be found quickly and simply. They happily scheduled their first meeting.

At the first meeting, Dan told Sara that she needed to keep better track of orders, that too often his staff received back orders on items in stock and orders for items that weren't in stock. Sara refused to be accountable, noting that the responsibility for

reordering rested with George. An argument broke out between Sara and George, who said he couldn't keep track of the inventory, since he received reports from her sporadically and always too late to help. Sara then attacked Tom, saying the computer generated the late or inaccurate reports.

Tom noted the "garbage in, garbage out" theory of data processing. Paula attacked the computer reports and Tom's handling of them. Sara left the meeting feeling she had been personally attacked, and Tom refused to discuss the computer output further. The two-hour meeting lasted only an hour. No progress had been made, and some fence-mending needed to occur before the managers met again.

Several months later, with no easy solutions in hand, the "team" dreaded each weekly meeting. They had only agreed that nothing had been accomplished, and all felt that the meetings were a waste of time. Territory that had been covered in the first meeting was re-covered endlessly, with each individual protecting his or her own turf. The team members distrusted each other and often attacked one another personally. The group was floundering, and inventory was still out of control.

Unfortunately, this team will continue to meet, possibly for many more months, until one of the members leaves for a different organization and the team dissolves. In the meantime, the team members' interactions outside of the team room have also deteriorated. All in all, this is not what management expected when it instituted the total quality management program and formed the team to look at the problem.

The disastrous effects could have been avoided had management provided the team with a qualified facilitator. The facilitator would have been able to defuse the personality issues, coach the team on the proper tools to use to examine the problem and provide solutions, and conduct refresher or minicourses on the quality tools. This issue of *Info-line* will outline the facilitator's role and his or her necessary skills. An upcoming issue will provide facilitators with techniques for both generating ideas and making decisions.

Facilitators and their Roles

Facilitators are usually individuals who assist teams in their meetings, to enhance the process—how the team works and comes to decisions. Generally, the facilitator is not involved in the process or task being examined: He or she is not a stakeholder and may begin team involvement knowing nothing about what is being discussed. Good facilitators ensure that teams don't get bogged down in personality or process issues and that every individual within the group is heard.

Don Aaron Carr, a consultant who specializes in team training, asserts that a good facilitator possesses "an attitude and philosophy that confirms a position of respect and admiration. Therefore, good facilitators display a high tolerance for ambiguity and conflict, patience and persistence."

Facilitators have a responsibility to both the team and the organization to support the team and integrate it into the organization's mainstream. Carr defines the facilitator's role as the following:

● coaching the team in process, roles, procedures, policies, and goals

● attending team meetings on an as-needed basis to provide feedback to the team leader and members

● acting as a regular consultant to the team leader

● monitoring team dynamics, diagnosing problems, and making appropriate interventions

● promoting the team concept

These roles contrast with those of the team leader, Carr says, noting that team leaders have the following roles:

● plan meeting agendas and conduct the meeting

● ensure through facilitation techniques that all members are involved in the team

● communicate with management about the team's progress

● consult with the facilitator on team issues

Since these two roles may overlap, the facilitator and the leader may negotiate which roles they want to play. A leader, for example, may want the facilitator to be present at every meeting to ensure that all team members participate if the leader feels uncomfortable in this team maintenance role. Or the leader may ask the facilitator to run or train the team in the processes involved in idea generation or decision making.

David Quinlivan-Hall and Peter Renner stress the use of a neutral facilitator who guides the group through its process stages. A neutral facilitator helps team leaders prepare the meeting and takes over the process. In this way, he or she allows the team leader to participate in the program.

Quinlivan-Hall and Renner list the following tasks facing facilitators:

Managing the Process

This includes the following:

● striving for consensus
● keeping members on task
● following the agenda
● focusing on problem solving
● controlling the flow of contributions
● rewarding and motivating group members

Acting as a Resource

This task includes:

- advising on problem-solving methods

- providing on-the-spot training in group-process techniques

- protecting group members from personal attacks

Remaining Neutral

This includes the following:

- keeping emotionally uninvolved

- keeping out of the spotlight

- becoming invisible when the group is facilitating itself

- keeping silent on content issues

Skills Required

The facilitator's role, while rather broad, is crucial to the success of the team. A good facilitator basically checks his or her personal concerns and causes at the door. Glenn Varney, president of Management Advisory Associates in Bowling Green, Ohio, suggests that facilitators should have the following skills:

■ Listening
The facilitator needs to be able to listen actively and hear what every team member is saying. "A day spent facilitating is as tiring as a day spent chopping wood," Quinlivan-Hall and Renner note. (For more on listening skills, see *Info-line* No. 8806, "Listening to Learn; Learning to Listen.")

■ Questioning
The facilitator should be skilled at asking questions. Good questions are open ended and stimulate discussion.

■ Sharing
The facilitator should be able to share his or her feelings and create an atmosphere in which team members are willing to share their feelings and opinions.

■ Problem Solving
Facilitators should be skilled at applying group problem-solving techniques. Group problem solving follows this process:

- defining the problem
- determining the cause
- considering alternatives
- weighing the alternatives
- selecting the best alternative
- implementing the solution
- evaluating the results

■ Resolving Conflict
Conflict among team members should not be suppressed. Indeed, it should be expected and dealt with constructively. This includes barring personal attacks. (For more information on conflict resolution, see *Info-line* No. 8909, "Coming to Agreement: How to Resolve Conflict.")

■ Using a Participative Style
The facilitator should be able to encourage all team members to participate in the meetings.

■ Accepting Others
The facilitator should maintain an open mind and not criticize the ideas and suggestions of the team members.

■ Empathizing
The facilitator should be able to "walk a mile in another's shoes" to understand the team members' feelings, and he or she should be able to express these feelings.

■ Leading
The facilitator must be able to keep the members focused and the discussion on target.

See the self-assessment instrument on the next page to assist facilitators in evaluating their skill levels.

Skill Inventory Self-Assessment Instrument

Glenn Varney provides the following inventory of team and interpersonal management skills to help you determine your strengths and weaknesses and chart your progress.

To What Extent Do You Need to Improve...

	1 (very little)	2	3 (somewhat)	4	5 (very much)

Relationships With Peers and Supervisors

1. Competing with my peers.
2. Being open with my seniors.
3. Feeling inferior to colleagues.
4. Standing up for myself.
5. Building open relationships.
6. Following policy guidelines.
7. Questioning policy guidelines.

Team Dynamics

8. Knowing other team members as individuals.
9. Meeting sufficiently often.
10. Supporting open expression of views.
11. Setting high standards.
12. Punishing behavior that deviates from the team norm.
13. Clarifying aims and objectives.
14. Giving information and views.
15. Using status to influence decisions of the team.
16. Delegating to reduce workload.

Relationships With Team Members

17. Helping others identify problems.
18. Practicing counseling skills.
19. Being distant with some people.
20. Intervening when things go wrong.
21. Being strong when reprimanding.
22. Giving energy to others.
23. Clarifying individuals' objectives.
24. Supporting others in difficulty.
25. Bringing problems out.
26. Supporting risk taking.
27. Being open in assessment of others.

Relationships With Employees

28. Being known as a person by employees.
29. Being available to employees.
30. Knowing how people feel.
31. Acting to resolve conflicts.

To What Extent Do You Need to Improve...	1 (very little)	2	3 (somewhat)	4	5 (very much)

Relationships With Employees *(continued)*

	1	2	3	4	5
32. Emphasizing communication.	☐	☐	☐	☐	☐
33. Passing information quickly.	☐	☐	☐	☐	☐
34. Emphasizing personal status.	☐	☐	☐	☐	☐
35. Bypassing management structure when communicating.	☐	☐	☐	☐	☐

Working in Groups

	1	2	3	4	5
36. Using a systematic approach.	☐	☐	☐	☐	☐
37. Developing others' skills.	☐	☐	☐	☐	☐
38. Being prompt.	☐	☐	☐	☐	☐
39. Using time efficiently.	☐	☐	☐	☐	☐
40. Listening actively.	☐	☐	☐	☐	☐
41. Openly expressing views.	☐	☐	☐	☐	☐
42. Dominating others.					
43. Maintaining good group climate.	☐	☐	☐	☐	☐
44. Dealing constructively with disruptive behaviors.	☐	☐	☐	☐	☐
45. Building informal contacts.	☐	☐	☐	☐	☐
46. Disparaging other groups.	☐	☐	☐	☐	☐
47. Sharing objectives with other groups.	☐	☐	☐	☐	☐
48. Identifying mutual communication needs.	☐	☐	☐	☐	☐
49. Arranging intergroup social events.	☐	☐	☐	☐	☐
50. Acting to resolve conflicts.	☐	☐	☐	☐	☐

Helping Others Improve

	1	2	3	4	5
51. Making time for counseling.	☐	☐	☐	☐	☐
52. Identifying the group's training needs.	☐	☐	☐	☐	☐
53. Setting coaching assignments.	☐	☐	☐	☐	☐
54. Allocating time and money for training.	☐	☐	☐	☐	☐
55. Giving feedback to others.	☐	☐	☐	☐	☐
56. Sharing parts of the job for others' development.	☐	☐	☐	☐	☐

Self-Development

	1	2	3	4	5
57. Setting aside time to think.	☐	☐	☐	☐	☐
58. Visiting other organizations.	☐	☐	☐	☐	☐
59. Discussing principles and values.	☐	☐	☐	☐	☐
60. Taking on new challenges.	☐	☐	☐	☐	☐
61. Attending training events.	☐	☐	☐	☐	☐
62. Knowing when and how to use specialists.	☐	☐	☐	☐	☐

Participant Guidelines

Don Aaron Carr presents the following guidelines for effective team facilitation:

- Contract with the team on your roles and responsibilities up front.

- Don't take on the team's work (for example, recording or scribing).

- Intervene to satisfy the team's needs, not your own desire to be heard.

- Give team members time to correct problems themselves before intervening.

- Once you've said your piece, be quiet.

- Do more asking than telling.

- Facilitate the leader so the leader can facilitate the team.

- Don't repeat feedback the team has already discussed.

- Be willing to take risks.

- Be willing to be wrong.

Appropriate Interventions

The word *intervention,* Carr says, is derived from a Latin word meaning to "interfere with the affairs of others." This is a good description of the kinds of actions facilitators are charged with taking. The facilitator, Carr notes, "performs an intervention whenever he or she decides to shift from that of a passive observer to that of an active participant or change agent."

Most frequently, interventions are focused on process, not on individuals or content. Carr maintains that there are four different types of interventions:

1. Interventions that cause the team to examine its dynamics and improve its performance.

2. Interventions that encourage member participation.

3. Interventions that encourage problem solving and decision making.

4. Interventions that ensure compliance with procedures, policies, ground rules, and requirements that define the process within the organization.

Active interventions alter the flow of events. They may quicken the development of the team, change the course of the discussion, increase the team's energy, or help the team become more aware of how it is functioning.

The facilitator should not intervene unless there is a reason for it—the intervention should alter what the team is doing or make available some additional information. Facilitators should intervene when the team wanders off track, when two team members are in conflict, when an individual isn't participating or is angry, or when the leader becomes autocratic.

Interventions, Carr continues, are made at four points in group process: before the meeting, during the meeting, at the end of the meeting with the team, and at a postmeeting coaching session with the leader. Timing an intervention depends on both the facilitator's style and the needs of the situation. Situational considerations include:

■ *Felt Need*

If the team is floundering and experiencing discomfort with its inability to move forward, the team may ask the facilitator to take some immediate action. If a felt need doesn't exist, Carr recommends not intervening, because the intervention might disrupt the group process. Carr also recommends that facilitators follow the "five-minute rule": Wait five minutes before intervening to see if the team corrects itself.

■ *Danger*

If an interaction occurs during a team meeting that would be difficult to repair later, the facilitator may intervene immediately—for example, if the team leader puts down a team member and the team shows no signs of addressing the interaction.

■ *Impact*

An immediate intervention has the greatest impact, but it may have to be repeated several times before the team begins to self-monitor. But beware of intervening every few minutes.

■ *Repeats*

If the facilitator intervenes with the same comment several times and the team doesn't act on it, the facilitator should mention the problem in a coaching session with the team leader.

How to Intervene

Knowing how to intervene in a group's process is key to the facilitator's success. David Quinlivan-Hall and Peter Renner in *In Search of Solutions* present 25 facilitator interventions and some guidance on when to use them. A few samples follow:

Describe process obstacles. If nothing is happening, the facilitator can describe the next step and perhaps encourage the contributions of several group members.

Encourage participation. The facilitator, Quinlivan-Hall and Renner note, should "establish a participative climate at the start of the meeting and maintain it throughout."

Stages and Phases

The work objective of an effective facilitator is to put himself or herself out of a job. It is easier to reach this end if the facilitator knows the stage of group development the team happens to be in. J. William Pfeiffer and Arlette C. Ballew have made several suggestions for the appropriate level of intervention in the various phases of group growth:

■ *Forming*

This is the "polite" phase. The facilitator's approach may be highly directive, instructing the group on what is to be done and how to do it. The facilitator intervenes by structuring getting-acquainted exercises, reviewing agenda items, and exploring similarities among members. During the later part of this phase, facilitators offer the group members the opportunity to set their own standards and identify each individual's reason for belonging to the team. Their task should be clarified, and the group members should be committed to it.

■ *Storming*

This is the "power" stage: who has it, who wants it, and who is doing what to get it. The facilitator's job in this stage is to create a common language and manage conflict: "Too little control can allow chaos, while suppression of all conflict can lead to apathy," Pfeiffer and Ballew point out. The facilitator engages in relationship-building activities, such as support, praise, encouragement, and simply paying attention.

■ *Norming*

This is the "positive" stage. The group comes together and works as a team. The team becomes self-monitoring. The facilitator can help the group share ideas, monitor or lead group problem-solving and decision-making tools, and provide feedback. Depending on the team, the facilitator may now become a consultant, attending only when the team feels his or her presence is needed, or working to blend in with the group.

■ *Performing*

This is the "proficient" stage. The facilitator turns over responsibility for decisions and implementation to the group and engages in both low-task and low-maintenance behaviors. He or she becomes "invisible."

■ *Adjourning*

This is the final phase. The team accomplishes its goal and disbands. The facilitator may help the team celebrate its success, debrief it on what worked and what did not, and help group members let go.

Roles Members Play

Team members can take on behaviors that hinder the group process. The following chart identifies several of these behaviors, explains why team members may behave that way, and tells what you can do about it.

Roles	Why It Happens	What to Do
Heckler	Probably good natured most of the time but is distracted by job or personal problems.	• Keep your temper under control. • Honestly agree with one idea, then move on to something else. • Toss a misstatement of fact to the group to turn down. • Talk privately with the person as a last resort to determine what is bothering him or her.
Rambler	One idea leads to another and takes this person miles away from the original point.	• When there is a pause for breath, thank him or her, refocus attention, and move on. • In a friendly manner, indicate that "We are a little off the subject." • As a last resort, use your meeting timetable. Glance at your watch and say, "Time is limited."
Ready Answer	Really wants to help, but makes it difficult by keeping others from participating.	• Cut it off tactfully by questioning others. Suggest that "we put others to work." • Ask this person to summarize. It keeps him or her attentive and capitalizes on his or her enthusiasm.
Conversationalist	Side chatter is usually personal in nature but may be related to the topic.	• Call by name and ask an easy question. • Call by name, restate the last opinion expressed, and ask his or her opinion of it. • Include in the discussion.
Personality Problems	Two or more individuals clash, dividing your people into factions and endangering the success of the meeting.	• Maximize points of agreement; minimize disagreements. Draw attention to the objective at hand. • Pose a direct question to an uninvolved member on the topic. • As a last resort, frankly state that personalities should be left out of the discussion.
Wrong Track	Brings up ideas that are obviously incorrect.	• Say, "That's one way of looking at it," and tactfully make any corrections. • Say, "I see your point, but can we reconcile that with our current situation?" • Handle tactfully since you will be contradicting him or her. Remember, all members of the group will hear how you respond to each individual, and you can encourage or discourage further participation.

Roles	Why It Happens	What to Do
Quiet One	Bored.	Gain interest by asking for opinion.
	Indifferent	Question the person next to him or her. Then, ask the quiet one to comment on the view expressed.
	Timid	Compliment this person the first time he or she contributes. Be sincere.
	Superior	Indicate respect for this person's experience, then ask for ideas.
Bungler	Lacks the ability to put good ideas into proper order; has ideas, but can't convey them and needs help.	Don't call attention to the problem. Say, "Let me see if we are saying the same thing." Then, repeat the idea more clearly.
Mule	Can't or won't see the other side; supports own viewpoint no matter what.	• Ask other members of the group to comment on the ideas. They will straighten him or her out. • Remind him or her that time is short, and suggest that he or she accept the group consensus presently. Indicate your willingness to talk with him or her later. Then, follow up.
Talker	Highly motivated	Slow this person down with some difficult questions.
	Show-off	Say, "That's an interesting point. Now, let's see what the rest think of it."
	Well informed	Draw upon his or her knowledge, but relay to the group.
	Just plain talkative	In general, for all overly talkative folks, let the group take care of them as much as possible.
Griper	Has a pet peeve, gripes for the sake of complaining, or has a legitimate complaint.	• Point out that the objective at hand is to operate as efficiently and cooperatively as possible under the present circumstances. • Indicate that you will discuss his or her personal problem privately at a later date. • Have another member of the group respond to his or her complaint.

Use body language. Facilitators can sit away from the table to indicate noninvolvement or move to the table when intervening in the process. "Moving closer to someone who is 'under fire' from the group gives this person support," they claim, while "moving close to a noisy, disruptive person usually results in a quieting down."

Discourage personal attacks. The facilitator may need to remind individuals of one of the first tenets of team building: "Examine the process, not the person." If one group member begins to attack another, the facilitator needs to step in to refocus the discussion on the issue.

Suggest a process. The facilitator should be able to instruct or run certain processes, such as idea generating and decision making, in order to move the group along.

Encourage equal participation. Facilitators need to observe the group to notice who is talking and who is being quiet. The trick is to draw out the wallflowers and shut up those who monopolize the conversation, without offending either.

Suggest a break. Taking a spontaneous break can end a deadlock or simply reenergize the group. Refreshment breaks are common, but others work just as well, including a "seventh-inning stretch," moving to small groups for several minutes, taking a five-minute "joke break," or bringing in a guest speaker.

Summarize. If the group has presented many alternatives, and those alternatives have generated much discussion, the group may get lost. Summarizing the problem and several of the alternatives may help the group refocus and keep moving.

Have the group manage the process. During the group's maturity, the facilitator may appropriately turn some of his or her duties over to the group. This indicates both trust and respect for the team and its interactions.

Debrief the group. A debriefing requires all team members to look at what is happening. It should be done at the end of the meeting and may be useful at natural breaks in the meeting agenda. Facilitators may take several approaches:

Objective: What happened here?

Reflective: How do you feel about what happened?

Interpretive: What did you learn from what happened?

Decision Making: What do you want to do with this information for the next time?

Search for common threads. If the group is wandering, the facilitator may stop the meeting and ask for members to search for what the solutions or problem definitions have in common. "With the common elements identified," Quinlivan-Hall and Renner assert, "focus is achieved for the next steps."

Present a straw man. During a break, the facilitator may develop, or suggest that someone else develop, a draft problem description or solution—the straw man. Encourage the team to criticize the plan, attack it, and pull it apart. "Only by picking it apart, adding to, and changing it, will the group develop ownership of it," the authors say.

Act stupid. Team members who are uninvolved may not understand what is happening or what someone else is saying, but may not, for many reasons, want to volunteer their ignorance. The facilitator may help these individuals by asking for clarification of issues, problems, terminology, or anything else that may get in the way of consensus later in the process. Remember, Columbo always got his criminal.

Get specific. Similar to acting stupid, getting specific can clear up hard-to-grasp issues, problems, and solutions.

The Power of Observation

All interventions have one thing in common: The facilitator has provided the proper feedback and timed the intervention to alter what the group is doing somehow. This means that the facilitator has paid careful attention to what the group as a unit is doing, as well as the interactions between individual team members.

The key tool in observing the group is listening. Listening shows interest in the individual speaking and respect for the other person's experience. According to Carr, there are three types of effective listening:

1. Passive listening, where one has no interaction with the speaker, such as listening to the radio or a cassette.

2. Attentive listening, where one has some interaction with the speaker, such as listening for content to lectures in class or taking notes in a meeting.

3. Active listening, where one has a high level of interaction with the speaker, listening for content, meaning, and feelings.

Facilitators listen actively throughout the meeting. They observe who talks and for how long, whom individuals look at when they talk, who supports whom, any challenges to group leadership, nonverbal communication, side conversations, and nonparticipation. They watch for individual reactions to what is being said in order to provide coaching. Facilitators may ask questions, restate what has been said, summarize positions, or reflect a speaker's feelings. They may also keep track of the different roles team members play.

Many facilitators find it helpful to develop a chart to "keep score" of the team members' different behaviors. Although these are helpful, the facilitator should get the team's permission to use it, especially in the early stages when team members may not trust each other completely. If the facilitator springs the results on the team at the end of

the meeting, team members may feel spied on and resent the tracking. A sample form with more detailed instructions is shown in the sidebar on the next page.

The chart attempts to quantify the contributions of team members in two broad areas: task and maintenance. Task functions facilitate the group in selecting, defining, and solving a common problem; maintenance functions alter or maintain the way in which group members interact. The chart also records any antigroup roles adopted by team members. Facilitators may want to chart the following behaviors:

Task Activity

Initiating. Proposing tasks or goals, defining the problem, suggesting a procedure or ideas for solving the problem.

Information seeking. Requesting facts, seeking relevant data about a problem, asking for suggestions or ideas.

Clarifying. Clearing up confusion, indicating alternatives and issues, giving examples.

Summarizing. Restating suggestions, synthesizing ideas, offering a decision or direction for the team to accept or reject.

Consensus testing. Setting up straw men to see if the team is near conclusion, checking to see how much agreement has been reached.

Maintenance Activity

Encouraging. Being friendly, recognizing others.

Expressing group feelings. Sensing moods, feelings, relationships with others, sharing feelings.

Harmonizing. Reconciling disagreements, reducing tensions, getting others to explore their differences.

Keeping Track

Many facilitators use checklists to track the behaviors—both good and bad—of team members. This allows the facilitator to provide accurate feedback at the end of the meeting. Keeping track of the team members' behaviors can make criticism specific, objective, and, therefore, easier to take. And it helps to know everyone on the team is receiving the same type of commentary.

But keep in mind that checklists could make team members uncomfortable. If you make such a list, do it with the team's approval and agreement on how the data will be used and discussed.

The checklists are generally a row-and-column grid. If group process is being monitored, the facilitator may put the team's rating in the second column. The facilitator then keeps a tally of how many times an individual engages in a particular behavior. For example, the team members may feel that, as a group, they interrupt each other too much. The facilitator may be asked to monitor that one aspect and report to the team members at the end of the meeting. Conversely, many facilitators use the tally sheet as a confidence-builder by tracking various desirable leadership behaviors and reporting them back. A sample grid follows:

Roles	Members											
Task Activity												
Initiator												
Information Seeker												
Clarifier												
Summarizer												
Consensus Tester												
Information Giver												
Maintenance Activity												
Encourager												
Expresser of Group Feelings												
Harmonizer												
Compromiser												
Gatekeeper												
Standard Setter												
Coach												
Collaborator												
Individual Activity												
Blocker												
Avoider												
Digressor												
Recognition Seeker												
Dominator												

Compromising. Admitting error, disciplining one-self to maintain group cohesion.

Gatekeeping. Trying to keep communication channels open, suggesting procedures to induce discussion of group problems.

Setting standards. Expressing standards to achieve, applying standards to evaluate the group and its output, evaluating frequently.

Coaching and consulting. Working with team members and management outside of meetings.

Individual Activity

Blocking. Interfering with group progress by arguing, resisting, disagreeing, or beating a dead horse.

Avoiding. Withdrawing from the discussion, day-dreaming, doing something else, whispering, leaving the room.

Digressing. Going off the subject, filibustering, discussing personal issues.

Other areas may also be observed that help the team function better. The facilitator may want to customize the list to suit the organization's culture or team environment. Among these other areas are:

- group rules
- clarity of ideas
- handling group problems
- favoritism
- group status
- sensitivity to needs of the group
- positive or negative body language
- seating arrangements
- tension
- program planning
- hidden agendas
- invisible committees
- making others aware of their own contributions

Feedback

These above categories also provide a framework for individual and group feedback. Gaining permission from the team members to keep track of their behaviors and explaining what impact these different behaviors have on the group will help the facilitator give useful feedback. In general, feedback should be:

■ **Descriptive**
Feedback is intended to provide others with a reading of what we are experiencing. For facilitators, this may mean pointing out someone's reaction to the action or statement of another, such as "What happened when you failed to post an agenda for the meeting?"

■ **Specific**
General feedback makes no value judgment of the person the facilitator is attempting to help: "I noticed you stared out the window when Bonnie was talking. It appears to me you may not be listening to Bonnie."

■ **Mindful of the Needs of Both Parties**
Feedback, especially when it is being given by the facilitator, should not be aimed at relieving one person's feelings or at relieving the facilitator's own feelings. Such feedback, Carr notes, tends to be destructive or hurtful, cuts off or reduces communication, and does little to change the behavior.

(See *Info-line* No. 9006, "Coaching and Feedback," for more information about feedback.)

Facilitators also observe how teams make decisions. Edgar H. Schein notes that observing how decisions are made helps the facilitator "assess the appropriateness of the method to the matter being decided on." Decisions made by groups are "notoriously hard to undo," Schein continues, adding that "often we can undo the decision only if we reconstruct it and understand how we made it and whether this method was appropriate." He lists some group decision-making methods:

Plop. Group decision by omission. "I think we ought to introduce ourselves." Silence.

Self-authorized agenda. Decision by one. "I think we should introduce ourselves. I'm John Smith."

Handclasp. Decision by two. "I wonder if it would be helpful if we introduced ourselves." "I think so. I'm John Smith."

Does anyone object? Decision by minority—one or more. "We all agree that introductions are appropriate."

Voting. Decision by majority.

Polling. "Let's see where everyone stands. What do you think?"

Consensus taking. Test for opposition, or find out if the opposition feels strongly enough to block the implementation of a decision. "Can you live with this?"

References & Resources

Articles

Allcorn, Seth. "Understanding Groups at Work." *Personnel*, August 1989, pp. 28-36.

Bettenhausen, Kenneth L. "Five Years of Group Research: What We Have Learned and What Needs To Be Addressed." *Journal of Management*, June 1991, pp. 345-381.

Cooper, Colleen, and Mary Ploor. "Challenges That Make or Break a Group." *Training & Development Journal*, April 1986, pp. 31-33.

Crapo, Raymond F. "It's Time To Stop Training…and Start Facilitating." *Public Personnel Management*, Winter 1986, pp. 433-449.

Driskell, James E., et al. "Task Cues, Dominance Cues, and Influence in Task Groups." *Journal of Applied Psychology*, February 1993, pp. 51-60.

Head, Thomas C. "Impressions on What Makes a Good Facilitator From a Frustrated Teamplayer." *Organization Development Journal*, Winter 1992, pp. 61-63.

Kaczmarek, Patricia S. "Planning and Conducting Facilitated Workshops— Part 2: Conducting the Session." *Performance and Instruction*, January 1993, pp. 31-34.

Kaye, Beverly. "Advisory Groups on the Seven Cs." *Training & Development*, January 1992, pp. 54-59.

Kochery, Timothy S. "Conflict Versus Consensus: Processes and Their Effect on Team Decision Making." *Human Resource Development Quarterly*, Summer 1993, pp. 185-191.

Levine, John M., and Richard L. Moreland. "Progress in Small Group Research." *Annual Review of Psychology*, 1990, pp. 585-634.

Rogelberg, Steven G., et al. "The Stepladder Technique: An Alternative Group Structure Facilitating Effective Group Decision Making." *Journal of Applied Psychology*, October 1992, pp. 730-737.

Sugar, Steve. "The RAT Race: An Exercise in Group Dynamics." *Performance & Instruction*, August 1990, pp. 13-17.

Thiagarajan, Sivasailam. "Secrets of Successful Facilitators." *Journal for Quality & Participation*, 1992, pp. 70-72.

Thornton, Paul B. "Teamwork: Focus, Frame, Facilitate." *Management Review*, November 1992, pp. 46-47.

Varney, Glenn H. "Helping a Team Find All the Answers." *Training & Development Journal*, February 1991, pp. 15-18.

Weingart, Laurie R. "Impact of Group Goals, Task Component Complexity, Effort, and Planning on Group Performance." *Journal of Applied Psychology*, October 1992, pp. 682-683.

Weingart, Laurie R., et al. "The Impact of Consideration of Issues and Motivational Orientation on Group Negotiation Process and Outcome." *Journal of Applied Psychology*, June 1993, pp. 504-517.

Williams, Bill. "Ten Commandments for Group Leaders." *Supervisory Management*, September 1992, pp. 1-2.

Books

Dimock, Hedley G. *Groups: Leadership and Group Development*. San Diego: University Associates, 1987.

Fox, William M. *Effective Group Problem Solving*. San Francisco: Jossey-Bass, 1987.

Heron, John. *The Facilitator's Handbook*. New York: Nichols Publishing, 1989.

Kayser, Thomas A. *Mining Group Gold: How to Cash In on the Collaborative Brain Power of a Group*. El Segundo, CA: Serif Publishing, 1990.

Mink, Oscar G., et al. *Groups at Work*. Englewood Cliffs, NJ: Educational Technology Publications, 1987.

Nutt, Paulo C. *Making Tough Decisions*. San Francisco: Jossey-Bass, 1989.

Quinlivan-Hall, David, and Peter Renner. *In Search of Solutions: Sixty Ways to Guide Your Problem-Solving Group*. Vancouver: PFR Training Associates, 1990.

Ulshak, Francis L., et al. *Small Group Problem Solving*. Reading, MA: Addison-Wesley, 1981.

Info-lines

Kirrane, Diane E. "Listening to Learn; Learning to Listen." No. 8806 (revised 1997).

Meyer, Kathy M. "Coming to Agreement: How to Resolve Conflict." No. 8909 (out of print).

"Coaching and Feedback." No. 9006 (revised 1998).

Job Aid

Intervention Starters

Interventions during facilitation often take the form of questions the facilitator asks of the group. The text discusses four forms of questions: objective, reflective, interpretive, and decision making. Following are suggested openers for each type of intervention.

Objective

What happened?

Do we need to get back on track?

Have we strayed from the topic?

Do we need to take a break?

Summarize the group's activity.

Reflective

How do you feel?

Would you like to say something?

Maybe we misunderstood
our roles.

I'm sorry it appears that way.

How would you like me to
provide feedback?

Hey, you wanted an enforcer!

Interpretive

What did you learn?

Is this what the team thinks?

What are the specifics?

What's our common ground?

Do you understand the other's
point of view or work process?

**Decision
making**

What do you want to do?

The material appearing on this page is not covered by copyright and may be reproduced at will.

Project Management: A Guide

Issue 9004

Project Management: A Guide

AUTHOR:

Connie Thompson

Editorial Staff for 9004

Editor
Barbara Darraugh

ASTD Internal Consultant
Cathy Fisk

Revised 1998

Editor
Cat Sharpe

Contributing Editor
Ann Bruen

Project Management Defined

Project management is a term that is used frequently—and sometimes incorrectly. By definition, project management is the planning, organizing, directing, and controlling of resources for a finite period of time to complete specific goals and objectives. In the day-to-day work environment, project management is one of the most efficient ways to do business: Change is constant, competition between companies is vital, and the need for new and better products is necessary. Today, companies are faced with increased costs and complexities, a scarcity of resources, and never-ending improvements in technologies and methodologies.

Project management has evolved as the answer to some management problems that result from today's complex systems. In the past, changes occurred more slowly, and a company could adjust and develop new products, processes, and systems through the use of the classical line organization. Now, however, as needs increase and the systems and processes used to develop responses to the changing environment become more complicated, the ability of functional organizations to respond effectively is even more difficult. To meet these challenges, companies are using the project approach for the management of more activities.

Project management allows a group to fulfill a specific task with a finite life span that will require company resources on a part-time basis. Usually, an organization institutes project management when a complex job that cuts across departmental lines needs to get done, and top management does not have the time to devote to the planning, execution, and completion of the effort. After several in-house meetings, management decides that the project approach, led by a project manager, is the preferred method of accomplishing the task. The expertise within the organization can be tapped, the project receives the assets—both human and monetary—it needs, and the project's budget can be projected and monitored.

This *Info-line* provides an overview of project management, step-by-step guidelines, and discussions of pertinent topics. The project management process described here is an extremely formal process used for a large project, such as building the space station. A less formal approach, using the same principles, is more likely to be employed on smaller projects.

Project Manager Selection

The selection of the right person for the job of project manager is very important. The project manager must work constantly with change and deal with problems across functional areas. His or her planning and actions must be directed toward attaining the performance, cost, and schedule goals of the project. The project manager's ability to get the job done through other people is another critical aspect of the job.

In their book, *Successful Project Managers*, Jeffrey K. Pinto and O.P. Kharbanda state: "The skills that separate successful project managers from those who are unsuccessful are rarely technical: They are almost always human skills." The successful project manager is able to do the following things:

- Plan, reiterate, organize, delegate, understand, communicate, and evaluate.

- Be energetic, realistic, self-confident, unpretentious, trustworthy, and systematic.

- Listen well.

- Be familiar with the operations of the company's line organization.

- Motivate and coordinate large groups of highly trained people.

The successful project manager also should be able to recognize the informal ties that exist in an organization, use those ties to his or her benefit, and be aware of the pitfalls of crossing organizational lines.

To choose a project manager, top management normally scans its line managers to determine how successful each person has been in the performance of his or her particular functional group and who has had previous experience in the same or similar projects. If the organization can find a person who is a successful line manager *and* has the "walk-on-water" characteristics listed above, that person is chosen as the project manager.

Management's responsibility, however, does not end with the selection and appointment of a project manager. Management needs to provide the

Case Study: Training Project Managers

Many organizations are realizing that project management can solve some of their headaches in the accomplishment of tasks and are committed to training their existing personnel. Finding the manager and team to perform these efforts successfully, however, is not easy.

To prepare for the future and deal with present requirements, companies are providing prospective project managers with systematic and structured methodologies for planning, tracking, documenting, and closing out projects. Project management training focuses on the performance factors necessary for the successful management of technical projects. Each project manager must learn:

- the elements of the project life cycle

- how each phase affects the completion of project objectives

- the people skills necessary for effective team building

- how to maintain and improve his or her knowledge of technology

In the 1980s, Xerox Corporation recognized that to stay competitive and increase productivity, their managers needed training. As they reorganized, they realized that a key factor to the organization's long-term success would be to increase the acceptance and commitment of a high-tech workforce to a large number of changes occurring at a rapidly increasing rate. To do this, Xerox retrained their managers to concentrate on task management, employee involvement, communications, and leadership.

Xerox used a three-phased approach that included an increased emphasis on innovation and risk taking and on developing an environment that encouraged greater workforce participation. The steps were as follows:

1. Unfreeze current ideas.

2. Change and train for the desired behaviors.

3. Refreeze the new behavior patterns through support mechanisms.

support and planning resources of the existing management structure, including a team of personnel from various functional areas, to accomplish the project objective.

Project managers need top management to cooperate with them and support their selection of a project team. Project managers determine, through the planning phase, the goals and objectives of the project, the characteristics required of the staff, the essential material resources, the cost of the venture, and the management tools necessary for control. Management should support and uphold the structure of the project and provide the managers with the necessary resources to fulfill the effort.

The "New" Project Manager

In the era of downsizing, it is likely that more and more employees will be asked to manage a project, but few have been trained to assume these duties. In his article "Essential Skills for Today's 'Instant' Project Managers," Michael Greer addresses the need for step-by-step guidelines for those employees who are thrust into project management roles. In Greer's words, "A new kind of manager has appeared in our organizations: an 'instant' project manager whose main interest and skill set, prior to acquiring project management responsibilities, is that of a specialist in a particular field."

Task specialists with little or no training in formal management are being asked to plan, execute, and control projects critical to their organizations' success. These managers need a framework for organizing their projects and a simple guide for their activities, as well as occasional mentoring by senior management to guide them along the path to success. They require "survival tools," such as checklists, worksheets, and models, so they will know what specific actions to take, when to take them, and how to know when they have achieved the proper results. These key project-management processes will be discussed in detail below.

Organizations need to develop the necessary skills in their employees so that they can be successful project managers. For an example of one organization's solution to this problem, see the case study at left.

Elements of Project Management

The term *project management* sounds "official"—and difficult. Yet everybody, at one time or another, manages projects. Small projects range from cooking dinner to building a bookcase. Large projects include planning a wedding or developing the space station. The project management process can be successfully used by a wide range of individuals, both inside and outside of business: students, homemakers, engineers, contractors, and supervisors.

Cooking dinner and developing the space station share a process—and that process is project management. Elements of project management include the following:

- definition
- planning
- implementation
- completion

Defining the Project

Once the project manager is selected, he or she and a group of people who are knowledgeable of the proposed areas (usually their line managers) come together to define the project plan. Each brings to the project his or her own particular knowledge base: execution of similar projects, personnel resources, technology availability, or quality and control. These components help the project manager define the proposed task.

The team must discuss and analyze the project and develop a firm grasp of the endeavor on which they are embarking. Planning will provide answers to most of the following questions:

- What are the specific goals and objectives of the project?

- How is the project going to be structured?

- What are the important tasks and events (milestones) of the project, and how should they be scheduled?

- What types of personnel are needed, and how will they be used?

A Project Management Glossary

Following are a number of terms that are used frequently in the project management field.

Budget: The financial or resource constraints under which the project will operate. It should be divided to reflect the major tasks to be performed, equipment or other material needs, and travel- or communications-related costs.

Critical Path: When a project has several tasks, some of them overlapping or dependent upon an earlier task, the critical path is the minimum time schedule for completing all the tasks.

Deliverables: The products that are to be delivered to the customer at the end of the project.

Gannt Chart: A floating bar chart, or series of lines that represent the beginning and end dates for each task in a project, placed on some form of time line.

Milestone: A key point (date) in a project when an event will occur.

Program Evaluation and Review Technique (PERT): A chart that visualizes the placement of cost-impacting elements and illustrates the interrelationships of activities and resources.

Work Breakdown Structure (WBS): The detailed subdividing of the project into tasks and subtasks in order to determine resources and schedules.

Adapted from "So You're Going to Manage a Project…" by Tom D. Conkright, Training, *January 1988.*

- How are other resources (money, equipment, materials, facilities) going to be distributed among the various tasks?

- How will the key elements of the project—cost, performance, and schedule—be estimated and controlled? What management tools will be used?

- What are the potential bottlenecks in carrying out the project, and how will they be handled?

The project planning team should take the time to answer these questions. A high degree of commitment to the planning effort will significantly benefit the undertaking. To be successful, the planning group should resist the urge to forge ahead with the implementation as rapidly as possible to attain "fast track" action. Doing it right the first time requires the formulation of a good plan, one that is not only flexible enough to adjust to change but also is defined adequately enough to provide a structured method of meeting project objectives.

Planning the Project

Once the project's objectives have been discussed and agreed upon, the project manager moves on to the next task—the establishment of a plan on how the project will be accomplished. These elements and steps include the following:

1. Selection of a strategy for achieving the objective.

2. Division of the project's tasks into subtasks and units (work breakdown structure).

3. Determination of the standards for measuring the accomplishment of each subtask (specifications).

4. Development of a time schedule and sequence for performing the tasks and subtasks (Gantt chart and Program Evaluation and Review Technique [PERT]—also known as the critical path method [CRT]).

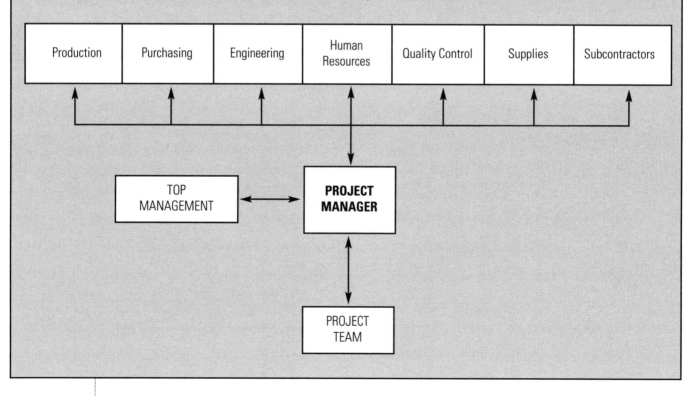

The Project Manager's Role

Resources

The project manager works across functional areas within an organization, tapping departmental resources on a part-time basis. This permits the project to receive the human and monetary assets it needs for success

| Production | Purchasing | Engineering | Human Resources | Quality Control | Supplies | Subcontractors |

TOP MANAGEMENT ◄──► PROJECT MANAGER

PROJECT TEAM

5. Estimation of costs of each task and subtask and compilation of the entire project's cost budget (if not predetermined).

6. Design of the staff organization needed to fulfill the tasks and subtasks, including the number and kind of people required, their duties, and any necessary training.

7. Development of policies and procedures that will be in effect during the project's life cycle.

8. Acknowledgement of predetermined parameters imposed by the customer or organization, such as military standards or specifications.

Each element should be carefully detailed and documented. Some methods of developing these project plan elements are contained in the following discussion.

Work Breakdown Structure

One of the most basic and effective tools in the planning and integration of a project is its work breakdown structure (WBS). The WBS is a tool many organizations use not only to identify the tasks, subtasks, and units of work to be performed but also to track the costs of each of these elements. (See example following.)

To develop a WBS, the project manager looks at each of the major tasks required to fulfill the project objective. He or she then identifies the next level of detail by delineating the steps necessary to perform the tasks. These steps or subtasks can be further defined into units and subunits, depending on the complexity of the task.

One method of dividing the tasks is for the project manager to look at the current company organization and segregate the tasks into these areas. For example, to develop an integrated data terminal, the project manager should look at hardware design, hardware production, software development, logistics, documentation, quality assurance, configuration management, and accounting as possible elements within the major task areas.

The project manager must be creative and meticulous in the development of a WBS to ensure that all possible subtasks, units, and subunits have been identified. There are no exact rules to follow in the generation of a WBS; good judgment and a general knowledge of the objectives of the project are the basic criteria. A general rule of thumb is that tasks should be divided into small enough terms to permit realistic estimates of cost and personnel required and to simplify control.

Of course, each project must be evaluated and structured on the basis of its own unique requirements and constraints. A project manager may decide that a tree diagram, flowchart, or a functional description can adequately define the parameters of a specific task. Whatever the size of the project, the project manager must chart the plan of action that the project should follow during its life cycle.

Schedules and Milestones

The time frame of a project can be derived from the plan and the WBS. The project manager lists the elements of the WBS, arranges them in the sequence of occurrence, and determines how the elements mesh into one another to form a milestone chart. Project managers should have some experience with similar activities to be able to estimate accurately the time required to perform certain functions. Many project managers find it more realistic to plan time intervals as a range rather than as a precise amount of time.

Time frame data are mapped onto a milestone chart, called a Gantt chart. The Gantt chart is a horizontal bar chart that graphically displays the time relationship of each step of the project. The Gantt chart has been used for many years and is a valuable tool for project managers in planning, monitoring, and controlling projects. For an example of Gantt and PERT charts, see *Tracking Techniques*.

In today's automated environment, there are several software packages for different computer systems that will provide the project manager with automated milestone charting. Data are entered for each element that can be traced, updates are made as schedules are adjusted, and costs and work-hour expenditures are added. By using one of these milestone-tracking software packages, the project manager has one source for actual versus projected charts for task performance and expenditures.

Sample Work Breakdown Structure

You have been asked to set up a work breakdown structure for installing an air filter at a construction site. After you determine the project objectives, identify all the necessary tasks in units small enough to track costs and personnel needs.

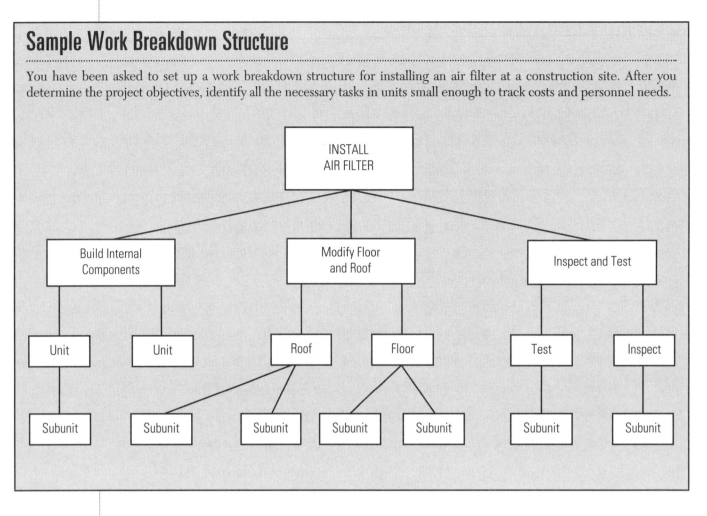

The project manager should investigate the automated tools currently being used by the company or packages of which he or she has prior knowledge. Learning a new software management package in addition to trying to manage a project may be too much of an endeavor to handle at one time.

Although milestone charts help planning by describing tasks and their associated time spans, there are disadvantages in relying only on these tools in managing complex projects. To assist with complex efforts, the project manager may require computer-based network-analysis tools as well. Some popular network-analysis tools are Program Evaluation and Review Technique (PERT), Critical Path Method (CPM), and Precedence Diagramming Method (PDM).

The applications of the network-based tools can be adapted to the specific needs of a company or organization. Some of the most widely used applications are:

- communication of interdependencies and involvement of the project team

- estimation of project length

- identification and resolution of conflicts and bottlenecks

- simulation of alternate plans of action

- project schedule acceleration

- optimum cost scheduling

- resource allocation

- cash-flow management

Tracking Techniques

A trainer for a mid-size service industry was asked to develop a training program to address a job performance problem. He devised a Gantt chart, showing the basic timeline for course development, and a PERT chart to illustrate the steps to be taken during the project implementation.

Gantt Chart

Time frame data for the project are mapped onto a milestone, or Gantt, chart. The Gantt chart is a horizontal bar chart that graphically displays the time relationship of each step of the project. The figure below shows the simple Gantt chart. The horizontal bar shows the initiation and completion of the task. The dashed extension provides an additional range of time (fudge factor) to allow milestone slippage without a negative impact on the project's deadlines. The Gantt chart has been used for many years and is a valuable tool for the planning, monitoring, and controlling of projects.

ACTIVITY	APRIL	MAY	JUNE	JULY	AUGUST
A. Determine goals					
B. Assemble resources					
C. Write objectives					
D. Determine contents					
E. Design sequence & training strategies					
F. Write instructional management plan					
G. Implement training plan					
H. Evaluate					

PERT Chart

Performance Evaluation and Review Technique (PERT) and Critical Path Method (CPM) are two widely used network techniques. Their advantage over the Gantt chart is their ability to illustrate the interrelationships between the activities and resources. PERT and CPM track predecessor activities and, using some statistical manipulations, can predict the "fudge factor."

ACTIVITY	DESCRIPTION	PREDECESSOR ACTIVITY	EXPECTED COMPLETION TIME (Weeks)
A	Determine goals	— —	2 (A)
B	Assemble resources	— —	2 (B)
C	Write objectives	A	3 (C)
D	Determine content	A, C	2 (D)
E	Design sequence & training strategies	A, C, D	5 (E)
F	Write instructional management plan	A, B, C, D, E	2 (F)
G	Implement program	A, B, C, D, E, F	1 (G)
H	Evaluate	A, B, C, D, E, F, G	2 (H)

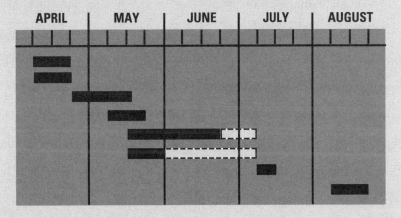

Again, the project manager should investigate currently available and known tools that will be the most helpful for the completion of the task. Gantt charts and network-based analysis methods are management tools; they are *not* substitutes for project management.

A major component of a project manager's job is the planning and controlling of costs. The success of the project will largely depend on correctly estimating the level of effort and expenditures required. For a more complete discussion, see *Estimating and Tracking Costs* opposite.

Staffing the Project

During the planning process, the project manager compiles the tasks and subtasks that need to be performed. One of the most important elements of planning is finding and using the correct personnel to perform these tasks. Most of the time, in the interests of cost, time, and availability, the personnel required for a project can be obtained from within the organization. The project manager, however, usually has the option of hiring specific expertise from outside the organization; a consultant, for example, may be the best way to obtain the required skills without hiring full-time employees.

When developing the project team, the project manager faces many of the following factors:

- current organizational structure

- commitment of management

- types of personnel needed

- number of hours necessary to complete the project

- other ongoing tasks for personnel

- cooperation of other line managers

- informal lines of communication within the organization

One method of developing a "perfect" team for the project is to compile a project summary sheet that describes the ideal qualifications for a job position required to perform a specific task. For example,

for the development of a hardware design of a ruggedized enclosure to be used in an aircraft environment, you would need a mechanical engineer with previous design experience, knowledge of the aircraft platform, and environment specifications (whether it is commercial or military).

The engineer should have a working knowledge of the components that are to be installed in the enclosure, and in-depth background in electrostatic discharge, electromechnical interference, installation procedures, test and evaluation techniques, and vibration and shock testing. By compiling an ideal job description, the project manager can look at the available personnel in the functional organization and easily ascertain whether or not the people needed to do the job are current employees and whether they can be "borrowed" either full- or part-time for the duration of the project.

As the investigation into personnel resources continues, the project manager should remember that he or she is not limited to the current personnel roster. The project manager may be able to request that current prospective employees receive some specialized training to meet the need; or hire a subcontractor or consultant for the duration of the particular task; or look into hiring new, full-time employees if the budget permits.

By developing the job description first, the project manager already has a general set of requirements to give the human resources department to begin the search for qualified applicants. One consideration that the project manager must remember, no matter what approach is used, is to reflect the cost of training, hiring, or subcontracting in the budget.

Each organization has its own methods of supplying personnel to work on projects. The project manager should be sensitive to these unwritten rules and coordinate access across the appropriate functional lines to obtain the personnel the project needs. In addition to the formal organization, there is usually an informal organization that grows within the operation of a company. Personal ties develop among personnel, and the ability to get a project done often relies on these informal relationships. The astute project manager should learn to recognize the informal ties that exist in the organization, try to use them, and be aware if their potential pitfalls.

Implementing the Project Plan

The project manager now has in place the objectives of the project, the plan and structure of its implementation, the management tools for tracking, the project team, the orders placed for materials and supplies, and the support and concurrence of top management. He or she is ready to undertake the project. The following elements are essential for a project to be successful:

- commitment to planning

- development and implementation of sound strategies

- establishment of meaningful objectives

- understanding the scope of the plan

- reliance on the project team's experience (to a certain degree)

- top management support
- clear delegation

- adequate control techniques and information

- realization that people resist change

Estimating and Tracking Costs

In today's competitive world, there is no room for cost overruns, project schedule slippage, or the inability to deliver. The project manager should be able to plan and control costs as a continuation of all the organizing and tracking functions. Careful planning for costs is extremely important for many reasons: Underestimating the level of effort and expenditures required produces cost overruns and loss of profit; overestimating expenses may make the overall cost of the job too high. Either scenario will threaten the life of the project.

A good plan includes the identification of the following elements:

- sources of supplies and materials
- direct labor hours
- overhead
- pay rates for the selected personnel
- equipment leases or purchases
- general and administrative expenses
- profit (if applicable)

Each project manager must carefully assess the cost requirements of his or her individual organization and add these elements into the budget. The accuracy of cost estimates is directly influenced by the type and level of WBS that has been developed. Each task, subtask, and unit should be carefully estimated for cost. Cost estimates can be generated in several different ways. For example, the project office can issue a statement of work to be accomplished, the specifications for the project, a preliminary master schedule, assumptions of performance (if any), and other special instructions. Each participating department or division and, in some cases, outside organizations can respond with labor estimates, travel, material, or other direct charges to fulfill the indicated objectives.

Other organizations rely on the project manager to develop these estimates. The success of this effort will depend on the experience and overall knowledge base of the manager. If the project manager is not experienced in these areas, he or she should definitely seek the assistance and guidance of other project managers and functional personnel performing the tasks. Top management will not accept excuses of the "I didn't know" type when costs are involved.

Regardless of how the costs are projected, all backup material and justifications for the cost estimates should be maintained in a safe—and recoverable—file. These can be invaluable when a cost-auditing trail is initiated or the project scope changes, and revised estimates need to be generated.

Automated packages for cost tracking, similar to those available for milestone tracking, will assist the project manager with cost spreadsheets, accumulation of costs, and accurate reporting of projections, budgets, and expenditures. The WBS, milestone charts, or network-analysis tools provide the project manager with concrete methods of tracking the cost of a project and alert the manager when areas do not fall with the projected budget. These factors are valuable not only during the planning phase but also through the implementation and completion phases of the project.

- encouragement of people involvement

- attention to detail

- ability to work with people, not against them

- interface with the customer (internal or external)

Working through people, effective team-building management techniques, and positive influences are the factors required for success. The intentional structure of roles and responsibilities of all concerned parties will provide the project team with attainable goals; only through teamwork and fulfillment of the plan's objectives can the project come to fruition.

During the project, the project manager is responsible for monitoring the progress of the tasks as well as controlling the financial and deliverable aspects of the project. He or she should refer to the standards and specifications that were developed during the planning state to ensure that the product being prepared meets those standards. On large manufacturing projects, the project manager should rely on inspectors and quality assurance personnel to conduct regular, predetermined checks on the programs of the product. Control points identified on Gantt or PERT charts can be monitored, and problems can be handled and corrected at those points.

The work breakdown structure provides each member of the project team with an outline of the portions of the task that need to be performed. When each task element is complete, the project team members can develop a concise progress chart or track progress on existing Gantt or PERT charts.

The project manager needs to keep the project team members aware of the progress of project activity that lies outside of their individual areas. Regular status meetings with a defined set of discussion items will fulfill this need. The project manager should also have an open-door policy to give the team the confidence to present new ideas, discuss problems, and solve unexpected difficulties.

Through the use of project management tools, the project manager is apprised of deliverable schedules and anticipated completion dates of tasks. The

project manager should make use of these aids to guide daily progress. Network-analysis tools, when used conscientiously, will alert the project manager when deadlines are in danger. Alternatives can be investigated and exercised before major problems occur. Bottlenecks and unexpected delays will invariably occur; however, if the planning process prepares for such problems, the success of the project will not be in jeopardy.

Throughout the project, the project manager should keep the customer, whether internal or external, aware of the project's progress. Predetermined progress-review meetings should be held with the customer. These reviews are established during the planning process. The customer may specify predefined periods of time for the reviews. For example, preliminary design reviews and critical design reviews for government contracts usually occur at 30 and 90 days after task initiation. Good relations with the customer, the adherence to customer specifications and standards, and the quality of the finished product will reflect the competence of both the team and the company.

Completing the Project

The goal of project management is to complete an effort and receive the customer's acceptance. Elements that are described in the work breakdown structure and the project plan to control the finished product include the following:

- test and evaluation
- acceptance testing
- review and delivery of documentation
- installation and inspections
- fulfillment of specifications
- fulfillment of product
- marketing considerations

The project manager and project team should be aware throughout the project of the final goals that must be attained. By meeting these goals, the team has collectively completed the project.

When the product has been delivered and the customer is pleased, the project team's work is still not done. The following tasks should be considered and performed after the physical completion of the project:

Prepare the Final Project Report

The project personnel should review the work that has been accomplished and prepare a report to management. The items to be included in this summary are the completion of goals and objectives, a summary of technological advances made, and recommendations for future projects in this discipline.

Prepare the Internal Project Report

The project team members should provide the project manager with a list of the lessons learned from interfaces with customers, suppliers, and subcontractors; feedback on the performance of personnel; recommendations for improvements for specific stages of development; and overall summary of the success or failure of exercised techniques.

Wrap Up Project

The project manager should compile a list of surplus equipment, materials, and supplies and recommend the disposal of these materials. He or she should also disband the project team and reallocate the personnel resources for other efforts.

Putting It All Together

Project management is the accomplishment of a task that has a definitive beginning and end. Here is a review of the phases in successful project management.

■ *Definition*

The definition of goals and objectives provides the project with an attainable end. The planning stage prepares all concerned parties to achieve that end. Implementation of the plans consists of the methods of accomplishing the project, and the completion of the project brings all the achievements and recommendations of the team together into a concrete package.

■ *Planning*

Not every project will require the same amount of planning and implementation time. Each type of project should be evaluated as to its size, scope, and type of organization that will best meet the goals. Effective planning focuses the attention of an organization on its future and to its success.

■ *Selection of the Project Manager*

The project manager is a very special person in an organization. He or she must possess the technological and human skills to compile a team and the physical resources to get the job done. The project manager needs the support of top management as well as the cooperation of line managers to be able to organize effectively and perform the task at hand.

■ *Staffing*

To perform the work, a project team is assembled and duties and responsibilities are assigned. Policies and procedures are delineated to clarify how the team is to function and how the project is to be prepared. The project manager is responsible for coordinating the work of individuals from various disciplines, monitoring the progress of the project, and measuring it against the plan. He or she keeps the project team and the customer informed of task status and resolves problems as they occur.

■ *Implementation*

Project management can be implemented with a minimum of trauma and organizational conflict. Through the structured set of plans, a project team can efficiently perform the tasks, achieve a level of quality, and maintain the cost and schedule parameters. The project manager monitors the progress of tasks, controls the functional performance, and keeps the team apprised of status, problems, and accomplishments.

■ *Completion*

The ultimate goal of project management is to deliver a product or service to a client that performs as expected, by deadline, and within cost limits. The quality of the product is defined by the schedule, and the costs are defined by a budget. At the completion of the project, the project manager and the team compile a summary of the accomplishments, recommendations for improvements, and ideas for future growth.

In today's competitive business climate, dramatic changes in corporate management and organizational structure are taking place. As companies downsize, streamline, and re-engineer the way they do business, they are placing greater emphasis on performance and profitability. Project-oriented planning is the major component of this streamlined organization, and successful project management has become a necessity. Companies must dedicate themselves to the project approach, however, and train their employees in the technical and strategic skills that will be required in the next century.

Four Phases of a Project

The four phases of a project are shown below, along with a time line that illustrates their interdependency.

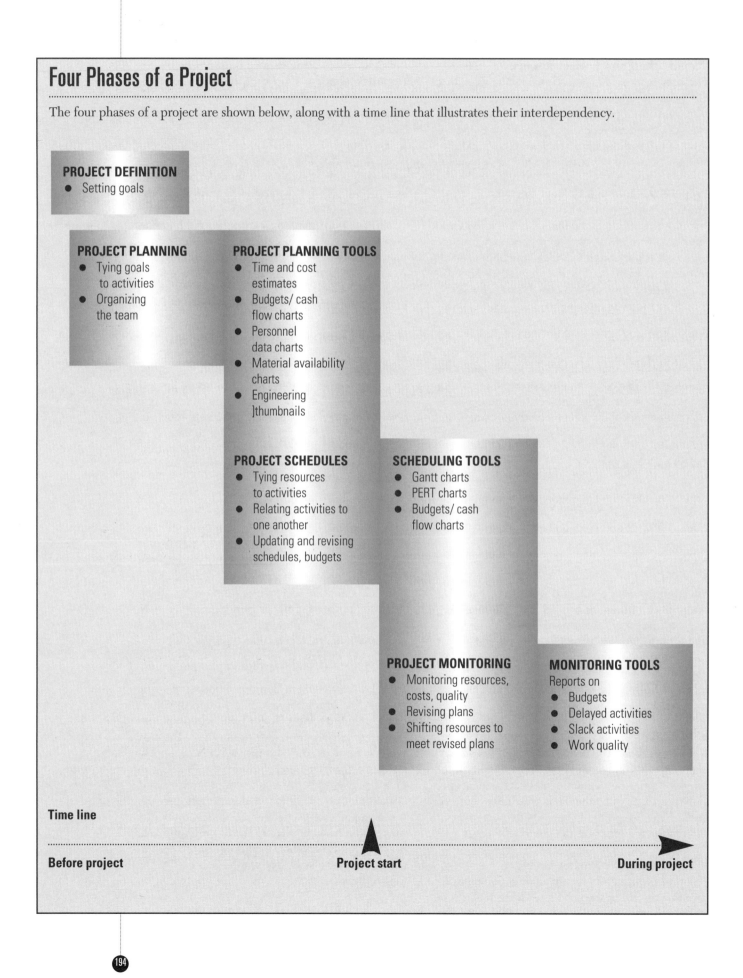

PROJECT DEFINITION
- Setting goals

PROJECT PLANNING
- Tying goals to activities
- Organizing the team

PROJECT PLANNING TOOLS
- Time and cost estimates
- Budgets/ cash flow charts
- Personnel data charts
- Material availability charts
- Engineering]thumbnails

PROJECT SCHEDULES
- Tying resources to activities
- Relating activities to one another
- Updating and revising schedules, budgets

SCHEDULING TOOLS
- Gantt charts
- PERT charts
- Budgets/ cash flow charts

PROJECT MONITORING
- Monitoring resources, costs, quality
- Revising plans
- Shifting resources to meet revised plans

MONITORING TOOLS
Reports on
- Budgets
- Delayed activities
- Slack activities
- Work quality

Time line

Before project   **Project start**   **During project**

References & Resources

Articles

Anderson, Scott, and Marcia Gibson. "Managing CBI Projects." *Journal of Interactive Instruction Development,* Winter 1994, pp. 32-37.

Bailey, Harold J., and Kathleen A. Ergott. "Project Management: Part 1—The Soft Skills." *Journal of Instruction Delivery Systems,* Winter 1998, pp. 3-7.

Bowen, H. Kent, et al. "Make Projects the School for Leaders." *Harvard Business Review,* September/October 1994, pp. 131-140.

Conkright, Tom D. "So You're Going to Manage a Project." *Training,* January 1998, pp. 62-67.

Deets, Norman, and Richard Morano. "Xerox's Strategy for Changing Management Styles." *American Management Association Management Review,* March 1986, pp. 31-35.

Dickson, Ron. "How to Salvage a Sunken Project." *Training & Development,* December 1995, pp. 12-13.

Fryer, Bronwyn. "Tools of the Trade: Teaching Project Management." *Inside Technology Training,* January 1988, pp. 13-18.

Garstang, Marlene. "Checklists for Training Project Management: The Team's Perspective." *Journal of Instruction Delivery Systems,* Winter 1994, pp. 29-33.

Greer, Michael. "Essential Skills for Today's 'Instant' Project Managers." *Performance Improvement,* February 1998, pp. 24-29.

Layng, Jacqueline. "Parallels Between Project Management and Instructional Design." *Performance Improvement,* July 1997, pp. 16-20.

Murphy, Charles. "Utilizing Project Management Techniques in the Design of Instructional Materials." *Performance & Instruction,* March 1994, pp. 9-11.

"Recipe for Success: Cross-functional Teams + Project Management Skills." *Getting Results . . . for the Hands-on Manager,* October 1996, pp. C1-2.

Stamps, David. "Lights! Camera! Project Management!" *Training,* January 1997, pp. 50-56.

Stevens, Larry. "The Right Mix." *Human Resource Executive,* April 1997, pp. 52-56.

Stewart, Thomas A. "The Corporate Jungle Spawns a New Species: The Project Manager." *Fortune,* July 10, 1995, pp. 179-180.

Thornley, James. "Tips for Project Management." *Performance & Instruction,* May/June 1996, pp. 6-8.

Books

DeWeaver, Mary F., and Lorie C. Gillespie. *Real-world Project Management: New Approaches for Adapting to Change and Uncertainty.* New York: Quality Resources, 1997.

Forsberg, Kevin, et al. *Visualizing Project Management.* New York: John Wiley & Sons, 1996.

Frame, J. Davidson. *Managing Projects in Organizations.* (rev. edition). San Francisco: Jossey-Bass, 1996.

Kerzner, Harold. *Project Management: A Systems Approach to Planning, Scheduling, and Controlling.* (6th edition). New York: John Wiley & Sons, 1997.

Kezsbom, Deborah, et al. *Dynamic Project Management.* New York: John Wiley & Sons, 1989.

Pinto, Jeffrey K., and O.P. Kharbanda. *Successful Project Managers.* Bonn, Germany: Van Nostrand Reinhold, 1995.

Pokras, Sandy. *Rapid Team Deployment: Building High Performance Project Teams.* Menlo Park, California: Crisp Publications, 1995.

References & Resources

Books

Stuckenbruck, Linn C. *The Implementation of Project Management: The Professional's Handbook.* Drexel Hill, Pennsylvania: Addison-Wesley, 1982.

Weihrich, Heinz, and Harold D. Koontz. *Essentials of Management.* (5th edition). New York: McGraw-Hill, 1990.

Wysocki, Robert K., et al. *Effective Project Management: How to Plan, Manage, and Deliver Projects on Time and Within Budget.* New York: John Wiley & Sons, 1995.

Info-lines

Bellman, Geoffrey. "How to Build a Successful Team." No. 9212.

Darraugh, Barbara (ed.). "How to Facilitate." No. 9406 (revised 1999).

Patterson, James G. "Leadership." No. 9402.

Ralphs, Lenny T. "Time Management." No. 9506.

"Team Building at Its Best." No. 8701.

Vrooman, Rona J. "Group Process Tools." No. 9407 (revised 1997).

Waagen, Alice K. "Task Analysis." No. 9808.

Younger, Sandra Millers. "How to Delegate." No. 9011 (revised 1997).

Pre-Project Management Checklist

If you are selected to be a project manager, ask yourself the following questions. The answers will identify any gaps in your training or your organization's support structure.

1. Does my organization already support and implement the concept of project management?

☐ Yes ☐ No

If not, what steps can I, as an individual, do to encourage the use of this management practice?

_____

_____

_____

2. How much planning time do I put into projects?

_____

_____

_____

3. Does top management support its project managers?

☐ Yes ☐ No

4. Does my organization have strict lines of expertise, a line organization, functional groups, or a matrix organization?

☐ Yes ☐ No

_____

_____

_____

5. What automated methods are available in my organization. Am I familiar with their applications?

_____

_____

_____

The material appearing on this page is not covered by copyright and may be reproduced at will.

Job Aid

6. As a project manager, do I have access to the personnel and physical resources to manage effectively?

☐ Yes   ☐ No

_____

_____

_____

7. A work breakdown structure (WBS) will help me to organize adequately and structure the processes of task performance. Am I familiar with the development of a WBS?

☐ Yes   ☐ No

8. Is financial control facilitated through the use of network-analysis tools and computer assets?

☐ Yes   ☐ No

_____

_____

_____

9. Is the project adequately planned?

☐ Yes   ☐ No

10. Am I, as the project manager, technically competent, as well as people oriented?

☐ Yes   ☐ No

11. Does my organization encourage its personnel to be flexible to work on projects, thus increasing their worth to the company?

☐ Yes   ☐ No

_____

_____

_____

12. At the completion of the project, did I compile lessons learned, project accomplishments, and problems encountered?

☐ Yes   ☐ No

_____

_____

_____

Fundamentals of HPI

Issue 9811

Fundamentals of HPI

AUTHORS:

Janice Dent
827 W. 38th Street
Baltimore, MD 21211
Tel: 410.467.6586
E-mail: janicedent@erols.com

Phil Anderson
Strategist
ASTD Market Development
1640 King Street
Box 1443
Alexandria, VA 22313-2043
Tel: 703.683.8114
Fax: 703.683.7259
E-mail: panderson@astd.org

Editor
Cat Sharpe

Associate Editor
Sabrina E. Hicks

Production Design
Anne Morgan

ASTD Internal Consultant
Pam Schmidt

Fundamentals of HPI

Without a doubt, many of the organizations we work for are in need of some improvement. Do any of these examples sound familiar?

A customer service representative (CSR) at a financial services company does not know what mailings went to the customer, so the customer (who is a little irate at this point) has to inform the CSR of new offerings.

The volume of claims at a large insurance company is so astronomical that there is a huge backlog of claims that need to be paid. Customers have to wait months before the company can process their claim.

Your non-profit organization has to struggle to get anything done, and it seems as if one person is doing all of the work.

The programmers at a software company continually produce programs that do not meet the customers' needs.

Examine what is wrong with your organization:

- Are you losing market share?
- Are you losing customers?
- Are you losing money?

Which of the following do you think will solve your organization's problems:

- more or better information
- the right people in the right jobs
- additional resources
- more motivated employees
- better incentives
- more highly skilled employees

Most organizations seem to take the "one size fits all" approach to addressing their organization's performance problems: **TRAINING.** The problem with haphazardly applying this approach is that training is the right answer only when the problem is caused by a lack of knowledge or skills. A clear understanding must exist that training does not solve problems associated with any of the following:

- inadequate information
- hiring the wrong person for the job
- old, out-dated tools and resources
- poorly designed incentive programs
- poor processes

But what if you had an objective, systematic way to fix what is wrong with your organization? There is a way: human performance improvement (HPI).

This issue of *Info-line* provides you with a detailed explanation of the HPI process and model. What follows is an overview of the roles associated with HPI and a description of the core competencies required of practitioners who want to join this very exciting and rewarding movement. Finally, this issue offers an overview for making the transition from trainer to HPI consultant.

Defining Performance

Imagine that you have just returned from attending a concert or play. When asked if you enjoyed the event, you reply, "It was good." What do you really mean by this statement? Do you want it understood that the musicians, actors, and support staff were talented or that the basic sheet music or script was entertaining? Or is it that the musicians or actors worked together with the proper leadership from the conductor or the director to produce something that you thought was valuable (and that is why you were willing to spend your hard-earned money on expensive tickets)?

Performance is about factors such as culture, mission, workflow, goals, environment, knowledge, and skills all working together to produce something that is valuable to the consumer. So performance, regardless of the organization that produces the performance (be it a baseball team, software company, girl scout troop, or law firm), is about *outputs* or *results.*

Three Levels of Performance

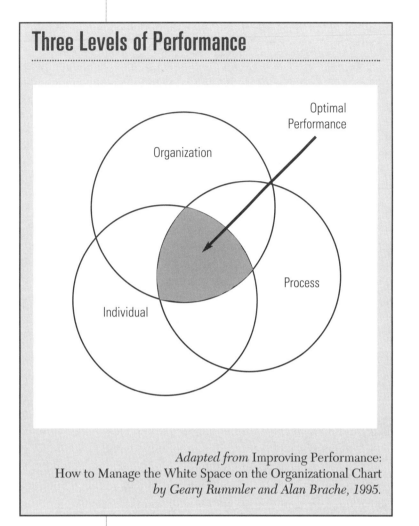

Adapted from Improving Performance:
How to Manage the White Space on the Organizational Chart
by Geary Rummler and Alan Brache, 1995.

When the sheet music or the script has potential, but the musicians or actors just are not talented, the performance fails. Perhaps the musicians or actors are talented individuals, but they just are not working well together. The performance just was not "good." Performance, therefore, needs to occur on many levels. Geary Rummler, author and well-known performance specialist, suggests that performance needs to occur on three levels:

1. The performer.

2. The process.

3. The organization.

Optimal performance is obtained when all three levels work in harmony. The *Three Levels of Performance* figure shown at left presents a visual rendition of this process. A breakdown at any one of the levels will prevent optimal performance, thereby requiring some type of planned action to improve performance.

According to Rummler, the organizational level establishes the necessary circumstances for the other levels of performance. When performance is not optimal, examine first the organization's culture, policies, mission, goals, and operating strategies. These factors delineate the boundaries by which we define processes and jobs.

The process level is where the actual work gets accomplished. When performance is not optimal, examine factors such as workflow, job design, required inputs and outputs, and the performance management procedures to see if these processes actually work and support the organizational goals.

The individual performers within the organization affect the processes. When performance is not optimal, determine if the individual performance goals, knowledge and skill, work environment, availability of support tools, coaching, and feedback support the processes.

Seldom is it true that only one set of factors (organization, process, or performer) are adversely affecting performance. When trying to identify why the performance problem exists, it is critical, therefore, to examine factors at all three levels of performance.

The reason for having a performance improvement need within an organization can usually be linked to one of the following three "trigger events":

1. Inadequate performance.

2. Introduction of something new (for example, a new process, system, technology, employee, or law).

3. Increased expectations.

What is Human Performance Improvement?

The concept of human performance improvement (HPI) or human performance technology is not new. In fact, much of the work that is the basis for the current focus on HPI was conducted in the late 1960s and early 1970s by individuals such as Thomas Gilbert, Joe Harless, Robert Mager, and Geary Rummler.

Much like instructional systems development (ISD) is a systematic process used to design and develop training programs, HPI is a systematic process used to address poor performance. In ASTD's publication *Models for Human Performance Improvement*, author William Rothwell states:

> HPI is the systematic process of discovering and analyzing important human performance gaps, planning for future improvements in human performance, designing and developing cost-effective and ethically justifiable interventions to close performance gaps, implementing the interventions, and evaluating the financial and non-financial results.

Systematic means that HPI is approached in an organized, rather than incidental way. It is based on open systems theory, or the view that any organization is a system that absorbs such environmental *inputs* as people factors, raw materials, capital, and information; uses them in such transformational *processes* as service delivery or manufacturing methods; and expels them as *outputs* such as finished goods or customer services. *Process* is a continuous activity carried out for a purpose.

Discovering and analyzing means identifying and examining present and possible future barriers that prevent an organization, process, or individual from achieving desired results. *Important* implies that priorities are established in the search for improvement opportunities. Importance is influenced by quantity, quality, cost, time, moral or ethical values, or some combination of these elements.

Human performance "denotes a quantified result or a set of obtained results, just as it also refers to the accomplishment, execution, or carrying out of anything ordered or undertaken, to something performed or done, to a deed, achievement, or exploit, and to the execution or accomplishment of the work" according to Harold Stolovitch and Erica Keeps in their book, *Handbook of Human Performance Technology*. Note that the quantifier *human* should be placed in front of *performance* to distinguish it from machine, capital, stock, or other forms of performance. *Gaps* are the differences between actual and desired results in the past, present, or future.

Planning for future improvements in HPI is meant to emphasize that HPI work is not focused solely on solving past or present problems; rather, it also can be focused on averting future problems or realizing improvement opportunities.

Designing and developing cost-effective and ethically justifiable interventions means finding and formulating optimal or desirable ways of solving past or present human performance problems or planning for future HPI opportunities. The word intervention implies a long-term, evolutionary, and progressive change effort. *Cost-effective* implies sensitivity to bottom-line improvements by those who perform HPI work. *Ethically justifiable* implies sensitivity to ethical and moral viewpoints.

Implementing the interventions means finding the optimal—most cost efficient and cost effective—way to plan for HPI. Sometimes called *deployment*, it refers to the installation process for an HPI intervention.

Evaluating the results focuses on accountability. Those who do HPI work must always remain keenly aware of the need to gather persuasive evidence of the economic and non-economic value of their efforts.

Adapted from ASTD Models for Human Performance Improvement *by William Rothwell, 1996.*

Inadequate performance results when part of the system breaks down. The organizational level is not producing the structure by which processes can be established. Or, the performers are not able to perform the processes.

Examples can include the following:

- Claims are processed incorrectly.
- The product breaks after the third use.
- The answers provided to customers are wrong.
- Deadlines are missed.

When something new is added or will be added to the organization, a performance opportunity exists. The new factor may affect the organizational, process, or performer level of performance.

Examples include the following:

- A new software package is installed.
- A new employee is hired.
- A new law is passed.

In our competitive work environments, today's acceptable performance is tomorrow's unacceptable performance. The organization that proactively identifies the need for an increase in performance will be the organization that beats out its competition.

Examples of proactive behavior include the following:

- Raising quality standards to out perform the competition.

- Increasing sale levels in anticipation of a new rival entering the market.

- Increasing production levels in preparation for launching a new product.

In each circumstance, whether inadequate performance, the introduction of something new, or increased expectations, the HPI process is the same.

The HPI Process Model

If you think of the performance improvement process in the context of your own health, it is easy to understand. When you are not feeling well and you go to the doctor, the physician asks you a number of questions and runs some tests to determine the cause of the problem. Once the cause is established, the physician selects the right treatment and prescribes it. Sometimes the treatment is simple ("take this pill"), but often the treatment involves many steps ("take this pill, drink plenty of fluids, and get plenty of rest").

Once you begin the treatment, you start to feel better. The doctor may even ask you to look for signs of improved health: "If you don't see a noticeable improvement in two to three days, call me—we could be on the wrong track." As a final step, the doctor sets up a follow-up appointment to ensure that your condition no longer exists. The physician may even order additional tests to compare against the original test.

HPI involves the same steps employed by the doctor. The HPI Process Model (refer to the diagram at right) illustrates the six-step process:

1. Performance Analysis.

2. Cause Analysis.

3. Intervention Selection.

4. Intervention Implementation.

5. Change Management.

6. Evaluation of Results.

Step 1: Performance Analysis

The performance improvement process starts with a two-step analysis phase. Imagine that when you walk into the examining room the doctor takes one look at you and says, "You have an ulcer." Sounds ludicrous. Why then, in the business environment, do we tend to make quick judgements in our organizations? Look at a simple example:

Sales manager to training manager: "Four of my sales people didn't meet their sales goals last quarter and I would like to send them to sales training."

HPI Process Model

The arrows between the steps in the model represent the system-aspects (inputs and outputs) of the process. For example, the output of the Performance Analysis phase is the input for the Cause Analysis phase.

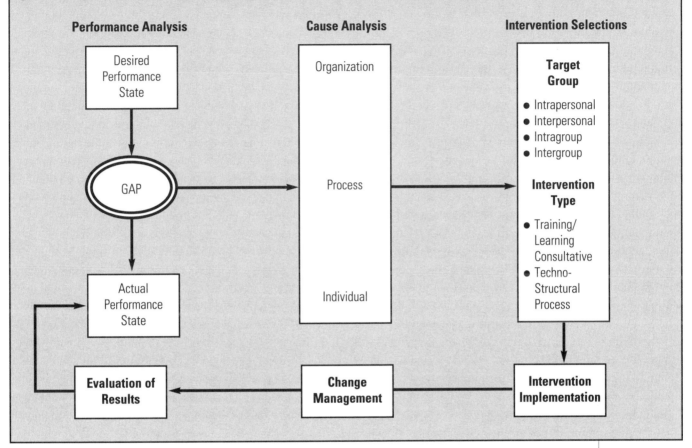

Training manager: *"Didn't we just send all of your people to sales training six months ago?"*

Sales manager: *"Yes, and these four attended that training, but ever since we introduced that new product, they haven't been doing real well."*

Training manager: *"Well how about we just send them to a refresher course. It shouldn't take as long, and it will be a lot cheaper."*

Sales manager: *"Sounds good. I can't afford to have them out of the office for an entire week anyway. Let me know when it is scheduled."*

As an HPI specialist you should ask yourself, "How do we know that training is the right answer to the performance problem unless we ask some questions? Listed below are some sample questions to help you get started:

- Do the sales people have the information they need to sell the new product?

- Have the sales people been given new performance goals that emphasize selling the new product?

- What is the sale person's level of knowledge about the new product?

- What incentives or disincentives are there for selling the new product?

Cause Analysis: Using a Fishbone Diagram

Follow these instructions to use a fishbone diagram for cause analysis.

1. Assemble stakeholders (individual workers, managers, division heads, executives, and so forth).

2. Draw this fishbone diagram on a flipchart or whiteboard.

3. Have stakeholders describe the performance gap in the box shown on the far right. Have stakeholders clarify what is actually happening (what can be seen and measured) and what results are desired.

4. Brainstorm causes of the gap by considering each performance category described in the boxes to the left of the performance gap box. (You will notice that the "bones" on the top of the diagram focus on the individual. The bottom-left "bones" focus on the process and the bottom-right "bones" focus on the organization.)

5. Ensure the group that there are no right or wrong answers. Challenge stakeholders to consider all the "bones."

6. Record their responses to uncover causes of the performance gap.

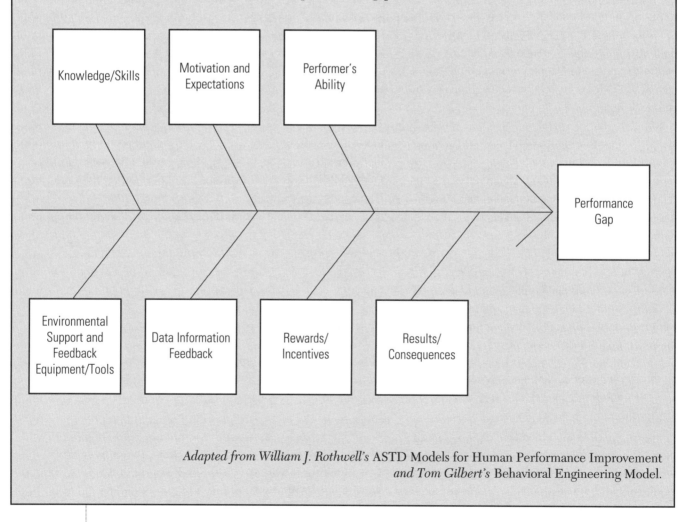

Adapted from William J. Rothwell's ASTD Models for Human Performance Improvement *and Tom Gilbert's* Behavioral Engineering Model.

Think of all the money that organizations waste on training, reorganization, or any other intervention because management thought it could not afford to spend the time and money to properly analyze the situation in the first place.

When conducting a performance analysis, you identify and describe past, present, and future human performance gaps. You collect information from key stakeholders (for example, executives, department heads, and line managers) as well as individual performers by asking questions that examine how existing performance compares to the desired performance. Then, you examine documents (such as annual reports or customer surveys) to find the consequences of the performance gap.

Other names for this phase—"performance gap analysis" or "up-front analysis"—refer to the same activity. As with any analysis, you can select a variety of methods to collect the information (such as surveys, interviews, or focus groups). Refer to *Info-line*s No. 9408, "Strategic Needs Analysis" and No. 8502, "Be a Better Needs Analyst" to acquire more information on how to conduct a needs analysis.

You will need to answer the following questions as a result of the performance analysis:

- What is the desired performance situation versus the actual situation?

- What is the gap or difference between the actual and desired performance?

- Who is affected by the performance gap? Is it one person, a group, an organization, or a work process?

- When and where did the performance gap first occur, or when is it expected to begin?

- When and where were the symptoms and the consequences of the performance gap first noticed?

- What has the performance gap cost the organization? Can the impact of the performance gap be measured?

The output of the performance analysis phase is a clearly defined problem or opportunity—complete with the existing and desired conditions that sur-

round performance. You may have also noticed that some of the questions presented to ask during the performance analysis are key to evaluating the success of the HPI process. You need to collect concrete examples of the consequences of the performance gap to measure the effects of the HPI process.

Step 2: Cause Analysis

Once you have adequately defined the performance gap, you can determine the cause of the gap through a cause analysis. Your goal is to answer one question: Why does the performance gap exist?

You are not simply addressing symptoms; you are getting to the root cause of the gap. First, you need to ask important questions that examine issues related to the organization, the process, and the performer. These questions should include the following issues:

- incentives
- flow of information
- equipment
- employee abilities
- motivation
- work environment
- knowledge and skills

Similarly, you will need to gather your information through a variety of methods. One cause analysis technique uses a *fishbone diagram*. Refer to the diagram at left for instructions on how to use this analysis technique.

Following are the types of questions you will need to answer as a result of a cause analysis:

- How well do performers see the results of what they do?

- How well are performers rewarded or provided with incentives for performing as desired?

- Are performers penalized for achieving desired work results?

Types of Interventions

Intervention Types	Possible Causes
Training Interventions Activities that focus on the acquisition of new knowledge and skills.	• lack of knowledge and skills
Consultative Interventions Activities that focus on helping clients to help themselves.	• lack of support and feedback • lack of results and consequences • performance ability
Techno-Structural Interventions Activities that focus on the performer's physical setting, available tools, or organizational structure.	• lack of rewards and incentives • lack of equipment and tools • environment support through organization structure • performer's ability
Process Interventions Activities that focus on how the performers complete their work.	• environmental support • ineffective job/process • design • lack of data information

Examples	Partners
<ul><li>classroom training</li><li>on-the-job training</li><li>computer-based training</li><li>web-based training</li><li>job aids</li><li>paper-based self-study</li><li>video-based training</li></ul>	<ul><li>subject matter experts</li><li>line supervisors, managers, executives</li><li>technical writers</li><li>programmers</li><li>workers</li><li>communication specialists</li><li>instructional designers</li></ul>
<ul><li>formal and informal coaching programs</li><li>feedback systems</li><li>mentoring programs</li><li>recognition programs</li><li>reward systems</li><li>incentive plans</li><li>career counseling centers</li><li>career ladders</li><li>tuition reimbursement</li><li>job rotation</li><li>promotion systems</li></ul>	<ul><li>line supervisors, managers, executives</li><li>HR specialists, generalists, and managers</li><li>survey design experts</li><li>communication specialists</li><li>compensation specialists</li><li>organization development experts</li><li>employee development staff</li><li>career development specialist</li></ul>
<ul><li>ergonomic improvements</li><li>work space redesign</li><li>equipment upgrade</li><li>electronic performance support systems</li><li>re-organization</li><li>employee selection</li><li>information systems</li><li>policies and procedures</li></ul>	<ul><li>line supervisors, managers, executives</li><li>HR specialists, generalists, managers</li><li>technology specialist</li><li>information systems staff</li><li>ergonomists</li><li>communication specialists</li><li>recruiters and staff specialists</li><li>workflow specialists</li><li>organization development experts</li><li>employee development staff</li><li>career development specialist</li></ul>
<ul><li>job redesign</li><li>competency modeling</li><li>quality systems</li><li>documentation systems</li><li>communication systems</li><li>management systems</li><li>team interventions</li></ul>	<ul><li>line supervisors, mangers, executives</li><li>workers</li><li>HR specialists, generalists, managers</li><li>team building experts</li><li>information systems staff</li><li>procedures writers</li><li>communication specialists</li><li>strategists</li><li>workflow specialists</li><li>quality control experts</li><li>organization development experts</li><li>employee development staff</li></ul>

- Do the performers have the ability to do the job?

- Are performers given the data, information, or feedback they need to perform at the time they need it?

- Do performers have the support tools and resources they need?

The output of the cause analysis phase is a clearly defined cause or list of causes that you can address by selecting and implementing the appropriate performance intervention. Also, you need to make sure that you have a clear sense of the target group that is involved in the cause.

Step 3: Intervention Selection

After determining root causes of the performance problem or performance opportunity, you must select the interventions that will address the situation. According to Wendell French and Cecil Bell in *Organizational Development: Behavioral Science Interventions for Organization Improvement,* an intervention is "a set of structured activities in which selected organizational units (target groups or individuals) engage in a task or a sequence of tasks where the task goals are related directly or indirectly to organizational improvement."

Before starting, determine the depth to which you will attack the problem or opportunity. Most performance problems or opportunities exist on several levels (organization, process, or performer). As you delve deeper, the potential benefits increase but so do the risks. Do not tackle more than you can deliver. In addition, you need to keep in mind that most performance improvement requires a combination of interventions.

To address the performance situation, you may need to implement a series of interventions. Perhaps you need an intervention for each of the following situations:

- to establish performance
- to maintain the established performance
- to extinguish incorrect performance

Begin the intervention selection process through divergent thinking. First, list all of the interventions that you can think of that might solve the root cause of the performance gap. Refer to the *Types of Interventions* chart on the previous pages for a categorized list of possible interventions. At this point in the process, do not worry about how plausible these interventions are—just make sure the intervention addresses the cause. Be sure to relate possible interventions to the target group. For example, if the target group is an individual, do not list interventions that only work with groups. (See the chart *Target Groups* sidebar at right.)

Next to the possible interventions, note the following elements associated with each:

- costs
- benefits
- potential obstacles

Also try to find opportunities where one intervention might solve two or more root causes of the problem. Always consider the organization's culture: which interventions could be effective without disrupting too many of the organization's norms and values? Pare down the list by eliminating ideas that have very little chance of success or are prohibitively expensive. Do not be too hasty—sometimes the craziest ideas start to have merit when considered carefully. At the end of the selection process, be sure that you have selected at least one intervention for each of the root causes.

Answer the following questions that result from the intervention selection process:

- What will a successful intervention be able to do?

- What are the costs and benefits associated with each intervention?

- Will one intervention address more than one cause?

- What are the concerns of stakeholders towards these interventions?

- What will be required to gain buy-in?

- How well do these interventions match what you know about the organization's culture?

The output of the intervention selection phase is a design document that includes intervention requirements, intervention components, and intervention specifications. You will need an action plan that lists the major tasks included for each intervention, the resources required to implement each intervention, and a plan for incorporating stakeholder support.

Step 4: Intervention Implementation

At this point, you are ready to help the organization implement the selected intervention. Implementation involves four parts: intervention, organization, leadership, and individuals affected.

■ *Intervention*
During the implementation phase, watch how people within the organization respond to the intervention. Observe for the following:

- Is it easy to implement? If not, you may need to find a way to implement it in stages.

- Is the intervention similar to past practices? You need to find a way to communicate the similarities to past success stories.

- Can the intervention be modified? Users like to make something their own. A successful implementer does not care if the user makes slight changes to the intervention, as long as it is still effective.

- Does the intervention have any social impact? Users do not want their relationships with other people to change. If it requires change, you will want to communicate these changes early.

■ *Organization*
An intervention will be successful only if the organization is ready for it. Prior to full blown implementation, look for the following:

- Are the interventions and the organization's culture in synch? If not, be prepared to fail.

- Does the strategic plan support the intervention? If so, communicate the similarities. If not, stop implementation until you find a way that it can.

- Are there external conditions that will influence the organization negatively? If so, consider postponing the implementation until you are prepared to deal with the external conditions.

Target Groups	
Target Group	**Intervention Examples**
Intrapersonal The performance is the function of an individual.	• career counseling • training • work space redesign
Interpersonal The performance is a function of the interaction of two or more individuals.	• job rotation • conflict resolution • role clarification
Intragroup The performance is a function of the interaction amount of team and group members.	• team building • process re-design • rewards systems
Intergroup The performance is a function of the interaction of two or more groups.	• process clarification • re-organization • strategic planning

■ *Leadership*
Organizational leadership can make or break an intervention. Perhaps the most important aspect of the implementation effort is the sponsor. When identifying and selecting a sponsor, look for someone who fits the following description:

- has the power to validate change within an organization

- is well-respected in the organization and believes in the suggested changes

- has the time to support the effort by writing letters, kicking-off training sessions, providing rewards for good performance, and so forth

- is someone you are comfortable working with—if he or she is not appropriate, you should be prepared to find another sponsor

What's Your Perspective?

Training Perspective	Performance Perspective
Assumptions	**Assumptions**
Training (giving employees more skills, knowledge, and abilities) is the solution to performance problems.	Training is one possible intervention when there are performance problems or opportunities.
The goal of training is to give employees more skills, knowledge, or ability.	The goal of performance improvement is to meet organizational performance goals.
A training department should deliver the training that customers ask for.	A performance improvement department should question whether training is needed.
A trainer's most important skill is to deliver training and facilitate learning.	A performance consultant's most important skill is to diagnose performance problems.
Roles	**Roles**
Training needs analysis	Performance analysis
Training design	Cause analysis
Training delivery	Intervention selection and implementation
Evaluation	Change management
Training management and coordination	Evaluation of results and feedback
	Project management
Tools	**Tools**
Assessment instruments	Organization's operating plan
Instructional design models	Strategy statement
Group process	Annual report
Classroom	Survey instruments
Learning technology	Process maps
Textbooks, workbooks, tests	Templates, models, matrices
Customers	**Customers**
Learner	Process owner
Learner's manager	Performer
Training purchaser	Performer's manager
	Organization's customers

Adapted from ASTD's Web site: www.astd.org.

■ *Individuals Affected*

Finally, you need to consider the individuals affected by the intervention. Below are some items for consideration:

● Some people adapt to change more quickly than others.

● You need to understand the characteristics of your audience to implement an intervention successfully.

● Are other changes occurring at the same time? If too many things are happening at once, you may need to change your time frames.

Note, however, that you are not necessarily responsible for implementing the selected intervention. Your responsibility is to identify the talent and resources needed to implement the interventions. The individuals who actually implement the intervention may be people within your organization (such as members of the human resources department, subject matter experts [SMEs], managers, or trainers). Or, you may get the help of outside consultants who specialize in compensation, ergonomics, management development, or computer programming.

The output of the intervention implementation phase is the occurrence of the actual intervention, such as the following examples:

● a new organizational structure
● an updated software program
● an incentive system
● a training program

A well-planned implementation is necessary for you to track the changes taking place as a result of your efforts.

Step 5: Change Management

During the change management phase, identify how people are reacting to the intervention, and address these reactions. Some things to consider are as follows:

● Although change management is positioned late in the HPI model, it is critical to begin thinking about change issues very early in the process.

- It is not necessary to have 100 percent of the population in favor of the change. It is actually beneficial to have some doubters.

- All of the planning in the world will not eliminate the discomfort associated with change that results from implementing interventions. As change agent, you need to anticipate the discomfort and make plans on how to address the discomfort.

Diane Dormant, in *Introduction to Performance Technology*, suggests incorporating the following change management strategies:

- Be a spokesperson for the change. Write newsletter articles or create other media events that introduce the change.

- Be credible and positive about the change. Enlist the help of the sponsor or key stakeholders.

- Empathize with the change concerns of the target group. Answer their questions and provide clear, reliable information.

- Emphasize the strengths of the intervention and its changes, and acknowledge the weaknesses too. Again, enlist the help of the sponsor or key stakeholders.

- Provide success images through relevant examples or successful demonstration of the change. If possible, promote discussion with others who have successfully changed.

- Provide incentives or rewards for changed behavior.

- Provide feedback and status reports as reinforcement and support for the change.

Many models represent the stages people go through as they experience change. Several *Info-line* issues address the change management process. Refer to *Info-line*s No. 9715, "The Role of the Change Manager," and No. 8910, "Managing Change," if you need additional help in managing your change effort.

The output of the change management phase is an on-going status report that tracks the following items:

- how well the intervention is working

- effect of the intervention on the target group

- modifications made to the original plan to address new concerns

Step 6: Evaluation of Results

During the final phase of the HPI process, determine how well the intervention met its desired outcome. To do this, you need to evaluate the intervention itself and the overall performance problem or opportunity. As with the change management phase, it is critical that you begin thinking about evaluation issues very early on in the process. Below are some issues to think about when focussing on evaluation:

- Be sure you are measuring against valid business results. An "increase in employee moral" is not a business result. A 10 percent decrease in production errors is a business result.

- Be sure you identify the desired business results prior to intervention selection.

- Be sure that the date you need to conduct your evaluation is available to you before you agree on how the intervention will be evaluated.

- An obvious link should exist between the selected intervention, the optimal performance, and the desired business result.

- Focus your HPI evaluation on the higher·levels of Donald Kirkpatrick's four levels of evaluation (namely, reaction, learning, behavior, and results).

As with analysis, much has been written about training evaluation. If you need additional help with your evaluation efforts, you may want to refer to other *Info-line* issues (such as No. 9801, "Benchmarking"; No. 9705, "Essentials for Evaluation"; No. 9813, "Level 1 Evaluation"; No. 9814,

HPI Process, Roles, and Skills

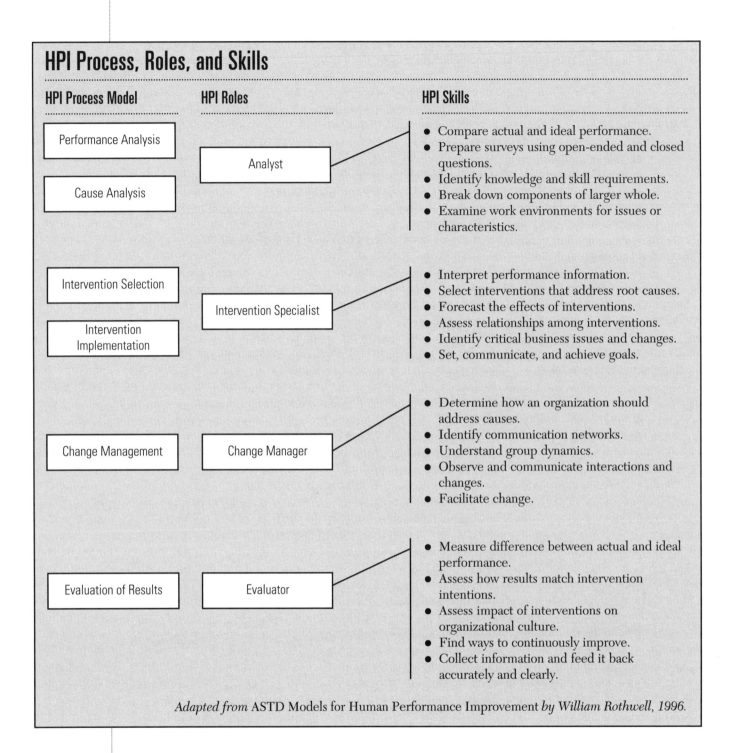

HPI Process Model	HPI Roles	HPI Skills
Performance Analysis Cause Analysis	Analyst	• Compare actual and ideal performance. • Prepare surveys using open-ended and closed questions. • Identify knowledge and skill requirements. • Break down components of larger whole. • Examine work environments for issues or characteristics.
Intervention Selection Intervention Implementation	Intervention Specialist	• Interpret performance information. • Select interventions that address root causes. • Forecast the effects of interventions. • Assess relationships among interventions. • Identify critical business issues and changes. • Set, communicate, and achieve goals.
Change Management	Change Manager	• Determine how an organization should address causes. • Identify communication networks. • Understand group dynamics. • Observe and communicate interactions and changes. • Facilitate change.
Evaluation of Results	Evaluator	• Measure difference between actual and ideal performance. • Assess how results match intervention intentions. • Assess impact of interventions on organizational culture. • Find ways to continuously improve. • Collect information and feed it back accurately and clearly.

Adapted from ASTD Models for Human Performance Improvement *by William Rothwell, 1996.*

"Level 2 Evaluation"; No. 9815, "Level 3 Evaluation"; No. 9816, "Level 4 Evaluation"; and No. 9805, "Level 5 Evaluation: ROI"). As you read these *Info-line* issues, remember that you need to work with the parts of the models that focus on measuring results.

The output of the evaluation of results phase is a well-documented account of the changes that took place in the organization with an emphasis on the benefits achieved as a result of the HPI process.

Basic HPI Competencies

Before leaping into the world of HPI, you may want to examine your own skill and knowledge level. William Rothwell in *ASTD Models for Human Performance Improvement* provides a detailed description of the roles, competencies, and outputs associated with the performance consultant. He begins by listing the core competencies associated with practitioners of HPI.

How do you rate yourself in relationship to these capabilities? From the following list, check the core competencies that you possess, and look for ways to improve in the areas that you feel you lack some capabilities.

- industry awareness
- leadership skills
- interpersonal relationship skills
- technological awareness and understanding
- problem-solving skills
- systems thinking and understanding
- performance and understanding
- knowledge of interventions
- business understanding
- organization understanding
- negotiating/contracting skills
- buy-in/advocacy skills
- coping skills
- ability to see "big picture"
- consulting skills

Rothwell also defines competencies for the separate roles effected by an HPI practitioner. Refer to the *HPI Process, Roles, and Skills* chart at left for a visual reference.

Moving to Performance Improvement

Much has been written about the transition from training to HPI. *Webster's Dictionary* defines "transition" as the "passage from one place, condition, or stage to another." We all know that a caterpillar transitions to a butterfly and a tadpole transitions to a frog. The idea that training professionals need to "transition" to HPI professionals is both scary and misleading.

The misleading part of the transition is the thought that an increased need for HPI specialists will eliminate the need for skilled instructors. While it is certainly true that HPI is not about a new way of training employees, it is also true that an organization's need to train its employees will never be eliminated. It follows logically that the need for skilled instructors will never be eliminated. Think about it, did the growth in the need for skilled instructional designers eliminate the need for skilled instructors? The apprehensive part of the transition is the thought that to be an HPI specialist, you need to be an expert in all the possible interventions.

Again, look at the role of an instructional designer. A skilled instructional designer knows how to partner with SMEs to design and develop a training program for which he or she is not a content expert. HPI specialists also need to partner with experts within a specific discipline to implement appropriate interventions.

A better way to look at the movement towards HPI is as an "expansion." Again using *Webster's*, expansion is defined as the "act of increasing the range, scope, volume, size, etc. of." This means that we, as HPI specialists, need to be prepared to offer more than just a training solution in our efforts to help our clients improve their individual and organizational performance.

References & Resources

Articles

Carr, C., and L. Totzke. "The Long and Winding Path (from Instructional Technology to Performance Technology)." *Performance & Instruction,* August 1995, pp. 4-8.

Elliot, P. "Power-Charging People's Performance." *Training & Development,* December 1996, pp. 46-49.

Galagan, P. "Reinventing the Profession." *Training & Development,* December 1994, pp. 20-27.

Gephart, M.A. "The Road to High Performance," *Training & Development,* June 1995, pp. 30-38.

Gill, S.J. "Shifting Gears for High Performance." *Training & Development,* May 1995, pp. 24-31.

Harless, J. "Performance Technology Skills in Business: Implications for Preparation." *Performance Improvement Quarterly,* vol. 8, no. 4 (1995), pp. 75-88.

Rummler, G. "In Search of the Holy Performance Grail." *Training & Development,* April 1996, pp. 26-32.

Smalley, K., et al. "Strategic Planning: From Training to Performance Technology within Three Years." *Performance Improvement Quarterly,* vol. 8, no. 2 (1995), pp. 114-124.

Sorohan, E.G. "The Performance Consultant at Work," *Training & Development,* March 1996, pp. 35-38.

Books

ASTD. *Introduction to Performance: A Primer for Trainers.* Alexandria, Virginia: ASTD, 1996.

Bassi, L.J., et al., *The ASTD Training Data Book.* Alexandria, Virginia: ASTD, 1996.

Browsher, J.E. *Revolutionizing Workforce Performance: A Systems Approach to Mastery.* San Francisco: Jossey-Bass Pfeiffer, 1998.

Dubois, D.D. *Competency-Based Performance Improvement.* Amherst, Massachusetts: HRD Press, 1995.

French, Wendell, and Cecil Bell. *Organizational Development: Behavioral Science Interventions for Organization Improvement.* New York: Prentice Hall, 1994.

Gilbert, T.F. *Human Competence Engineering Worthy Performance.* New York: McGraw-Hill, 1978.

Harbour, J.L. *The Basics of Performance Measurement.* New York: Quality Resources, 1997.

Kaufman, R. *Strategic Planning: An Organizational Guide (revised edition).* Newbury Park, California: Sage Publications, 1992.

Kaufman, R., et al. *The Practitioner's Handbook on Organization and Human Performance Improvement.* San Diego, California: University Associates/Pfeiffer, 1995.

Kirkpatrick, D.L. *Evaluating Training Programs: The Four Levels.* San Francisco: Berrett-Koehler, 1994.

Robinson, D.G., and J.C. Robinson. *Performance Consulting.* San Francisco: Berrett-Koehler, 1995.

Rothwell W. *ASTD Models for Human Performance Improvement.* Alexandria, Virginia: ASTD, 1996.

———. *Beyond Training and Development: State-of-the-Art Strategies for Enhancing Human Performance.* New York: AMACOM, 1996.

Info-lines

Rummler, G., and A. Brache. *Improving Performance: How to Manage the White Space on the Organization Chart.* San Francisco: Jossey-Bass, 1995.

Smith, Martin (ed.) *Introduction to Performance Technology.* International Society for Performance Improvement, 1986.

Stolovitch, Harold D., and Erica J. Keeps. *Handbook of Human Performance Technology: A Comprehensive Guide for Analyzing and Solving Performance Problems in Organizations.* San Francisco: Jossey-Bass, 1992.

Swanson, R.A. *Analysis for Improving Performance: Tools for Diagnosing Organizations & Documenting Workplace Expertise.* San Francisco: Jossey-Bass, 1992.

"Be a Better Needs Analyst." No. 8502 (revised 1998).

Bricker, B. "Basics of Performance Technology." No. 9211 (out of print).

Carr, D.A. "How to Facilitate." No. 9406 (revised 1999).

Callahan, M. "From Training to Performance Consulting." No. 9702 (revised 1999).

———. "The Role of the Performance Intervention Specialist." No. 9714.

Kirrane, Diane. "The Role of the Performance Needs Analyst." No. 9713.

Koehle, Deborah. "The Role of the Performance Change Manager." No. 9715.

Gill, S. "Linking Training to Performance Goals." No. 9606 (revised 1998).

Sparhawk, Sally, and Marian Schickling. "Strategic Needs Analysis." No. 9408 (revised 1999).

Job Aid

HPI Process Checklist

Use this checklist as you advance through the phases of the performance improvement process.

Phase 1: Conduct a Performance Analysis

Technique: Use a variety of methods (such as interviews, focus groups, and surveys) to determine the performance gap. Answer the following questions:

☐ What is the desired performance verses what is actually happening?

☐ What is the difference (gap) in performance?

☐ Who is affected?

☐ What is the impact?

Output: A clearly defined problem or opportunity, complete with conditions that surround the performance and concrete measurements that can be used in the evaluation phase.

Phase 2: Conduct a Cause Analysis

Technique: Use a variety of methods (such as a fishbone diagram) to determine why the performance gap exists. Consider all of the causes that may apply, such as the following:

☐ knowledge	☐ motivation	☐ rewards
☐ skills	☐ expectations	☐ incentives
☐ tools	☐ performer's ability	☐ consequences
☐ environmental support	☐ feedback	☐ results

Output: A clearly defined list of causes that includes the target group involved.

Phase 3: Select, Design, and Develop Interventions

Technique: Use the following guideline to help determine intervention requirements.

☐ What results should be seen?

☐ What is important to stakeholders?

☐ What are limitations to budget, time, and resources?

☐ Brainstorm possible interventions and then choose appropriate interventions based on benefits and advantages verses costs and disadvantages.

   Hint: More than one intervention may be required to establish and maintain correct performance while extinguishing incorrect performance.

☐ Create a project plan that includes major tasks, resources required, and timing/dates for each intervention.

☐ Develop a pilot intervention and test it, prior to producing the final intervention.

Output: A selection/design document that includes intervention components, major tasks, resources required, and timing. A development project plan that indicates development dates, pilot tests, and revision time.

Phase 4: Implement the Intervention

Technique: Use the following strategy to implement an intervention that affects the four parts of the implementation phase: intervention, organization, leadership, and individuals.

☐ Gather implementation team and gain support from the intervention sponsor.

☐ Determine implementation strategy.

☐ Prepare the implementation team, target group, and organization by clarifying expectations.

☐ Identify possible intervention implementation weaknesses (such as those listed below) and create strategies to address the weaknesses.

- The intervention is hard to learn.
- The external workload increased.
- Users were not involved in the process.

Output: An implemented intervention (such as a new computer system, reorganization, a new process, a training program, or an incentive system).

The material appearing on this page is not covered by copyright and may be reproduced at will.

Job Aid

Phase 5: Manage Change

Technique: Using the statements below, identify how people are reacting to the change, and address those reactions.

☐ Identify the target group's change stages.

☐ Determine strategy to address change states:

- Be a spokesperson for the intervention or change.
- Provide clear, reliable information about the intervention or change.
- Provide incentives or rewards.

Output: An on-going status report (often newsletter articles, videos, or peer discussions) of how well the intervention is working, the effect on the target group, and modifications made.

Phase 6: Evaluate the Results

Technique: Use the following strategy to evaluate how well the intervention met its desired outcome.

☐ Reaction: Use an intervention satisfaction survey.

☐ Learning: Use assessments, interviews, focus groups, or surveys to determine if "they got it."

☐ Behavior: Use observations, interviews, focus groups, or surveys to determine if the performance gap no longer exists.

☐ Results: Use observations, interviews, documents, or surveys to determine if the impact of the performance gap no longer exists.

Output: A report of the measurable changes taking place in the organization with an emphasis on the benefits associated with the HPI process.